GEORGIA ON MY MENU

A Medley Of Southern Hits

from
family, friends
and
fellow Georgians

The Junior League of Cobb-Marietta, Inc.

The Junior League of Cobb-Marietta is an organization of women committed to promoting voluntarism and to improving the community through the effective action and leadership of trained volunteers. Its purpose is exclusively educational and charitable.

Copyright© 1988
League Publications
Junior League of Cobb-Marietta, Inc.
Marietta, Georgia

1st Printing	April, 1988	10,000
2nd Printing	October, 1988	10,000
3rd Printing	November, 1989	10,000
4th Printing	February, 1991	10,000
5th Printing	May, 1992	10,000

Copies of **Georgia On My Menu** may be obtained by sending $15.95 plus $2.00 postage and handling to the address below. (Georgia residents pay $.80 sales tax).

League Publications
P.O. Box 727
Marietta, Georgia 30060
Phone: (404) 422-5266

Library of Congress Catalog Card Number: 87-83654
ISBN   0-9619983-0-X

Printed in the USA by
WIMMER BROTHERS
A Wimmer Company
Memphis • Dallas

THANK YOU FOR YOUR SUPPORT

Your purchase of **GEORGIA ON MY MENU** helps support the following projects and activities of the Junior League of Cobb-Marietta, Inc.

MINI GRANTS
Enrichment resources for area teachers

YWCA BATTERED WOMEN'S SHELTER
An emergency shelter for abused women

MARIETTA/COBB MUSEUM OF ART—KIDS' PLACE
An environment where the love of art can begin to grow

CHILDCARE PROJECT
Development of a childcare center for low income families

KIDS ON THE BLOCK
Puppet shows focusing on substance abuse and divorce

GIRLS INCORPORATED OF COBB COUNTY
Assistance with adolescent pregnancy prevention program

COOKBOOK CHAIRMEN

1987 – 1988	Meredith Webb Dykes
	Ginger Byrd McPherson
1988 – 1989	Anna Tucker
1989 – 1990	Cheryl McColl
1990 – 1991	Rehnea Kemble
	Denise Riester
1991 – 1992	Rebecca Breedlove
	Polly Burson
1992 – 1993	Keli Davies

PAST COOKBOOK COMMITTEE MEMBERS

Carolyn Campbell

Kathryn Coffee

Cathy Colquitt

Anresa Davis

Martha Franks

Charlene Gates

Judy Gorrell Harper

Louise Hetherwick Hunter

Darlene Huggins

Dell Cochran James

Elise Johnston

Karen Jones

Suzanne Lambert

Betty Neel Cobb Lawton

Laura Phillips Lewis

Patricia Rusinek Macchia

Marilyn Simon Massey

Shelley Mayes

Judy Melton

Lisa Moraitakis

Vicky Murphy

Ginny Northcutt

Claudia Mitchell Owens

B. P. Pope

Donya Smith Rickman

Mary Risley

Donna Cates Robinson

Mindy Rohrbach

Melanie Speed

Peggy Spillane

Marcia Thompson

Lynn Tinsley

Shelley Trousil

Ellen Woodruff

Melissa Worley

Jan Youngberg

INTRODUCTION

Georgia on my Menu: A Medley of Southern Hits truly can be said to represent two areas of life with which Georgians are intimately acquainted—the appreciation of fine Southern cooking and the desire to have music in one's life. This collection of recipes does justice to a state which boasts a varied and rich historical and cultural background. From the era of the Cherokee and Creek Indians of the early sixteenth century through the founding of the Thirteen Original Colonies and the beginning of the Gold Rush of 1828 to the present day hustle and bustle of a state which has the largest land area east of the Mississippi River—Georgians can be proud of their heritage.

Instrumental to their awareness of a rich heritage is a willingness to share the secrets of that elusive, but vital, quality of life known as "Southern Hospitality." Georgians from all parts of the state and from different backgrounds maintain a common desire to have their past accomplishments reflected in the prosperous future that is theirs.

Food has long been a barometer in Georgia for the true test of gracious entertaining that is a part of our Southern legacy. *Georgia on my Menu* offers a collection of the best recipes of our state which may be used to orchestrate a truly musical and magical gastronomic experience.

The host might begin with the Overtures and Preludes—appetizers, beverages and soups and salads which set the tone for a gracious repast. The Accompaniments (fruits and vegetables) and the Melodies (entreés) are enjoyed fully in the presence of the Harmonies (breads). The Finale (desserts) merely signifies the fitting end to a truly enjoyable event. There you have it—an example of "Southern Hospitality" as Georgians see it.

Two special sections of the score need yet to be performed. The Encore section offers a delicious array of Sunday night suppers which will enable all samplers to appreciate the subtle delicacy of "supper" in the Southern sense. The Celebrities portion offers unique hints and selections from Georgia celebrities and restaurants; these recipes could make you a culinary star in your own right!

As is customary when one considers "Southern Hospitality", a true sense of community is prevalent. This commitment to a better world is the underlying theme of this work. Through the funds generated from the sale of the book, the Junior League of Cobb-Marietta will continue to improve its community through such projects as Open Gate, a temporary emergency shelter for children and youth; Mini Grants, an enrichment program for area teachers; Woman to Woman, a project dealing with the critical issues of women and alcoholism; continued support of the Cobb County Youth Museum, a unique hands-on children's museum; and GATE, substance abuse program presented to local students. These programs and others, coupled with a sincere desire to make a difference in one's community, will enable all to enjoy the delicious array presented here and to experience "Southern Hospitality" in the fullest sense.

Ingredients ready…
    Recipes at hand…
        Let the music begin!

Beverly Webb McCollum, President
Junior League of Cobb-Marietta, 1985-86
Board of Directors, Association of Junior Leagues 1987-89

Special thanks go to Mr. Tim McCabe of Tim McCabe Productions, who was instrumental in soliciting the famous Georgian celebrities who appear in the celebrity section of the cookbook. This section of the cookbook would not have been possible without his support and efforts.

About our artist: Heather Smith, a native of Columbus, Ohio, spent her childhood and formative years in Florida. After receiving a degree in art form Florida State University, she spent six years in England where she married and began her career as a teacher. Upon her return to the United States, she took further courses in order to specialize in the area of commercial art. In 1982, the family moved to Marietta, Georgia where she started her own business; after much success, she expanded her operation and formed a new partnership, *Creative Solutions, Inc.*

A note about methodology: The recipes in this book have been carefully collected by the cookbook committee. All of the efforts have been made possible by the submission of "favorite" or "special" recipes by friends of the league. Submitters were found among the membership and in the community, locally and on a statewide level. Extensive testing of these recipes was begun in order to test for accuracy and the resulting effect has been the compilation of the very best of these selections. Note that all of these choices were submitted as "tried and true" by the contributors; no one claims complete originality—only that these particular selections are indeed their favorites. We regret that due to space limitations and similarity in recipes, we were unable to use all the recipes submitted.

CONTENTS

Appetizers And Beverages

Antipasta
As featured in Inside Cobb Magazine

2 (6½-ounce) cans white
  albacore tuna, packed in
  water, drained well
1 pound of muenster
  cheese, cubed
1 large red onion, thinly
  sliced and separated
1 medium cauliflower, cut
  into florets
1 pound fresh
  mushrooms, sliced
1 (15-ounce) can of chick
  peas, drained
2 packages snow peas,
  thawed
1 small carton cherry
  tomatoes, halved

1 small jar capers
1 (15-ounce) can sliced
  black olives
1 small can chopped
  green chilies, drained
6 to 8 ounces pepperoni,
  sliced
6 to 8 ounces salami,
  sliced
2 bottles of prepared
  Italian dressing
Lemon juice to taste
Salt and pepper to taste
Lettuce to garnish

Arrange vegetables, meat and tuna in two separate 13 x 9-inch dishes and pour dressing over to cover. Let marinate overnight. To serve: Drain the marinade from the vegetables, meat and tuna. Arrange the lettuce on a large serving platter and place the meat and vegetables around the tuna. Serve with tooth-picks. Serves a very large crowd.

Betty Parrott Barnett

Cocktail Grapes
Surprise your guests

8 ounces cream cheese,
  softened
¼ pound Roquefort
  cheese, softened

1 pound seedless grapes
10 ounces almonds,
  toasted and finely
  chopped

Combine cream cheese and Roquefort cheese in mixing bowl and blend well. Stir dry grapes into cheese mixture, stirring with hands until each is coated. Remove and roll each grape in the chopped, toasted almonds. Refrigerate until ready to serve. These cannot be prepared more than six hours in advance. Do not stack for serving until the last minute.
Yield: 5 dozen

Leckie Kern Stack

Caviar Supreme
For a special treat

3 envelopes unflavored gelatin

¼ cup water

First Layer:
4 boiled eggs, chopped
½ cup mayonnaise
1 large spring onion, chopped
Dash of hot sauce

Salt to taste
White pepper to taste
¼ cup fresh parsley, chopped
1 tablespoon gelatin mixture

Second Layer:
1 medium avocado, diced
1 medium avocado, puréed
2 tablespoons mayonnaise
1 tablespoon lemon juice

Dash cayenne pepper
Fresh ground black pepper to taste
¼ teaspoon salt
1 tablespoon gelatin mixture

Third Layer:
1 (8-ounce) carton sour cream

1 medium onion, chopped
1 tablespoon gelatin mixture

Fourth Layer:
1 (3-ounce) jar of caviar

Fresh lemon juice

Crackers

Dissolve gelatin in water in microwave for 20 seconds. Set aside.

First Layer: Combine all ingredients and place in a spring form pan or a soufflé dish lined with plastic wrap. Let set.

Second Layer: Combine the diced avocado and toss with half of lemon juice. Combine the puréed avocado with remaining lemon juice and mayonnaise. Combine both avocado mixtures with remaining ingredients; layer over first layer. Let set.

Third Layer: Combine all ingredients; layer over second layer. Let set.

Fourth Layer: Just before serving, drain caviar and sprinkle with fresh lemon juice. Run water over caviar; drain. Sprinkle caviar over third layer. Remove from spring form pan and serve with crackers. If using soufflé dish, remove from dish before sprinkling with caviar.

Yield: 15 to 20 servings

Pat Holden Mozley

Easy Spiced Pecans

1 cup sugar	¼ cup hot water
¼ teaspoon cinnamon	½ teaspoon vanilla
⅛ teaspoon cream of	flavoring
tartar	1½ cups pecan halves

Mix sugar, cinnamon, cream of tartar, and hot water together in pot. Heat until boiling. Continue boiling mixture, stirring constantly until mixture forms a softball when a small amount is allowed to drip into a glass of cold water. Add vanilla and nuts and stir until mixture "sugars." Pour out on a flat surface and separate nuts. When cooled, place pecans in a container.
Yield: 2 cups   *Cynthia Crain Wheeler*

Jezebel Sauce

Stores indefinitely in individual small jars in the refrigerator.

1 (16-ounce) jar apple jelly	1 (1½-ounce) can dry
1 (16-ounce) jar pineapple	mustard
preserves	Cream cheese
1 (5-ounce) jar horseradish	Assorted crackers

Mix first four ingredients, cover and refrigerate. Spread over cream cheese and serve with assorted crackers. Also good with meatballs, sliced ham or sausage.
Yield: 3½ cups   *Linda Allen Milligan*

Phyllis' Pickled Shrimp

2 pounds of shrimp,	Dash of Tabasco sauce
cooked and cleaned	1 teaspoon sugar
2 cups sliced onions	1 cup oil
1 (2¼-ounce) bottle of	1 cup vinegar
capers and juice	¾ cup water
4 tablespoons fresh lemon	Bay leaves
juice	2½ teaspoons celery
1½ teaspoons salt	seeds

Layer shrimp, onions, and capers in a jar. Mix all remaining ingredients and pour over the shrimp mixture. Add more salt and lemon juice if needed. Marinate in the refrigerator before serving. Drain and serve in a pretty bowl with toothpicks.
Yield: 12 servings   *Phyllis Royster Rivers*

Mexican Roll-Ups

1 (8-ounce) package cream cheese, softened
1 (4-ounce) can chopped black olives
1 (4-ounce) can chopped green chilies
1 (14-ounce) jar picante sauce
Garlic powder to taste
Flour tortillas

Combine cream cheese, olives, chilies and one teaspoon picante sauce. Spread on flour tortillas and roll up. Refrigerate at least one hour. Slice in ¾-inch slices. Insert toothpick and dip in picante sauce.
Yield: 10 to 12 servings   *Sheryl Neiheiser Turner*

Macadamia Hors D'Oeuvres

1 (8-ounce) package cream cheese
½ cup macadamia nuts, chopped
¼ cup cinnamon sugar (may use less)
Flaked coconut

Soften cream cheese at room temperature and mix with chopped nuts and cinnamon sugar. Chill, then shape into bite-size balls. Roll in coconut.
Yield: 24   *Deborah Grosser Anthony*

Nancy Varella's Cheesies
Mouth watering

1 egg white
1 teaspoon water
¼ cup fresh Parmesan cheese, grated
1½ cups Swiss cheese, grated
½ cup butter or margarine, softened
¾ cup flour
¾ teaspoon salt
⅛ teaspoon ground nutmeg

Preheat oven to 425°. Mix egg white and water, beat lightly, and set aside. Combine Parmesan, Swiss cheese and butter. Add flour, salt and nutmeg. Stir with a fork until stiff dough is formed. Cover and chill at least 15 minutes. Shape dough into ¾ inch balls and place on greased cookie sheet. Flatten with a fork and brush with egg white mixture. Bake at 425° for 10 minutes.
Yield: 3 dozen   *Marsha Brown Thomas*

Poppy Cheese Sticks

These freeze well and are great to have on hand.

1 pound corn oil
   margarine
8 ounces Italian Parmesan
   cheese
2 tablespoons poppy
   seeds

1 teaspoon celery salt
1 teaspoon paprika
1 large loaf thin sliced
   bread

Preheat oven to 325°. Trim bread edges and cut into thirds; set aside. Lightly grease a cookie sheet. Melt margarine completely. Mix cheese, poppy seeds, celery salt, and paprika in shallow dish. Brush strips of bread with melted butter. Roll bread strips in cheese mixture and place on cookie sheet. Bake at 325° for 15 to 20 minutes or until crisp and brown. Cool on paper towel.

Yield: 30 to 34 servings   *Patricia Wilson George*

A Crowd Pleasin' Shrimp Dip

1 (10¾-ounce) can cream
   of shrimp soup
1 (8-ounce) package cream
   cheese
⅓ cup celery, chopped
½ small onion chopped
   finely
1 cup mayonnaise
½ pound shrimp, cooked
   and diced

Season to taste with the
   following:
Dried parsley
Garlic powder
Onion salt
Lemon juice
Salt
Tabasco
Worcestershire sauce
Assorted crackers

Combine soup and cream cheese in double boiler over medium heat. Stir until cheese melts and mixes well with the soup. Add remaining ingredients and season to taste with the spices. Stir well. Place in a bowl and refrigerate for two hours before serving. Serve with assorted crackers.

Yield: 18 to 20 servings   *Bruce Goode Boling*

Almond Broccoli Dip

2 (10-ounce) packages
frozen chopped broccoli
1 cup butter
1 large onion, chopped
2 (10¾-ounce) cans
mushroom soup,
undiluted
2 (6-ounce) rolls garlic
cheese, cubed

Salt and pepper to taste
1 (8-ounce) can mushroom
pieces, drained
1 (2¼-ounce) package
slivered almonds
Corn chips or crackers

Cook broccoli according to directions. Drain well. Sauté onions in butter. Add all ingredients except mushrooms and almonds. Simmer until cheese is melted. Add mushrooms and almonds. Serve in chafing dish with crackers or dip-size corn chips.
Yield: 20 servings   *Cathy Colquitt*

Artichoke-Bacon Dip

1 (14-ounce) can artichoke
hearts, drained well
8 pieces bacon, cooked
and crumbled
1 small onion, chopped

¾ cup mayonnaise
1½ teaspoons lemon juice
1½ teaspoons
Worcestershire sauce
Ritz crackers

Chop artichoke hearts and combine with remaining ingredients and chill. Serve with Ritz crackers.
Yield: 8 servings   *Lindy Suhr Wyche*

Parmesan Crowns
Fit for a king

7 to 8 slices white bread
1 cup mayonnaise

½ cup Parmesan cheese
1 tablespoon onion, grated

Remove crusts from bread and cut each slice into quarters. Bake 2 hours at 225°. Mix next three ingredients. Spread cheese mixture on toast squares being sure to cover edges so they will not burn. Broil until brown and bubbly, watching constantly.
Yield: 8 servings   *Lanier Scott Hoy*

Chili Con Queso

1 large onion, chopped
1 clove garlic, minced
1 tablespoon vegetable oil
1 tablespoon flour
1 tablespoon chili powder
1 (10-ounce) can Rotel
 tomatoes
1 pound Velveeta, cut into
 ½-inch cubes
1 pound bag taco or
 tortilla chips

Sauté onion and garlic in oil in a large heavy pan, until tender but not brown. Stir flour and chili powder into onion mixture; add tomatoes. Cook over low heat stirring constantly until thick and bubbly. Add cheese and cook over low heat, stirring frequently until cheese is melted. Serve warm in a chafing dish with taco or tortilla chips.
Yield: 8 to 12 servings   *Sharon McPherson Gordon*

Crabmeat In Chafing Dish
(Artichokes make the difference)

2 (6½-ounce) cans
 crabmeat, drained
2 (8-ounce) packages
 cream cheese, softened
½ cup sherry
Juice of 3 lemons
Curry powder, salt and
 pepper to taste
1 (14-ounce) can artichoke
 hearts, quartered
Melba rounds

Preheat oven to 300°. Drain crabmeat. Combine all ingredients and heat in 300° oven until bubbly. Serve with melba rounds.
Yield: 12 servings   *Phyllis Royster Rivers*

Hot Chicken Dip
This is also good served over rice as a main course.

1 can chunk chicken
1 can mushroom soup,
 undiluted
1 (4-ounce) can sliced
 mushrooms
1 (8-ounce) package cream
 cheese, softened
1 teaspoon Worcestershire
¼ teaspoon garlic powder

Mix together and serve warm in chafing dish. Serve with assorted crackers of chips.
Yield: 10 to 12 servings   *Cathy Colquitt*

Cucumber Dip
Refreshing

1 (8-ounce) package cream cheese, softened
1 (.4-ounce) package Original Hidden Valley Ranch mix
2 tablespoons mayonnaise
1 teaspoon lemon juice
½ cup pecans, chopped
1 cucumber, peeled and chopped
Raw vegetables for dipping

Combine all ingredients and mix well. Refrigerate for several hours. Serve with raw vegetables.
Yield: 2 cups   *Judy Thomas Ballard*

Curry Chutney Dip

3 (8-ounce) packages cream cheese, softened
½ box crystallized ginger, chopped
3 tablespoons Madras curry
1 tablespoon garlic powder
1 (20-ounce) can crushed pineapple, drained
1 (8-ounce) jar Bengal hot chutney
1 (8-ounce) jar Mango chutney
1 (6-ounce) can cashews
1 (8-ounce) carton sour cream
King size corn chips

Whip cream cheese with a fork until smooth. Add spices, pineapple and chutneys. Mix well. Add nuts and sour cream at the last. Serve with corn chips.
Yield: 12 to 14 servings   *Ansley Hurst Pascoli*

Everyone's Favorite Crab Dip

1 (8-ounce) package cream cheese, softened
2 tablespoons milk
1 tablespoon horseradish
½ pound fresh crabmeat
2 tablespoons green onions, minced
Salt and pepper to taste
⅓ cup sliced almonds, toasted

Preheat oven to 350°. Mix all ingredients except almonds. Pour into a baking dish and top with almonds. Bake at 350° for 20 minutes. Serve with assorted crackers.
Yield: 8 servings   *Lanier Scott Hoy*

Taco Dip
This is great for a patio party or picnic.

1 (15-ounce) can jalapeno bean dip
¼ cup sour cream
¼ cup mayonnaise
1 package taco seasoning mix
1 medium avocado, mashed
1 tablespoon lemon juice
1 cup Cheddar cheese, shredded
1 cup tomatoes, diced
½ cup ripe olives, chopped
¼ head lettuce, shredded
Tortilla chips

Spread bean dip evenly on the bottom of a 9-inch glass pie plate. Combine sour cream, mayonnaise and taco seasoning. Spread over bean dip. Mix avocado and lemon juice and spread over sour cream mixture. Layer remaining ingredients in order listed. Serve with nacho or tortilla chips.

Yield: 20 to 24 servings   *Margaret Seawell Barfield*

Artichoke Delights
Indeed they are

2 (6-ounce) jars of marinated artichoke hearts, drained and quartered
1 small onion, chopped
1 clove garlic, mashed
2 tablespoons butter
4 eggs, beaten
2 tablespoons parsley
¼ cup bread crumbs
¼ pound sharp Cheddar cheese, grated
½ loaf hot pepper cheese, grated
¼ teaspoon salt
¼ teaspoon pepper
⅛ teaspoon ground oregano
Dash of Tabasco

Preheat oven to 325°. Sauté artichoke hearts, onion, and garlic in butter. Remove from heat. Beat eggs in separate bowl. Add bread crumbs, grated cheeses and spices. Combine egg mixture with artichoke mixture. Pour into greased 9 x 12-inch glass baking dish. Bake at 325° for 30 minutes. Cool and cut into 1-inch squares.

Yield: 10 to 12 servings   *Patricia Moore Caltabiano*

Tipsy Fruit Dip

4 ounces butter or
margarine
1 (14-ounce) can
sweetened condensed
milk
1 cup dark brown sugar

2 tablespoons coconut
cream
½ teaspoon rum extract
½ cup dark rum
Assorted fresh fruits

Heat butter, condensed milk and brown sugar stirring constantly until melted. Remove from heat and let cool. Once cooled, add the remaining ingredients and serve with fresh fruit.

Yield: 4 cups   *Louise Hetherwick Hunter*

Blue Cheese Stuffed Mushrooms
A tangy taste

24 large fresh mushrooms
2 (3-ounce) packages
cream cheese, softened
¼ package dry blue
cheese salad dressing
mix

¼ cup walnuts, finely
chopped
Paprika

Preheat oven to 425°. Remove stems from mushrooms. Chop enough stems to make one half cup. Blend cream cheese and dry dressing mix. Stir in nuts and chopped stems. Spoon into mushrooms caps. Place stuffed caps in shallow baking pan. Sprinkle with paprika. Bake uncovered in 425° oven for 6 to 8 minutes.

Yield: 6 servings   *Roddy Thomas Hiser*

Bacon Cheddar Mushrooms

1½ pounds fresh
mushrooms
¾ cup mayonnaise
10 slices bacon, cooked
and crumbled

1 medium onion, chopped
finely
1½ cups sharp Cheddar
cheese, grated
Seasoned salt

Preheat oven to 325°. Wash mushrooms and remove stems. Chop stems and mix with mayonnaise, bacon, onion, Cheddar cheese and seasoned salt to taste. Generously stuff mushrooms and bake at 325° for 15 to 20 minutes. Serve hot.

Yield: 8 to 10 servings.   *Nancy Finke Rambasek*

Bacon Wrapped Shrimp

For those who like to cook "elegant" but fast!

32 large shrimp,
  uncooked, shelled and
  deveined

1 (8-ounce) bottle French
  dressing
16 pieces of bacon

Marinate shrimp in French dressing over night. Drain. Wrap each shrimp in half a slice of bacon and secure with wooden toothpick. Place on a rack over shallow pan and bake at 375° for 15 to 20 minutes or until bacon is crisp.
Yield: 8 servings   *Thalia V. Eden*

Buffalo Style Chicken Wings

Hot and crispy

6 pounds chicken wings
4 tablespoons melted
  butter

½ bottle hot sauce
Dash of garlic salt

Clip off chicken wing tip at first joint. Wash and pat dry. Cook chicken wings over medium heat on gas or charcoal grill for 25 minutes or until done. Mix butter, hot sauce and garlic salt in a bowl. Place ¼ of the cooked wings in the bowl, cover and shake. Place wings on a tin foil covered cookie sheet and let hot sauce mixture dry. Repeat using the rest of the chicken wings. When ready to eat, bake at 400° for 15 minutes.
Yield: 4 servings   *Nancy Jane Smith*

Crab Canapé Pie

1 pound backfin or lump
  crabmeat, picked
1 tablespoon horseradish
½ bottle capers, drained
1 teaspoon grated lemon
  rind
½ teaspoon Accent

1 dash Tabasco or hot
  pepper sauce
2 cups mayonnaise
¾ cup sharp cheese,
  grated
Melba toast

Preheat oven to 350°. Mix all ingredients except cheese and pour into 10-inch pie pan. Place grated cheese on top. Bake 350° for 20 to 25 minutes. Serve with melba toast.
Yield: 8 servings   *Mariam Thomas Richardson*

Crab Stuffed Mushrooms

20 to 24 large fresh
mushrooms (about 1
pound)
1 cup Italian salad
dressing
¾ cup soft bread crumbs,
divided
1 (6½-ounce) can
crabmeat, drained,
picked and flaked

2 eggs, beaten
¼ cup mayonnaise
¼ cup onion, minced
1 teaspoon lemon juice
Salt to taste

Preheat oven to 375°. Clean mushrooms. Remove stems. marinate mushrooms in salad dressing 1 to 2 hours. Drain well. Combine ½ cup bread crumbs and remaining ingredients. Mix well. Spoon mixture into mushroom caps and sprinkle with remaining bread crumbs. Place in an 8-inch square baking dish. Bake at 375° for 15 minutes.
Yield: 8 to 10 servings   *Ginger Colquitt Autry*

Pizza Dip
Outstanding

1 (8-ounce) package cream
cheese, softened
1 (14-ounce) jar pizza
sauce
⅓ cup onions, chopped
1½ cups mozzarella
cheese, grated

1 (6-ounce) can ripe
olives, drained and
chopped
2 ounces sliced pepperoni,
chopped
Light corn chips

Preheat oven to 350°. Press cream cheese in bottom of 9-inch glass pie pan. Spread pizza sauce over cream cheese and layer remaining ingredients in order listed. Bake at 350° for 25 minutes. Serve with light corn chips.
Yield: 8 to 10 servings   *Linda Allen Milligan*

Mock Boursin Cheese

8 ounces whipped butter
2 (8-ounce) packages
  cream cheese
2 cloves garlic, minced
½ teaspoon oregano
¼ teaspoon basil
¼ teaspoon dill weed
¼ teaspoon marjoram
¼ teaspoon black pepper
¼ teaspoon thyme
Assorted crackers

Place the butter and cream cheese in large bowl of mixer or food processor. Beat at high speed until the mixture is smooth and fluffy. Add the remaining ingredients and continue beating until well combined. Pack mixture in container and refrigerate at least 12 hours before serving. Serve cold with crackers (a stoned wheat type is especially good). Stored airtight, it will keep for a month. Do not freeze.

Yield: 3 cups   *Patricia Pope Chilton*

Hot Cheese And Asparagus Puffs
May be frozen

1 (3-ounce) package blue
  cheese, softened
1 (8-ounce) package cream
  cheese, softened
1 egg
1 large loaf thin sliced
  white bread
1 (16-ounce) can
  asparagus spears
1 pound of butter or
  margarine, melted

Mix blue cheese, cream cheese and egg. Remove crust from bread and roll the bread flat. Spread each slice with the cheese mixture. Put one asparagus spear on each slice. Roll and rest on the seam. Cut into bite size pieces. Roll pieces in melted butter. Place on cookie sheet with sides so butter will not drip over sides. Bake at 400° 10 to 15 minutes. These may be frozen, then baked for 20 minutes.

Yield: 18 to 20 servings   *Pam Duncan Balsley*

Mushrooms Florentine

½ pound fresh spinach or
1 (10-ounce) package
  frozen chopped spinach
1 tablespoon butter
Juice of ½ lemon
18 large mushrooms
¼ cup onions, chopped
  finely
¾ cup butter, divided
¼ cup fine bread crumbs
Dash of garlic salt and
  pepper
¾ teaspoon salt
½ cup Parmesan cheese

Cook spinach until barely wilted. Drain. Add 1 tablespoon butter and lemon juice. Chop well. Wash mushrooms. Remove stems and chop. Sauté chopped mushrooms stems and onions in ¼ cup butter. Melt ½ cup butter and dip the mushroom caps in the melted butter. Combine spinach, onion and mushroom mixture, bread crumbs and spices. Mix well. Stuff mushroom caps with spinach mixture. Sprinkle with cheese. Bake at 350° for 20 to 25 minutes.
Yield: 6 servings   *Julia Branham Stokes*

Mushroom Logs
May be made ahead.

2 (8-ounce) cans crescent
  dinner rolls
1 (8-ounce) package cream
  cheese, softened
1 (4-ounce) can mushroom
  pieces, drained and
  chopped
1 teaspoon seasoned salt
1 bunch scallions,
  chopped
1 tablespoon
  Worcestershire sauce
1 teaspoon lemon pepper
1 egg, beaten
2 tablespoons poppy
  seeds

Separate crescent dough into eight rectangles. Press perforations to seal. Combine cream cheese, mushrooms, salt, scallions, Worcestershire and lemon pepper. Spread mushroom mixture in equal portions over each rectangle of dough. Starting at long side, roll up each rectangle jelly-roll fashion. Pinch seams to seal. Slice logs into one-inch pieces. Place seam-side down on ungreased baking sheet. Brush each log with beaten egg and sprinkle with poppy seeds. Bake at 375° for 10 to 12 minutes.
Yield: 4 dozen   *Meredith Webb Dykes*

Mushroom Tarts

Tart Shells:
3 loaves thin sliced
  sandwich bread

Filling:

1 pound fresh
  mushrooms, chopped
  finely
3 tablespoons scallions,
  chopped finely
½ stick butter or
  margarine
1½ tablespoons flour
1 cup heavy cream

½ teaspoon salt
Juice of ½ lemon
1½ tablespoons parsley,
  chopped
1 tablespoon chives,
  chopped
¼ teaspoon cayenne
Parmesan cheese

Tart Shells: Butter or spray miniature or regular size muffin tins. Using a glass as a cutter cut circle of bread 2½-inches for small tarts 4-inches for large tarts. Press bread into muffin tins and bake 375° for 10 minutes. Shells can be frozen and thawed before use.

Filling: Preheat oven to 375°. Sauté mushrooms and scallions in butter 20 minutes until most water is cooked from mushrooms. Add flour sprinkling to thicken. Slowly add cream, stirring until it comes to a low boil. Remove from heat and add remaining ingredients, except Parmesan cheese. Place tarts on cookie sheet, fill to top with mushroom filling and sprinkle with Parmesan cheese. Bake at 375° for 10 minutes.

Yield: 25 large or 60 small tarts   *Dell Cochran James*

Ripe Olive Snack

2 cups Cheddar cheese,
  grated
2 tablespoons onions,
  ground

1 (4-ounce) can ripe
  olives, chopped
1 cup mayonnaise
1 loaf party rye

Combine cheese, onion, olives, and mayonnaise. Spread on party rye. Bake at 300° for 18 minutes.

Yield: 6 to 8 servings   *Judy Gorrell Harper*

Pizza Hors D'Oeuvres

1 pound sausage
1 medium onion, diced
Oregano to taste
1 (8-ounce) can tomato
  sauce

1 loaf party Rye bread
2 (8-ounce) packages
  mozzarella cheese slices
Parmesan cheese

Combine sausage and onion in a skillet; sprinkle with oregano. Cook well and drain. Add tomato sauce. Place Rye bread under broiler until crisp. Turn to unbrowned side and top with mozzarella slices. Top with sausage mixture and sprinkle with Parmesan cheese. Bake at 375° until hot and bubbly. These may be frozen and reheated at 400° for 20 minutes.
Yield: 10 to 12 servings   *Cathy Colquitt*

Saucy Sausage Balls
An easy "do ahead"

1 pound hot sausage
1 pound medium sausage
½ cup ketchup
½ cup wine vinegar

1 tablespoon soy sauce
½ teaspoon ginger
½ cup brown sugar

Open both packages of sausage and mix together either by hand or in food processor, being careful not to purée. Form into bite-size balls and place on broiler tray. Bake at 375° for 20 to 30 minutes. Drain and place in airtight container. Heat remaining ingredients to boiling point, stirring frequently. Remove from heat. Pour sauce over sausage balls and refrigerate overnight. When ready to serve, heat and serve in chafing dish.
Yield: 6 dozen   *Stephanie Threlkeld Gill*

Shrimp Wheels

1 (4½-ounce) can shrimp,
drained and mashed
¼ cup mayonnaise
2 tablespoons stuffed
green olives, diced

1 tablespoon celery,
chopped finely
1 (8-count) package
crescent rolls

Preheat oven to 375°. Combine first four ingredients. Unroll crescents to form four rectangles, pinching together at the seams. Spread one fourth of mixture on each rectangle and roll up jelly roll style. Refrigerate 30 minutes. Slice each rectangle into 10 to 12 pieces. Bake on ungreased cookie sheet at 375° for 12 minutes.
Yield: 6 servings   *Subie Schuessler Espy*

Spiced Meatballs
Perfect cocktail fare for a hungry crowd

1 pound ground chuck
½ pound ground pork
¾ cup bread crumbs
2 tablespoons onion,
chopped finely
1 tablespoon ketchup
4 drops of hot sauce
½ teaspoon prepared
horseradish
2 eggs, well beaten
½ teaspoon salt
¼ teaspoon pepper
1 tablespoon Parmesan
cheese
2 to 3 tablespoons butter
or margarine

½ cup ketchup
½ cup chili sauce
¼ cup cider vinegar
½ cup brown sugar, firmly
packed
2 tablespoons onion,
chopped, finely
1 tablespoon
Worcestershire sauce
4 drops of hot sauce
½ teaspoon dry mustard
3 drops Angostura Bitters
1 teaspoon salt
¼ teaspoon pepper
Chopped green onion,
optional

Combine first 11 ingredients in a large mixing bowl. Mix well and shape into 1-inch balls. Sauté in butter until browned. Drain well and set aside. Combine remaining ingredients, except green onion, in a large saucepan. Bring to a boil. Reduce heat and simmer 5 minutes. Add meatballs and simmer another 10 minutes. Transfer to a chafing dish and serve warm. Garnish with green onion if desired. *This recipe can easily be doubled or tripled.*
Yield: 4 dozen   *Laura Powell Whitlock*

Spinach Cheese Squares

4 tablespoons butter
3 eggs
1 cup plain flour
1 cup milk
1 teaspoon salt
1 teaspoon baking powder

1 pound Monterey Jack cheese, grated
2 (10-ounce) packages chopped spinach, thawed and drained

Preheat oven to 350°. Melt butter in 9 x 13 x 2-inch glass baking dish. In large bowl, beat eggs. Add flour, milk, salt, and baking powder. Mix well. Add cheese and spinach. Pour into buttered baking dish. Bake at 350° for 35 to 40 minutes. Cool one hour to set. Cut into bite-size pieces.
Yield: 60 squares   *Betsy Lee McNair Holladay*

Swiss Bacon Pleasers
Also good for a breakfast dish

1 (8-ounce) can crescent rolls
3 slices Swiss cheese
3 eggs, slightly beaten
¾ cup milk
1 tablespoon minced onion

6 slices bacon, fried and crumbled
1 tablespoon parsley flakes

Separate dough into four rectangles. Place in the bottom of an ungreased 9 x 13 x 2-inch glass baking dish. Press over bottom and 1 inch up the sides of the dish. Place cheese slices over dough. In a small bowl, combine eggs, milk and onion. Pour over cheese slices. Sprinkle with bacon and parsley flakes. Bake at 425° for 20 minutes until crust is golden. Cool before cutting into squares.
Yield: 24 squares   *Patricia Wilson George*

Tipsy Chicken Wings

Pack for a picnic, a concert in the park or a ballgame.

**36 chicken wings or
drumettes
1 cup soy sauce**

**½ cup Vodka
1 tablespoon garlic salt**

Combine soy sauce, Vodka and garlic salt. Pour over chicken pieces and marinate for four hours or overnight. Bake on a large cookie sheet at 350° for 40 minutes, turning occasionally and baste with soy sauce marinade. *These can be made ahead and frozen.*

Yield: 6 servings   *Betty Parrott Barnett*

Zucchini Zips

**4 cups zucchini, thinly
sliced
1 cup onion, chopped
½ cup butter
2 tablespoons, parsley,
chopped
½ teaspoon salt
½ teaspoon black pepper
¼ teaspoon sweet basil**

**¼ teaspoon garlic powder
¼ teaspoon oregano
2 eggs, well beaten
8 ounces mozzarella
cheese, grated
2 teaspoons Dijon mustard
1½ (8-ounce size cans)
refrigerated crescent
rolls**

In a large skillet, cook zucchini and onion in butter until tender. Stir in parsley and seasonings. In a large bowl, blend eggs and cheese. Stir into vegetable mixture. Preheat oven to 375°. Separate dough into sections and press over the bottom and up the sides of an ungreased 9 x 13-inch glass pan. Spread this "crust" with mustard. Pour vegetable mixture evenly over the dough. Bake at 375° for 20 to 23 minutes. Let sit in dish for 10 to 15 minutes before cutting into bite size squares.

Yield: 8 to 10 servings   *Laura Phillips Lewis*

Salmon Ball

1 (1-pound) can red salmon
1 (8-ounce) package cream cheese
2 tablespoons freshly squeezed lemon juice
3 teaspoons grated onion
2 teaspoons horseradish
½ teaspoon salt
Dash of Worcestershire sauce
Several dashes cayenne pepper
¼ teaspoon liquid smoke
½ cup pecans, chopped
3 tablespoons fresh parsley, minced

Drain salmon, remove skin and bones; flake with a fork. In small bowl of electric mixer, cream cheese and blend in lemon juice, onion, horseradish, salt, Worcestershire sauce, cayenne pepper, and liquid smoke. When well blended, stir in the flaked salmon. Check seasonings; it may require a little more salt. Combine pecans and parsley; spread on wax paper. Turn salmon out onto this mixture; roll salmon in the mixture until well coated on all sides. Wrap in wax paper and chill thoroughly before serving. This is not a sliceable dish, but will spread nicely after chilling.

Yield: 10 servings
Dona Owenby Harbin

Marinated Skewered Beef

2 pounds flank steak
5 tablespoons brown sugar
1 teaspoon fresh ginger, minced
½ cup soy sauce
3 cloves garlic, minced
1 tablespoon oil
Mushrooms, (optional)
Green pepper, (optional)

Slice the meat into very thin strips. Combine next five ingredients and marinate the mixture for 4 to 5 hours or overnight. Soak wooden skewers in water for about 20 minutes to prevent burning while cooking. Arrange beef on skewers and broil for 2 to 4 minutes. Mushrooms and green peppers can be used as an optional garnish.

Yield: 12 to 16 servings
Thalia V. Eden

Shrimply Divine

1 (4¼-ounce) can shrimp,
reserve liquid
1 (8-ounce) package cream
cheese, softened
2 to 3 tablespoons
mayonnaise
¼ cup onion flakes
¼ cup celery, diced
1 teaspoon lemon juice
Dash of Tabasco
Salt and pepper to taste
Crackers or assorted fresh
vegetables

Drain Shrimp. Mash with fork. Combine remaining ingredients including liquid from shrimp. Form into desired shape and chill. Spread on crackers or serve as a dip for fresh vegetables. This is better if prepared a day ahead.
Yield: 8 servings   *Kathy Chiles Pilcher*

Smoked Salmon Pâté
Savor this show piece!

12 ounces cream cheese,
room temperature
4 ounces butter, room
temperature
2 tablespoons sour cream
4 ounces smoked salmon
2 teaspoons minced onion
2 teaspoons horseradish

Topping:
1 to 2 tablespoons caviar
2 eggs, boiled and
chopped finely
1 tablespoon parsley,
chopped
Crackers

Blend first 6 ingredients together with mixer. Shape into a mound on a serving plate. Chill. When ready to serve, sprinkle with caviar. Mix parsley and chopped eggs together and place in a circle around the mold. Serve with crackers.
Yield: 6 to 8 servings   *Judy Thomas Ballard*

Ranch Cheese Spread
A snap to make!

1 (8-ounce) package cream
cheese, softened
1 (.4-ounce) package
Ranch dressing mix
½ cup pecans, chopped
Assorted crackers

Mix all ingredients and shape into a ball. Serve with assorted crackers.
Yield: 6 to 8 servings   *Glynda Sanders Chalfant*

Sombrero Spread

½ pound ground beef
¼ cup onions, chopped
¼ cup ketchup
1½ teaspoons chili
  powder
½ teaspoon salt
1 (8-ounce) can kidney
  beans

½ cup sharp Cheddar
  cheese, grated
¼ cup green olives,
  chopped
¼ cup onions, chopped
Tostados or large corn
  chips

Brown meat and onions. Stir in ketchup, chili powder and salt. Mash in beans with the liquid from the can. Heat well. Serve in a chafing dish. Garnish with cheese, olives and onions. Serve with tostados or large corn chips.
Yield: 4 to 6 servings   *Cathy Colquitt*

Three-Cheese Cheese Ball

½ pound Roquefort or
  Blue cheese, softened
2 (5-ounce) jars sharp
  cheese spread, softened
4 (3-ounce) packages
  cream cheese, softened
2 tablespoons onion,
  grated
1 teaspoon Worcestershire
  sauce

1 cup pecans or walnuts,
  chopped finely
½ cup fresh parsley,
  chopped finely
¼ to ½ cup sherry
  (optional)
Black or green olives
  (optional)

Blend softened cheeses, onion and Worcestershire sauce until smooth. Stir in one-half of the nuts and parsley. Divide in half and pack into 2 small foil-lined bowls. Cover and chill. One hour before serving, roll cheese ball in remaining mixture of nuts and parsley. Serve on platter ringed with crackers. Decorate with olives, if desired. May be frozen for later use.
Yield: 2 cheese balls   *Rebecca Edenfield Lingerfelt*

Tuna Mold
Unique way to serve tuna

2 (6½-ounce) cans tuna,
  drained
2 boiled eggs, chopped
½ cup green olives,
  chopped
2 tablespoons capers

1 tablespoon onion,
  minced
1 package unflavored
  gelatin
¼ cup cold water
2 cups mayonnaise

Combine tuna eggs, olives, capers, and onion. Dissolve gelatin in water. (It may need to be heated in order to dissolve the gelatin.) Add dissolved gelatin to mayonnaise, stirring constantly. Combine the two mixtures and put into a 5-cup mold. Chill at least 6 hours. Unmold and serve with crackers.
Yield: 5 cups   *Elia Ellis Thomas*

Vegetable Mold
"A wonderful sandwich spread too"

3 large tomatoes, chopped
  finely
1 large cucumber,
  chopped
1 large green pepper,
  chopped

½ onion, chopped
1 pint mayonnaise
1 tablespoon cold water
¼ cup boiling water
1 package Knox
  unflavored gelatin

Mix vegetables and mayonnaise. Add 1 tablespoon cold water to the gelatin and stir. Then add ¼ cup boiling water to the gelatin and stir to dissolve. Add gelatin to the vegetable mixture and mix well. Pour into a 2-quart mold and chill until set. Serve with butter flavored crackers.
Yield: 10 to 12 servings   *Lynn Stiles Foster*

Velvet Hammer
May be doubled or tripled easily.

1 pint vanilla ice cream
1 ounce Cointreau
1½ ounces brandy

1 ounce white Crème de
  Cacao

Combine all ingredients in blender and blend well.
Yield: 2 servings   *Karen Brown*

Back Porch Lemonade

1 cup granulated sugar
1 cup water
8 cups cold water
1⅓ cups fresh lemon juice

1 tablespoon lemon zest,
    grated fine
Lemon slices and fresh
    mint leaves for garnish

Combine sugar and one cup water in small saucepan over medium heat and bring to a boil. Reduce heat and simmer five to six minutes, stirring occasionally. Remove from heat and cool completely. Combine rest of ingredients and stir well. Serve over ice and garnish.
Yield: 2½ quarts.   *Michelle Wallace Wyant*

Bloody Mary Mix
A real morning pick me up!

2 (46-ounce) cans cocktail
    tomato juice
6 ounces lemon juice
½ cup Worcestershire
    sauce
20 shakes Accent
    seasoning

20 shakes lemon pepper
20 shakes seasoned salt
20 drops Tabasco
Vodka (optional)

Combine all ingredients in a large container and mix well. This will keep in the refrigerator for several weeks. Add vodka to the individual glasses prior to serving.
Yield: Approximately ½ gallon   *Mary Mayes Suhr*

Brandy Alexander
Sinful

2½ cups ice
3 ounces Brandy
3 ounces dark Cremè de
    Cacao

8 ounces milk
1 cup ice cream
Nutmeg

Fill blender with ice; add remaining ingredients except nutmeg. Blend until smooth. Pour into four glasses and sprinkle with nutmeg.
Yield: 4 servings   *Robert Alexander Hunter*

Cocktail Punch
Strong, but good!

1 quart Southern Comfort
1 cup lemon juice
1 (6-ounce) can frozen
   lemonade, undiluted
1 (6-ounce) can frozen
   orange juice, undiluted
3 (28-ounce) bottles 7-Up

Mix all ingredients together, adding the 7-Up last. May add food coloring, if desired. Serve from punch bowl, cooling it with an ice ring. Freeze lemon, lime or orange slices in ice ring.
Yield: 3 quarts   *Carol Armbrust Fey*

Coffee Punch
Easy for large groups

1 gallon water
½ cup plus 3 tablespoons
   instant coffee
1 cup sugar
1 quart milk
1 tablespoon vanilla
   extract
½ gallon vanilla ice cream

To make coffee, bring water to boil, add instant coffee and stir until dissolved. Add sugar to hot coffee and stir until dissolved. Cool. Add milk and vanilla extract. Refrigerate. (This may be done 1 to 2 days in advance.) Spoon ice cream into a punch bowl and add coffee mixture. Stir gently to mix.
Yield: 25 servings   *Patricia Pope Chilton*

Cranberry Tea
No caffeine and loaded with vitamin C.

1 bag cranberries
2 quarts water
2 cups water
2 cups sugar
3 cinnamon sticks
2 cups orange juice
4 tablespoons lemon juice

Boil cranberries in 2 quarts water until cranberries burst. Strain and discard berries. Add remaining ingredients and simmer 20 minutes. *This can be kept for several weeks in refrigerator and reheated or served over ice. This makes a very colorful and nutritious Christmas drink.*
Yield 20 to 24 serivngs   *Lanier Scott Hoy*

Holladay Shrub
(Shrub is an old fashioned name for punch)

1 (750-milliliter) bottle
  white port wine
1 (12-ounce) can frozen
  limeade concentrate
Juice of 1 lemon

12 ounces water
2 tablespoons sugar,
  optional
8 strawberries (optional)
8 mint sprigs (optional)

Mix the first five ingredients together. Freeze over night in plastic pitcher. Place in refrigerator 15 minutes before serving and stir with spoon to make drink slushy. Pour in old fashion glasses or large wine glasses. Garnish with strawberries and mint sprigs for special touch.
Yield: 8 (4-ounce) servings   *Betsy Lee McNair Holladay*

Hot Cranberry Punch

9 cups cranberry juice
9 cups pineapple juice,
  unsweetened
4½ cups water
4 tablespoons whole
  cloves

4 sticks cinnamon
1 cup brown sugar
¼ teaspoon salt

Pour first four ingredients into the bottom of a percolator. Place cloves, cinnamon, sugar and salt in percolator tray. Perk until percolator stops perking. Serve hot.
Yield: 30 cups
                                  Cheryl Tilley Briscoe

Hot Spiced Wine
Drink by the fire

2 cups cranberry juice
½ cup sugar
6 strips lemon peel, 2
  inches by ¼ inch
1 cinnamon stick

10 whole cloves
1 (4/5 quart) burgundy
  wine
Nutmeg, optional

Simmer first 5 ingredients in a large pot over low heat for 10 minutes. Strain. Return liquid to pot and add wine. Heat just until warm. Serve in punch glasses with a dash of nutmeg, if desired.
Yield: 10 to 12 servings   *Susan Smith Phillips*

Iced Tea Punch

1 quart hot water
4 level tablespoons tea
2 cups sugar
4 lemons, juice and rind
3 quarts cold water

2 (6-ounce) cans
sweetened pineapple
juice (may adjust
pineapple juice to your
taste)

To 1 quart boling water add tea. Let steep 5 to 8 minutes. Strain. Add sugar while hot. Add juice and rind of lemons and let this stand for several hours. Strain. Add 3 quarts of cold water. Just before serivng, add pineapple juice. Do not make tea in aluminum container. Garnish with pineapple, sage or mint.
Yield: 1 gallon   *Pamela Croy Newton*

Mock Champagne
A New Non-Alcoholic Punch

½ cup sugar
1½ cups water
2 cups cranberry juice

1 cup pineapple juice
2 (10-ounce) bottles
lemon-lime soda

Boil sugar and water until sugar is dissolved. Cool. Add juices. Chill until slushy. Before serving add soda.
Yield: 6 servings   *Cathy Godwin Menendez*

Mormon Punch
*This is an excellent punch for brunch
garnished with fresh mint.*

2 (6-ounce) cans frozen
orange juice concentrate,
thawed
1 (6-ounce) can frozen
lemonade concentrate,
thawed
1 cup sugar

6 ounces water
1 teaspoon vanilla extract
1 teaspoon almond extract
1 to 3 ounces Amaretto
liqueur (optional)
Mint for garnish

In a gallon container combine orange juice and lemonade. Mix sugar with 6 ounces of water and add to juices. Add vanilla and almond extracts. Fill container with water to equal one full gallon. Shake well and serve chilled garnished with mint. Amaretto is optional but quite tasty.
Yield: 15 servings   *Karla Ward Self*

Orange Smoothie

1 (6-ounce) can frozen
  orange juice, undiluted
1 cup milk
1 cup water
½ cup sugar
1 teaspoon vanilla
10 to 12 ice cubes

Combine all ingredients in blender. Cover and blend until smooth. Serve immediately.

Yield: 6 cups   *Beverly Perkins Jones*

Pat's Frozen Margaritas
Deadly!

1 (6-ounce) can frozen
  limeade concentrate
6 ounces tequilla
2 ounces triple sec
4 ounces water
Ice

Place all ingredients in blender and blend until smooth. Pour into glasses that have been chilled and rimmed with salt.

Yield: 4 to 6 servings   *Patsy John Marino*

Peach Fuzz Buzz

2 large or 4 small peaches,
  peeled and sliced
1 (6-ounce) can lemonade
  concentrate
4 ounces Vodka
1 ounce grenadine

Place all ingredients in blender and mix. Add ice and blend to desired consistency. Serve in wine glasses.

Yield: 4 servings   *Kathy Chiles Pilcher*

Southern Mint Tea
A Tara favorite

2 quarts boiling water
10 individual-size tea bags
1½ to 2 cups sugar
Juice and rind of 1½ to 2
  lemons
Fresh mint sprigs

Combine water, tea bags, sugar, juice and rind of lemons and 12 mint sprigs. Cover and steep 45 minutes to one hour. Strain and cool. Serve over ice. Garnish each glass with a sprig of mint.

Yield: 2 quarts   *Becky Worthington Dorsett*

Spiced Tea
Serve from crock pot.

6 individual tea bags
2 teaspoons whole cloves
2 sticks cinnamon
4 quarts boiling water
2 cups sugar
2 cups pineapple juice, unsweetened

1 (6-ounce) can orange juice concentrate, thawed
¾ cup lemon juice
Dark rum (optional)

Pour boiling water over tea bags, cloves, and cinnamon. Steep 10 to 15 minutes. Remove tea bags and add remaining ingredients. Heat and serve. Stores well or may be frozen. Spike with dark rum, if desired.

Yield: 5 quarts

Carol Armbrust Fey

Sangria
Perfect with Sombrero Spread.

1 (12-ounce) can frozen grape juice concentrate
1 (6-ounce) can frozen lemonade concentrate

1 quart Burgundy wine
Sprite
Sliced oranges for garnish
Sliced lemons for garnish

Mix grape juice and lemonade according to directions on can. Add Burgundy. Put one part Sprite to three parts Burgundy mixture in each glass. Garnish with orange and lemon slices.

Yield: 20 to 24 servings

Louise Hetherwick Hunter

Frozen Lime Slush
Great on a hot summer day

2 cups cracked ice
1 (6-ounce) can frozen limeade
¼ cup lemon juice
1¼ cups vodka

1 (10-ounce) bottle club soda, chilled
Strawberries or mint for garnish

Combine first three ingredients in blender and mix until slushy. Add vodka and blend well. Add soda and mix gently. Serve in wine glasses and garnish with strawberries or mint.

Yield: 4 servings

Louise Hetherwick Hunter

Wassail
Christmas Merriment

6 stick cinnamon
16 whole cloves
1 teaspoon ground
  allspice
¼ cup sugar
2 cups cranapple juice

6 cups apple juice (frozen
  concentrate, diluted is
  best)
1 teaspoon bitters
¼ cup rum (optional)

Combine spices in a cloth bag. Combine sugar, juices and bitters in a large sauce pan. Simmer spices in juices for 10 minutes, then remove spice bag. Add rum before serving. Serve hot.

In a large electric percolator: Place spices in basket. Place juices, sugar, and bitters in pot. Percolate until done. Add rum to liquid.

To multiply: Use same amount of spices and only multiply sugar, juices and bitters times 4 for a 30 cup percolator.
Yield: 8 servings   *Dianne Davison Isakson*

White Cargo
A rich after dinner drink

½ ounce brandy
½ ounce Galliano
½ ounce Triple Sec

½ ounce Cointreau
4 heaping spoons vanilla
  ice cream

Mix all ingredients in a blender and serve immediately.
Yield: 2 servings   *Bonnie Wooten Wagoner*

Fruit Punch

1 quart sweetened tea
1 pint grape juice
1 pint orange juice

1 pint pineapple juice,
  unsweetened

Combine all ingredients. Chill and serve over ice. Lemonade, cranberry, apple, or other juices may be substituted.
Yield: 8 to 10 servings   *Connie Heidt Kirk*

Soups And Salads

Apricot Wine Soup
Fancy

2 (16-ounce) cans apricots
  with peel and juice
1 cup sour cream
¾ to 1 cup white wine
¼ cup apricot liquer
2 tablespoons lemon juice
2 teaspoons vanilla extract
¼ teaspoon cinnamon
Extra sour cream and
  cinnamon for garnish

Mix all ingredients in blender or food processor. Chill until very cold. Serve garnished with a dollop of sour cream sprinkled with cinnamon.

Yield: 4 servings   *Leckie Kern Stack*

Asparagus Soup

1 large onion, chopped
½ stick margarine
1 pound potatoes, pared
  and sliced
2 (13¾-ounce) cans
  chicken broth
2 pounds fresh asparagus
  (can use frozen)
1 cup half and half
Salt and pepper to taste

Sauté onions in margarine for two minutes; stir in broth and potatoes. Bring to a boil. Cover and simmer for 20 minutes until potatoes are cooked. Cut asparagus into one inch pieces and add to soup. Cook until tender, about 5 minutes. Add cream and blend the soup in the blender or food processor. Season to taste. Serve hot or cold.

Yield: 6 to 8 servings   *Carol Armbrust Fey*

Aunt Joyce's Cabbage Chowder

2 tablespoons butter
1 pound Polish sausage
2 cups carrots, sliced
4 teaspoons caraway
  seeds
2 cans celery soup
1 can milk
1 can water
3 cups cabbage, shredded
  in long shreds

Cut Polish sausage in thin slices. Brown sausage, carrots and caraway seeds in butter until tender. Mix the soup, milk and water together and add the sausage mix and the cabbage. Bring to a slow boil and simmer ten minutes or until cabbage is tender.

Yield: 4 to 6 servings   *Roddy Thomas Hiser*

Broccoli Cheese Soup
Freezes beautifully

1 pound Velveeta cheese
2 (10-ounce) packages
frozen chopped broccoli
1 tablespoon butter or
margarine
¾ cup onions, chopped
6 cups water

6 chicken bouillon cubes
1 (8-ounce) package fine
egg noodles
1 teaspoon salt
6 cups milk
⅛ teaspoon garlic powder
Pepper to taste

Heat butter and sauté onion. Add water and bouillon cubes. Bring to boil and gradually add noodles and salt. Cook uncovered for three minutes. Stir in garlic powder and chopped broccoli. Cook three more minutes. Lower temperature and add pepper, milk and cheese. Stir constantly until all cheese melts. Serve immediately. *Will keep for a few months in the freezer. To reheat, use a double boiler.*
Yield: 4 quarts   *Kaye Armitage DeJarnett*

Canadian Cheese Soup
A sure hit

4 small carrots, grated
3 celery stalks, grated
1½ cups chicken stock (or
1½ cups water with 2
chicken bouillon cubes)
¼ cup butter, melted
¼ cup flour
2 tablespoons onion,
grated

2 cups sharp Cheddar
cheese, grated
4 ounces cream cheese
3 cups chicken stock (or 3
cups water with 4
bouillon cubes)
½ cup dry white wine
1½ cups evaporated milk
Parsley for garnish

Cook carrots and celery in 1½ cups of chicken broth over medium heat for 15 minutes. Sauté onions in butter; add flour and cook 5 minutes, whisking constantly. In a large pot, over medium heat, add cheese and melt with the 3 cups of chicken stock. Add carrot mixture and flour mixture to the melted cheese. Add milk and wine 5 minutes before serving; heat thoroughly. Garnish with parsley if desired. Carry this soup in a large thermos to fall football tailgate picnics.
Yield: 1½ quarts   *Ann Konigsmark Johnson*

Cheesy Potato Soup

5 pounds potatoes, pared
and sliced
2 medium onions,
chopped
Garlic powder

Parsley flakes
Salt and pepper
2 pounds Velveeta cheese
½ cup wine or cooking
sherry

Wash, peel and slice potatoes and onions. Place in a large kettle, covering with water. Add garlic powder, parsley, salt and pepper to taste. Cook until tender. Do not drain water. In a blender, blend about two cups of the soup and return to the kettle (this makes the soup thicker). Add cheese and continue to cook over low heat until cheese is melted. Add wine just before serving. Serve hot. This recipe will halve easily. May freeze any leftovers.

Yield: 10 to 12 servings   *Jeanne Powell Orman*

Clam Bisque

2½ tablespoons onion,
minced
1 stick plus 1 tablespoon
butter
9 tablespoons flour
4 (7½-ounce) cans minced
clams, reserve liquor

4½ cups bottled clam
juice
Paprika, to taste
Salt and pepper to taste
2½ cups half and half

Sauté onions in butter until golden. Stir in flour using a whisk. Add liquor from drained clams, clam juice and seasonings. Heat, stirring constantly, until slightly thickened. Add cream and clams. Heat throughly.

Yield: 8 to 10 servings   *Jane Hughson McLauglin*

Clam Chowder

4 slices bacon, chopped
2 tablespoons butter
½ cup green onion, chopped
½ cup onion, chopped
1 cup celery, chopped
1 clove of garlic, chopped
1 cup carrots, chopped
½ cup green pepper, chopped
3 tablespoons flour
3 cups hot chicken stock
1½ to 2 cups potatoes, cubed
1 teaspoon salt
¼ teaspoon white pepper
1 teaspoon caraway seed
1 (10-ounce) can whole clams and juice
1 (6½-ounce) can minced clams, drained
2 tablespoons butter, melted
2 tablespoons flour
2 cups half and half
1 whole pimento, chopped
3 tablespoons fresh parsley or 2 teaspoons dried parsley

Cook bacon; add 2 tablespoons butter to bacon and grease. Add onions, carrots, celery, garlic, and green pepper; sauté a few minutes. Add 3 tablespoons flour and sauté until dry. Slowly add chicken stock and cook 10 minutes. Add salt, pepper, potatoes, clams and juice and caraway seeds. Cook an additional 10 minutes. In another saucepan make a roux with 2 tablespoons butter and 2 tablespoons flour. Add 2 cups half and half and cook until thickened. Blend in pimento and parsley; heat until just before boiling. Cool. Combine the two mixtures and store overnight in refrigerator. Before serving warm thoroughly.
Yield: 2 quarts   *Pam Roukoski Webb*

Cold Cucumber Soup
Great to take to Chastain Park

3 to 5 medium cucumbers, peeled and chopped
1 quart chicken bouillon
1 pint sour cream
1 cup half and half
1 tablespoon onion, grated
Salt and pepper to taste
Fresh dill for garnish

Remove some of the cucumber seeds and cook in bouillon until soft. Cool. Blend half of the onion and half of the cucumber stock with half of the sour cream. Then blend in the other half. Add the half and half and seasonings. Chill throughly. Before serving, stir well and sprinkle with fresh dill.
Yield: 8 servings   *Lanier Scott Hoy*

Corn and Sausage Chowder
A winter favorite

1 pound sausage meat
1 large onion, chopped
3 large potatoes, sliced
2 teaspoons salt
1 teaspoon basil
½ teaspoon pepper
2 cups water

1 (16½-ounce) can cream
  style corn
1 (16½-ounce) can whole
  kernel corn, undrained
1 (12-ounce) can
  evaporated milk

Crumble sausage in a skillet and brown. Drain off fat. Put sausage into a deep pan. Return 2 tablespoons of the fat to the pan and sauté the onion with the sausage. Add potatoes, salt, pepper, basil and water. Cover and simmer 15 minutes. Stir in the cream corn, corn, corn liquid and evaporated milk. Cover and heat almost to boiling. Serve with French bread and a salad.
Yield: 6 to 8 servings   *Marsha Brown Thomas*

Cream Crab Soup

1 small onion, chopped
2 tablespoons butter
1 (8-ounce) can cream of
  potato soup
1 (8-ounce) can cream of
  celery soup
1 soup can of milk
1 soup can of half and half
  (or 2 soup cans half and
  half)

1 (5 to 7½-ounce) can of
  crabmeat
¼ cup sherry
Salt and pepper to taste
2 teaspoons parsley,
  chopped

In a large saucepan, sauté onion in melted butter. Add soups, milk and cream. Drain crabmeat and add. Heat just to boiling; add sherry, salt and pepper. Heat again and add parsley.
Yield: 4 to 6 servings   *Dianne Davison Isakson*

Creamy Artichoke Soup
Quick and easy

2 (9-ounce) packages
  frozen artichoke hearts
  or 2 (12-ounce) cans
  artichokes
1½ cans cream of
  mushroom soup
1 cup heavy cream

1 cup half and half
½ cup chicken broth
¼ cup white wine
Tabasco to taste
1 teaspoon lemon pepper
Sour cream

If using frozen artichoke hearts, cook according to the package directions, until tender. Blend all ingredients in a blender or food processor. Serve hot or refrigerate and serve cold garnished with a dollop of sour cream.
Yield: 6 servings   *Leckie Kern Stack*

Crock-Pot Vegetable Soup

2 pounds stew meat,
  cubed
1 (16-ounce) can tomatoes
2 carrots, sliced
3 stalks of celery, sliced
2 medium onions, diced
2 medium potatoes, diced
1 (7-ounce) can green
  beans

1 (7-ounce) can whole
  kernel corn
3 cups water
1 teaspoon salt
4 peppercorns
3 beef bouillon cubes

Put all ingredients in a crock-pot. Cover and cook on low for 24 hours. Serve with Cream Style Cornbread.
Yield: 6 to 8 servings   *Anna Ferguson Tucker*

Cuban Black Bean Soup

1 pound black beans
2 quarts water
2 tablespoons salt
5 cloves garlic, peeled
½ tablespoon oregano
½ tablespoon cumin

1 ounce white vinegar
5 ounces Spanish oil
½ pound onions, chopped
½ pound green peppers,
  chopped
Cooked rice

Soak beans in water overnight. Add salt and boil until soft. Crush, in a mortar, the garlic, oregano, cumin and vinegar. Heat the oil in a pan, adding the onions and peppers and fry until the onions are brown. Add the crushed ingredients, frying slowly. Drain some of the water off the beans before adding them to the onions and peppers. Cook slowly until ready to serve. This is best served with rice.

Yield: 6 servings

Ann Hite Benson

French Onion Soup

2 medium onions, thinly
  sliced
2 tablespoons butter,
  melted
4 cups beef broth
½ cup water

½ cup Madeira (optional)
½ cup Swiss cheese,
  shredded
Salt and pepper to taste
Croutons

Cook onions in butter, covered, until tender (about 5 minutes). Uncover and cook until well browned. Stir in broth and water, cover and simmer 30 minutes. Add salt and pepper to taste, stir in Madeira. Ladle soup into oven proof bowls, place croutons and Swiss cheese on top. Bake at 400° for 15 minutes.

Yield: 4 servings

Donya Smith Rickman

Gazpacho

1½ cups tomato juice
1 teaspoon beef bouillon
or 1 cube
1 small tomato, chopped
¼ cup unpared cucumber,
chopped
2 tablespoons green
pepper, chopped
2 tablespoons onion,
chopped

1 tablespoon red wine
vinegar
1 tablespoon salad oil
½ teaspoon salt or garlic
salt
½ teaspoon
Worcestershire sauce
3 drops Tabasco
Croutons for garnish

Heat tomato juice until boiling, add bouillon and stir until dissolved. Cool, add other ingredients and chill several hours. Sprinkle croutons on top.
Yield: 4 servings

Lanier Scott Hoy

Hearty Beef Chowder

1 pound ground chuck
2 large onions, chopped
1 tablespoon oil
3 tablespoons converted
rice
5 potatoes, cut into ½ inch
cubes

1 tablespoon sugar
1 tablespoon salt
1 (28-ounce) can
tomatoes, cut up
2 cups carrots, diced
1 zucchini, diced (optional)

Brown meat and onions in oil, pour off fat. Stir in remaining ingredients. Add water to almost cover and simmer for two hours. Stir often during last hour of cooking to avoid burning. Add seasonings to taste. Freezes great. Serve with cornbread on a cold winter night.
Yield: 8 servings

Patricia Weaver Bringardner

Homemade Minestrone Soup

2 tablespoons margarine
1 pound stew meat, cubed
4 beef bouillon cubes,
  crumbled
7 cups hot water
1 medium onion, chopped
½ cup celery, chopped
2 tablespoons dried
  parsley flakes
¼ teaspoon pepper
1 teaspoon salt
½ teaspoon thyme
1 (14½-ounce) can
  tomatoes, cut up

4 (8-ounce) cans tomato
  sauce
2 cups cabbage, shredded
1 cup zucchini, sliced thin
1 cup carrots, sliced thin
1 (15-ounce) can garbanzo
  beans, drained
1 cup small macaroni,
  uncooked
3 to 4 tablespoons
  Parmesan cheese

Melt margarine in a 5 quart kettle. Brown beef in margarine. Stir in bouillon cubes, hot water, onion, celery, parsley flakes, salt, thyme, pepper, tomatoes and tomato sauce. Cook over medium heat until mixture comes to a boil; reduce heat to low. Cover and simmer 1 to 1¼ hours, or until beef is tender, stirring occasionally. Add cabbage, zucchini, carrots, garbanzo beans and macaroni. Increase heat and cook until it boils again, then reduce heat to low. Cover and simmer until vegetables are tender and macaroni is done (approximately 20 to 25 minutes). Spoon soup into bowls and top each with a generous sprinkling of Parmesan cheese. Do not overcook but good reheated. Serve with hot bread and fruit salad for an easy supper!
Yield: 8 to 10 servings   *Carol Armbrust Fey*

Ice Storm Soup
Great way to hide vegetables from picky children!

1 pound mild sausage
3 onions, chopped
3 stalks celery, chopped
3 carrots, chopped
1 bell pepper, chopped
1 Idaho potato, chopped
4 to 5 cloves garlic, chopped

1 (48-ounce) can tomato juice
2 (12-ounce) cans pinto beans, with juice
1 tablespoon taco seasoning
1 (4-ounce) can chopped chilies

Fry sausage until brown. Add vegetables and sauté five minutes. Add tomato juice. Bring to a boil, then simmer, uncovered 45 minutes, stirring occasionally. Purée some (or all) of soup in blender. (The more puréed thicker the soup and less visible the vegetables.) Add pinto beans, chopped chilies and taco seasoning. Heat thoroughly. May be served with a dollop of sour cream. This recipe is from Ursula's Cooking School and has become a family favorite.
Yield: 6 to 8 servings   *Ann Coleman Wolf*

Hot Cheese Beer Soup

4 tablespoons butter
1 medium onion, chopped
2 stalks celery, chopped
1 carrot, chopped
4 tablespoons flour
2 cups chicken stock
7 ounces beer

1 cup heavy cream
¾ cup Cheddar cheese, grated
2 tablespoons fresh parsley, chopped
Salt and pepper

Sauté onion, celery and carrots in butter until soft. Stir flour into vegetables and add chicken stock slowly. Continue to stir until well blended. Bring to a boil, add beer and simmer until vegetables are tender. Add cream and cheese. Cook until cheese is melted. Taste for seasoning.
Yield: 6 servings   *Paula Finley Grayson*

Mr. O's Brunswick Stew
A must for every Georgia family reunion or barbecue

1 large frying chicken,
  quartered
1½ pounds lean pork
4 medium Irish potatoes,
  peeled
1 large onion, peeled
1 (1-pound 14-ounce) can
  tomatoes
4 (14½-ounce) cans cream
  style corn
3 tablespoons
  Worcestershire sauce

1 tablespoon liquid smoke
  (hickory flavored)
½ cup butter
1 (32-ounce) bottle tomato
  ketchup
2 tablespoons prepared
  mustard
Salt, black and red pepper
  to taste

Boil fryer and pork separately until tender and meat can be easily removed from bones. Remove chicken from stock and reserve. Bone chicken and chop meat (may use food processor). Remove pork from pork stock and bone meat. Grind pork meat. Discard pork stock. Using the course blade in the food processor, grind potatoes . Add to chicken stock and cook slowly for 20 to 30 minutes. To the stock add the ground chicken and pork. Grind the tomatoes, corn and onion. Add to the stock. Add the remaining ingredients. Cook slowly for 30 minutes, stirring often. If the stew is too thin, add Ritz cracker crumbs.
Yield: 1 gallon   *Joanna Owens Conyngham*

Oyster Stew
Warm and easy on a chilly evening

¼ cup butter
1 pint oysters with liquor
2 cups half and half
½ teaspoon salt

⅛ teaspoon freshly
  ground pepper
2 green onions sliced,
  tops included

Melt butter in the top of a double boiler. Add the remaining ingredients. Heat, over medium heat until oysters float on top and soup is steaming.
Yield: 4 servings   *Linda Hiller LeSueur*

Lentil Soup

2 cups dried lentils
2½ quarts water
¼ cup salt pork, diced
¾ cup carrots, sliced
¾ cup onions, chopped
¾ cup celery, sliced
1 clove garlic, minced

1 ham bone
1 bay leaf
2 whole cloves
1½ teaspoons salt
¼ teaspoon freshly
  ground black pepper
Dash of cayenne pepper

Combine lentils and water in large soup pot. Sauté pork for five minutes in a large skillet. Add carrots, onions, celery and garlic, sauté for 10 minutes. Add sautéed mixture to lentils in water. Add ham bone, bay leaf, cloves, salt and pepper. Bring soup to a boil. Cover, reduce heat and simmer gently for about 2 hours. Skim off bay leaf, cloves, ham bone. Dice lean meat from ham bone and return to soup. Correct seasonings if necessary and serve with French bread for a hearty supper.
Yield: 6 to 8 servings   *Linda Hiller LeSueur*

Savannah She Crab Stew

½ cup celery
1 cup potatoes
2 cans cream of celery
  soup
1½ cups water

2 cans white crabmeat,
  drained
2 cups half and half
¼ teaspoon lemon pepper

Dice potatoes and celery. Cover with water and boil for 8 minutes. Pour water off. Mix celery soup with 1½ cups water, pour over potatoes and celery. Bring to a boil, then reduce to low. Add crabmeat, half and half and lemon pepper. Simmer for 20 minutes. Stir often, it is very thick. Serve with sherry on the side.
Yield: 6 to 8 servings   *Dorothy M. Elletson*

Vichyssoise

½ small onion, sliced
1 (14-ounce) can clear
  chicken broth, chilled
1 teaspoon salt
Dash of pepper

1½ cups potatoes,
  cooked, diced, chilled
1 cup sour cream
Chopped chives for
  garnish

In blender container, combine onion, chicken broth, salt, pepper, sour cream and potatoes. Cover; blend at high speed about 8 to 10 seconds. Add sour cream and blend another 10 seconds. Refrigerate soup until well chilled, about one hour. Serve in chilled bowls. Garnish with chives. *Note:* This recipe improves with real chicken broth.
Yield: 4 servings   *Helen Clayton Shingler*

Apricot Nectar Salad

1 (12-ounce) can apricot
  nectar
1 (3-ounce) package lemon
  gelatin
⅓ cup water
1 tablespoon lemon juice

1 (11-ounce) can mandarin
  oranges
½ cup seedless grapes,
  halved
¼ cup apples, chopped
  and unpeeled

Bring nectar to a boil; add gelatin and stir until dissolved. Stir in water and lemon juice; chill until consistency of unbeaten egg whites. Stir in next three ingredients. Pour into oiled four-cup mold. Chill until firm. Unmold and garnish with apples, grapes and oranges.
Yield: 6 to 8 servings   *Donna Cates Robinson*

Congealed Asparagus Salad

2 envelopes gelatin
½ cup cold water
1 cup water
¾ cup sugar
½ cup white vinegar
1 teaspoon salt
1 (10½-ounce) can cut
  asparagus

1 (2-ounce) jar chopped
  pimento
1 cup celery, chopped
1 small onion, grated
½ cup pecans or water
  chestnuts, chopped

Soften gelatin in cold water. Mix 1 cup water, sugar, vinegar, and salt in pan; bring to a boil. Add softened gelatin and stir until dissolved. When mixture cools and begins to thicken, add asparagus, pimentoes, celery, onions and nuts. Chill until firm.
Yield: 6 servings   *Deborah Grosser Anthony*

Congealed Coca-Cola Cranberry Salad

A Georgia Thanksgiving Classic

1 (16-ounce) can whole
  cranberry sauce
1 (3-ounce) package
  orange gelatin
1 cup boiling water
1 envelope gelatin,
  softened in ½ cup cold
  water
1 (20-ounce) can crushed
  pineapple, undrained

1 tablespoon lemon juice
1 tablespoon grated
  orange rind
1 cup pecans or walnuts,
  chopped
6 ounces Classic
  Coca-Cola

Dissolve orange gelatin in boiling water; add cranberry sauce and blend well. Add plain gelatin. Add remaining ingredients and stir just to blend. Spray an 8-cup mold with non-stick cooking spray. Pour mixture into mold. Chill. When mixture begins to gel, stir to distribute nuts evenly. Continue to chill until firm.
Yield: 8 servings   *Bebe Moor Meaders*

Cool As A Cucumber Salad

1 (3-ounce) package sugar
free gelatin, lime flavor
¼ teaspoon salt
¾ cup boiling water
1 tablespoon lemon juice
½ cup cold water

Ice cubes
½ cup sour cream
1 cup cucumber, chopped,
seeded and peeled
1 teaspoon minced onion
½ teaspoon dillweed

Dissolve gelatin and salt in boiling water; add lemon juice. Combine cold water and ice cubes to make 1½ cups. Add to gelatin, stirring until slightly thickened. Remove any unmelted ice. Blend in sour cream. Add remaining ingredients. Pour into individual dishes or square glass dish and chill until set (about 30 minutes).
Yield: 4 to 6 servings   *Roddy Thomas Hiser*

Creamy Coleslaw

4 cups cabbage, shredded
½ cup carrots, shredded
2 medium tomatoes,
coarsely chopped

½ cup mayonnaise
1 tablespoon vinegar
2 teaspoons sugar
1 teaspoon celery salt

In a large bowl, combine cabbage and carrots. To prepare dressing, stir together mayonnaise, vinegar, sugar and celery salt. Pour dressing over cabbage mixture. Toss lightly to coat vegetables. Fold in chopped tomatoes. Cover and chill.
Yield: 8 servings   *Suzanne Gayton Lambert*

Frozen Banana Salad

2 cups sour cream
1 (8-ounce) can crushed
pineapple
1 tablespoon lemon juice
½ cup pecans, chopped
¾ cup sugar

4 medium bananas,
mashed
1 teaspoon salt
1 (8-ounce) jar maraschino
cherries, quartered

Mix all ingredients. Pour into 9 x 9-inch glass pan; freeze. Remove from freezer 15 minutes before serving. *Note:* Whole or jellied cranberry sauce may be substituted for cherries.
Yield: 9 servings   *Sharon Wilson Carson*

Frosty Fruit Loaf

1 (30-ounce) can fruit
  cocktail
1 envelope unflavored
  gelatin
½ cup mayonnaise
1 (10-ounce) package
  frozen sweetened
  strawberries, thawed

½ cup light corn syrup
1 (8-ounce) carton plain
  yogurt

Drain fruit cocktail, reserving ½ cup syrup. Pour reserved syrup into saucepan and sprinkle gelatin on top. Stir over low heat until dissolved. Beat in mayonnaise, stir in strawberries and corn syrup. Chill until mixture mounds slightly when dropped from spoon. Fold in fruit cocktail and yogurt. Spoon into loaf pan. Cover and freeze until firm.

Yield: 10 to 12 servings   *Dorothy Thompson Woodruff*

Frozen Cherry Salad

1 envelope unflavored
  gelatin
¼ cup sugar
Juice of ½ lemon
½ cup mayonnaise
1 pint whipping cream,
  whipped
2 dozen small
  marshmallows

1 (6-ounce) bottle red
  cherries with juice,
  halved
1 (16-ounce) can fruit
  cocktail, drained
1 banana, chopped
  (optional)
½ cup pecans, chopped
  (optional)

Soften gelatin in 1 tablespoon cold water. Add 1 cup hot water and ½ cup cold water; stir to dissolve. Add sugar and lemon juice. Combine remaining ingredients; stir in gelatin mixture. Pour into large casserole dish and freeze. May cut into squares before serving. If using individual salad molds, spray with non-stick oil. Remove from freezer shortly before serving.

Yield: 24 servings   *Pamela Croy Newton*

Grandmother's Cranberry Salad
This is a family favorite that my Grandmother brings to holiday gatherings.

2 (3-ounce) packages
  cherry jello
2 cups boiling water
2 cups crushed pineapple,
  drained and reserve
  juice
1 bag cranberries, washed
  and ground *

1 orange, sectioned,
  seeded and ground
2 small stalks celery,
  ground
½ cup sugar

Dissolve jello in boiling water. Add the juice plus enough water to equal 2 cups. Add remaining ingredients and pour into 1 large mold or 12 individual molds. Refrigerate until set. * Can use the food processor to grind cranberries, orange sections and celery (all together or separately).
Yield: 10 to 12 servings   *Ginger Byrd McPherson*

Strawberry Pretzel Salad

2 cups pretzels, coarsely
  crushed
3 tablespoons sugar
¾ cup margarine, melted
1 (8-ounce) package cream
  cheese, softened
1 cup sugar
1 (8-ounce) carton frozen
  whipped topping, thawed

1 (6-ounce) package
  strawberry gelatin
1 cup boiling water
2 (10-ounce) packages
  frozen sliced
  strawberries, thawed

Mix togther pretzels, margarine and 3 tablespoons sugar; press into a 9 x 13-inch pan. Bake at 400° for 8 minutes, cool. Beat cream cheese and 1 cup sugar until well blended. Stir in whipped topping and spread on crust. Dissolve gelatin in boiling water; stir in strawberries. Let stand for 10 minutes. Pour on top of cheese mixture and chill.
Yield: 12 servings   *Jean Jones Warren*

Orange Lemon Salad

Salad:

1 (3½-ounce) package orange gelatin
1 (3½-ounce) package lemon gelatin
2 cups boiling water
1½ cups cold water
3 ice cubes

¼ cup orange juice
1 (20-ounce) can crushed pineapple, drained and juice reserved
3 to 4 bananas
1 (12-ounce) package mini marshmallows

Topping:

½ cup pineapple juice
¾ cup sugar
1 egg, beaten
2 tablespoons flour
1 (8-ounce) package cream cheese, softened

1 envelope whipped topping, prepared as directed
Pecans, chopped
Sharp cheese, grated

Salad: In 3-quart casserole, dissolve orange and lemon gelatin in 2 cups boiling water. Add 1½ cups cold water, ice cubes, and orange juice. Add pineapple. Slice bananas over top; cover with marshmallows. Chill until set.

Topping: Mix flour and sugar together; gradually add pineapple juice stirring carefully so mixture won't become lumpy. Add egg and cook until thick, stirring constantly over low heat. Remove from heat; add cream cheese; beat until smooth. Chill. When chilled add the whipped topping. Spread the entire topping mixture over the firm gelatin mixture. Sprinkle with pecans and cheese.

Yield: 12 to 16 servings
Pamela Croy Newton

Tomato-Artichoke Aspic
An elegant luncheon salad

4 cups cocktail vegetable juice, divided
2 (3-ounce) packages lemon flavored gelatin
1 teaspoon Worcestershire sauce
1 (14-ounce) can artichoke hearts, drained and halved
3 green onions with tops, cut into 1-inch pieces
1 (8-ounce) package cream cheese, cut in 1-inch pieces
1 (12-ounce) carton small curd cottage cheese
2 cups mayonnaise
½ cup capers
Bibb lettuce
1 (2-ounce) jar black caviar

Bring 2 cups vegetable juice to a boil in a medium saucepan; remove from heat and add all of the gelatin, stirring until dissolved. Stir in remaining 2 cups of juice and Worcestershire sauce. Pour 2 cups gelatin mixture into an oiled 11-cup ring mold. Let the remaining juice mixture stand at room temperature. Chill mixture in mold until the consistency of unbeaten egg whites. Press artichoke halves into thickened mixture around outside of mold; chill until firm. Position knife blade in food processor bowl; add green onions. Process, pulsing 5 or 6 times until onions are chopped. Add cream cheese and cottage cheese; process 15 seconds, or until smooth. Spread cheese mixture evenly over chilled aspic, spreading to edge of ring mold. Gently pour remaining gelatin mixture over cheese layer. Chill until firm. Combine mayonnaise and capers; mix well. Chill until serving time. Run a thin spatula between ring mold and aspic all the way around; unmold aspic onto serving platter. Surround aspic with Bibb Lettuce leaves. Place caper mayonnaise in a small serving bowl; place in center of the aspic mold. Place caviar onto the center of the mayonnaise.

Yield: 14 servings   *Betty Bickerstaff McRae*

Aloha Salad

Salad:

1 (6-ounce) package
   apricot jello
2 cups water, boiling
2 cups water, cold
2 cups crushed pineapple,
   drained (reserve juice)

1 cup miniature
   marshmallows
2 cups bananas, diced
1½ cups nuts, chopped

Topping:

½ cup sugar
1 egg, beaten
½ cup pineapple juice
2 tablespoons flour
2 tablespoons butter,
   melted

1 (3-ounce) package cream
   cheese
1 cup whipped topping

Prepare jello and pour into a 9 x 12-inch baking dish; let thicken slightly in refrigerator. Add pineapple, marshmallows, bananas, and nuts. Stir to mix well. Chill.

For topping: Combine sugar, beaten egg and pineapple juice. Add flour and melted butter. Cook over low heat, stirring constantly until thick. Add cream cheese. Cool. Fold in whipped topping and pour over top of salad. Garnish with nuts and pineapple if desired.

Yield: 10 to 12 servings   *Carla Carroll Rice*

Chinese Chicken Salad

2 cups cooked chicken,
   chopped
1 cup celery, diced
1 tablespoon onion,
   minced
1 cup green grapes
1 small can mandarin
   oranges, drained

1 teaspoon salt
⅓ cup toasted sliced
   almonds
1 cup whipped topping
1 cup salad dressing (not
   mayonnaise)
1 cup chow mein noodles

Mix the first seven ingredients together in a large bowl. Fold in the salad dressing, whipped topping and noodles just prior to serving. Mix well.

Yield: 8 servings   *Beth Miller*

Chicken Cashew Salad

⅔ cup wild rice
2 chicken breasts, cooked and cubed
1 (8-ounce) can water chestnuts, chopped
⅔ cup mayonnaise
⅓ cup milk
⅓ cup lemon juice
2 tablespoons onion, grated
1 cup cashew nuts, chopped
2 cups seedless green grapes, halved

Cook rice according to package directions. Mix rice with chicken, water chestnuts, and onion. Blend together mayonnaise, milk and lemon juice. Add to chicken mixture and toss well. Refrigerate 1 hour or longer. Immediately before serving, fold in cashews and grapes; toss and serve.
Yield: 4 to 6 servings   *Leckie Kern Stack*

Cork Screw Salad

8 ounces cork screw macaroni
1 cup celery
½ cup green onions, chopped
½ cup radishes, sliced
1 cup sour cream
2 tablespoons white vinegar
2 teaspoons spicy mustard
2 teaspoons salt
⅛ teaspoon pepper

Cook macaroni according to package. Rinse several times and drain. Add celery, onions, and radishes. In separate bowl, combine remaining ingredients and pour over macaroni. Toss and refrigerate several hours.
Yield: 6 to 8 servings   *Bonnie Mullen Murphy*

Curried Seafood Salad

1 (6½-ounce) can white tuna
1 cup shrimp, cooked and deveined *
½ cup mayonnaise
2 tablespoons lemon juice
1 teaspoon curry powder
½ cup celery, chopped
3 cups yellow rice, cooked and chilled
2 to 3 tablespoons French dressing
½ cup snipped parsley
¼ cup ripe olives, sliced (optional)

Drain tuna well. In large bowl, combine tuna and shrimp. Cover with foil; refrigerate until chilled. Just before serving, blend mayonnaise, lemon juice and curry powder. Add celery to shrimp and tuna. Pour curried mayonnaise over all and toss. Toss cold cooked rice with French dressing and parsley. Spoon onto serving platter. Arrange seafood mixture on top. Sprinkle with sliced olives for garnish. * May use all tuna.
Yield: 4 to 6 servings   *Laura Phillips Lewis*

Gourmet Chicken Salad

1 (10-ounce) package frozen artichoke hearts
1 pound chicken breasts, cooked and cut into bite size pieces
2 or 3 scallions, chopped
1 or 2 ribs celery, chopped
½ teaspoon sweet basil
½ teaspoon black pepper
½ teaspoon garlic powder
⅛ teaspoon tarragon
⅛ teaspoon thyme
⅛ teaspoon poultry seasoning
2 to 3 tablespoons parsley
½ cup mayonnaise
½ cup sour cream
1 cup walnut pieces

Cook artichoke hearts according to package directions. Drain well. Cool. Cut artichoke hearts into bite-size pieces. (Refrigerate to make slicing easier.) Combine with chicken pieces, scallions, celery, all spices, mayonnaise and sour cream. Add nuts and stir well. Chill for several hours to blend flavors. Serving suggestion: Serve on a bed of lettuce surrounded by tomato wedges, pickle spears and deviled eggs. Sprinkle parsley on top for a festive touch.
Yield: 4 to 6 servings   *Susan Guess White*

Layered Chicken Picnic Salad

2 cups chicken cooked
and cubed
½ teaspoon curry powder
¼ teaspoon salt
¼ teaspoon paprika
Dash of pepper
2 cups lettuce shredded
2 cups Romaine lettuce,
shredded
1 large cucumber, sliced
1 cup macaroni, cooked
and drained

1 large green pepper,
chopped
1 (16-ounce) package
frozen English peas
1½ cups mayonnaise
2 tablespoons milk
2 tablespoons lemon juice
½ teaspoon salt
2 tomatoes, cut in wedges
2 tablespoons snipped
parsley

Combine chicken, curry, salt, paprika and pepper. Toss to coat well. In a clear salad bowl, layer lettuce, Romaine, chicken, peas, cucumber, macaroni and green pepper. Stir together mayonnaise, milk, lemon juice, ½ teaspoon salt, and pepper; spread over top of layered ingredients. Cover and chill several hours or overnight. Garnish with tomato wedges and parsley.
Yield: 8 servings   *Carolyn Cobb Anderson*

Luncheon Chicken Salad

4 cups chicken, cooked
and coarsely chopped
1 cup celery, sliced
1 pound seedless green
grapes
1 (8-ounce) can water
chestnuts, drained and
diced
1 (15-ounce) can pineapple
tidbits, drained

¾ cup sour cream
¾ cup mayonnaise
1 tablespoon soy sauce
2 teaspoons lemon juice
1½ teaspoons curry
powder
Lettuce leaves
⅓ cup slivered almonds,
toasted

Combine chicken, celery, grapes, water chestnuts and half of the pineapple tidbits. Combine next five ingredients and stir well. Add to chicken mixture and toss. Refrigerate. Serve salad on a bed of lettuce. Top with remaining pineapple and sprinkle with almonds.
Yield: 8 servings   *Lucy Rush McBee*

Mexican Chicken Salad

2 pounds chicken breasts, boiled and shredded
¾ cup scallions, chopped, green tops and all
1 (16-ounce) can kidney beans, drained
¾ cup olive oil
¼ cup red wine vinegar
1 teaspoon sugar
1 tablespoon tomato paste
1 tablespoon chili powder
2 cloves garlic, chopped
6 cups mixed salad greens
2 cups Cheddar cheese, grated
½ cup pitted black olives
1 large avocado, sliced lengthwise

In a large bowl mix olive oil, wine vinegar, sugar, tomato paste, chili powder and garlic to make dressing. Combine chicken, scallions and beans with dressing and chill overnight. Toss mixed salad greens in a salad bowl. Layer marinated chicken and beans on top of lettuce. Top with Cheddar cheese. Garnish with black olives and avocado slices. Serve using salad tongs.
Yield: 6 to 8 servings   *Lynn Stiles Foster*

Macaroni Shrimp Salad

1 pound fresh shrimp, cooked
1 pound elbow macaroni (small size), cooked
½ cup fresh onion, chopped
½ cup green pepper, chopped
½ cup pimentos, sliced thin
¼ cup fresh parsley
1 cup mayonnaise *
⅓ cup Thousand Island dressing
Salt and pepper to taste

Mix drained macaroni, onion, pepper, pimento and parsley with mayonnaise and dressing. Salt and pepper to taste. Add shrimp and toss gently. Garnish with sliced ripe olives, Spanish olives, sliced green pepper and a sprinkle of paprika for color.
* Add more mayonnaise if necessary.
Yield: 6 to 8 servings   *Lynn Stiles Foster*

Neptune Salad

1 pound sea fingers or
    pollock
1 bunch green onions,
    diced
1 cup celery, finely diced
Black or white pepper, to
    taste

Salt to taste
Mayonnaise to blend
1 tablespoon lemon juice
Parsley

Squeeze all juice out of meat. Pull meat apart - don't chop. Add celery, lemon juice and seasonings. Add mayonnaise slowly to blend together . Cover with parsley and chill. Good served with artichokes or ripe avocados.

Yield: 4 servings *Ann Hite Benson*

Oriental Chicken Salad

1 large head Romaine
    lettuce
2 bunches spinach
6 to 7 large chicken
    breasts, cooked and
    diced
5 green onions, chopped
    fine
1 (8-ounce) can water
    chestnuts, drained

½ pound fresh
    mushrooms, sliced
½ pound fresh bean
    sprouts
1 (3-ounce) can Chinese
    noodles

Dressing:
8 tablespoons sugar
4 teaspoons salt
6 teaspoons Accent
1 teaspoon pepper

8 tablespoons white
    vinegar
1 cup salad oil

Break up lettuce and spinach in large bowl. Add chicken, onions, mushrooms, bean sprouts and water chestnuts. Cover and chill. Mix all dressing ingredients and store in refrigerator until ready to serve. Shake well before serving. Pour over salad and mix well. Add the noodles and toss again.

Yield: 12 servings *Beverly Daniels Bentley*

Pasta Salad
Well worth the effort

2 cups fresh snow peas
2 cups broccoli flowerets
2½ cups cherry tomatoes, halved
2 cups fresh mushrooms, sliced
1 (8-ounce) can whole pitted ripe olives, drained

1 (8-ounce) package cheese stuffed tortellini, cooked and drained
3 ounces fettuccine, cooked and drained
1 tablespoon grated Parmesan cheese

Dressing:

½ cup green onions, sliced
½ cup red wine vinegar
½ cup vegetable oil
½ cup olive oil
2 tablespoons chopped parsley
2 cloves garlic, minced
2 teaspoons dried whole basil

1 teaspoon dried whole dillweed
1 teaspoon salt
½ teaspoon pepper
½ teaspoon sugar
½ teaspoon dried oregano
1½ teaspoons Dijon mustard

Combine all dressing ingredients in a jar and cover tightly. Shake vigorously until well mixed. Drop snow peas into boiling water; boil one minute and remove. Place broccoli in boiling water; boil one minute and remove. Combine peas, broccoli, tomatoes, mushrooms and olives. Combine cooked pasta and vegetables with the dressing. Toss well. Garnish with additional Parmesan cheese, if desired. Chill several hours before serving.

Yield: 12 to 14 servings   *Pam Roukoski Webb*

Salmon Salad

2½ cups seashell
  macaroni, uncooked
1 (17¾-ounce) can salmon
½ cup mayonnaise
1 tablespoon lemon juice
1 tablespoon dry mustard
¼ teaspoon salt

½ cup celery, chopped
½ cup cucumber, chopped
1 small onion, finely
  chopped
Lettuce
Tomato wedges

Cook macaroni in boiling water for 10 to 12 minutes. Drain well and cool. Wash and drain salmon. Blend mayonnaise, lemon juice, mustard, salt, and salmon. Add celery, cucumber and onion. Toss with shells; chill for several hours. Serve on a bed of lettuce with tomato wedges.

Yield: 6 servings   *Becky Worthington Dorsett*

Shrimp Salad Masterpiece

1 (6-ounce) package
  curried rice mix
2 cups shrimp, cooked,
  cleaned, halved
  lengthwise (about 1½
  pounds of shrimp)
1 cup celery, diced
½ cup green pepper, diced

4 slices of bacon, cooked
  crisp and crumbled
½ cup whipping cream
½ cup mayonnaise
1 teaspoon curry powder
Grated coconut (optional)
Cashews (optional)
Chutney (optional)

Cook rice according to package directions, cool. Reserve 6 shrimp halves for garnish. In a bowl, combine remaining shrimp, cooked rice, celery, green pepper and bacon. Whip cream into soft peaks. Combine whipped cream with mayonnaise and curry. Fold into rice mixture. Cover and chill. Serve in lettuce leaves or in ½ chilled cantalope. Top with reserved shrimp. Serve with grated coconut, cashews and chutney.

Yield: 4 to 6 servings   *Jill White*

Super Seafood Salad

¾ cup sour cream
¾ cup mayonnaise
1 tablespoon mustard
2 teaspoons dillweed
1 teaspoon lemon pepper
½ teaspoon salt

1 medium onion, diced
(preferably Vidalia)
1 (8-ounce) can water
chestnuts, sliced
12 ounces cooked shrimp
10 ounces crabmeat

Mix together first seven ingredients. Fold in seafood and water chestnuts. Chill at least four hours. Good stuffed in pretty summer tomatoes or garnished with sliced seedless cucumbers.

Yield: 6 to 8 servings

Janice Gamel Tucker

Zesty Pasta Salad

1 (12-ounce) package
spiral medley pasta
1 large onion, chopped
1 large green pepper,
chopped
1 (12-ounce) can
unseasoned artichoke
hearts or 1 package
frozen artichoke hearts,
cooked as directed
1 (4-ounce) can black
olives, pitted and sliced
1 tomato, chopped

1 cup mozzarella cheese,
grated
½ cup Parmesan cheese,
grated
1 tablespoon oregano
¼ pound deli ham, bite
size pieces
¼ pound deli salami, bite
size pieces
1 teaspoon garlic powder
Salt and pepper to taste
1 (8-ounce) bottle Zesty
Italian salad dressing

Cook noodles as directed. Cool. Mix with remaining ingredients. Refrigerate for several hours before serving. Keeps well several days.

Yield: 10 servings

Mary Ann Dickerson Maloy

Charlie's Caesar Salad

2 cloves garlic
1 tablespoon red wine
  vinegar
2 tablespoons lemon juice
1 glass dry red wine
1 egg
½ teaspoon anchovy
  paste

⅓ cup olive oil
½ cup box seasoned
  croutons
1 medium size head of
  Romaine lettuce
⅓ cup Parmesan cheese,
  grated

Break garlic in large wooden salad bowl. Add vinegar and lemon juice; soak for two hours. Drink wine. Remove garlic from liquid and rub sides of bowl. Dice half of one clove and leave in liquid. Add egg, olive oil and anchovy paste. Tear Romaine into one inch squares. Toss with croutons and sprinkle with Parmesan cheese.

Yield: 4 servings
Anna Ferguson Tucker

Corn Salad

2 cups shoe peg corn
¾ cup cucumber, chopped
1 medium tomato,
  chopped
¼ cup onion, chopped
½ teaspoon dry mustard

½ teaspoon celery seed
4 tablespoons mayonnaise
2 tablespoons vinegar
2 teaspoons salt
½ cup sour cream

Combine corn, cucumber, tomato, and onion; set aside. In small bowl, combine remaining ingredients and mix well. Pour over vegetables and toss. Cover and marinate in refrigerator for 12 hours.

Yield: 6 to 8 servings
Susan Bolen Sappington

Dilly Rice Salad

2 cups chicken broth
1 cup regular rice,
  uncooked
⅓ cup green onions,
  chopped
⅓ cup green pepper,
  chopped
⅓ cup stuffed green
  olives, sliced

1 (7-ounce) jar marinated
  artichoke hearts, drained
  and chopped
⅓ cup celery, chopped
½ cup mayonnaise
¾ teaspoon dillweed
Salt and pepper to taste
Lettuce
Green olives for garnish

Bring chicken broth to boil. Add rice and cook as directed. Cool. Combine rice and next 8 ingredients. Chill well. Serve on lettuce and garnish with sliced olives.
Yield: 6 servings

Flay MaCaskill Keys

Fresh Broccoli Salad

1 bunch broccoli, chopped
⅔ cup green olives,
  chopped
1 small onion, chopped or
  grated
4 hard boiled eggs,
  chopped

1 cup mayonnaise
1 tablespoon lemon juice
½ teaspoon sugar
Salt and pepper to taste
Fresh mushrooms, sliced
  for garnish

Cut broccoli, including stalks, into cubes. Add olives, onion and eggs. Combine mayonnaise, lemon juice, sugar, salt and pepper; toss with broccoli mixture. Garnish with mushrooms. Chill before serving.
Yield: 4 to 6 servings

Cheryl Tilley Briscoe

Fruit Salad With Yogurt Dressing

3 cups Boston lettuce
3 cups Iceberg lettuce
2¼ cups grapefruit
  sections, drained
1½ cups mandarin
  oranges, drained
1½ cups avocado, cubed
2 teaspoons lemon juice
1 medium banana, halved

1 tablespoon frozen
  orange juice concentrate,
  thawed and undiluted
2 teaspoons honey
⅛ teaspoon ground ginger
⅛ teaspoon ground
  cinnamon
1 carton low fat orange
  yogurt

In a bowl, place the lettuces, grapefruit and oranges. Mix avocados and lemon juice. Add to fruit and lettuce mixture. In a blender, add banana, orange juice, honey, ginger and cinnamon. Blend until smooth. Fold in yogurt and chill. Just before serving, place dressing over salad and toss.
Yield: 6 to 8 servings   *Susan Thomas Burney*

Garden Potato Salad

2 pounds small red
  potatoes, scrubbed, and
  quartered
1 medium cucumber,
  peeled and sliced
2 medium celery ribs,
  chopped
1 medium green pepper,
  chopped

2 small scallions, thinly
  sliced
4 medium radishes, sliced
⅓ cup mayonnaise
⅓ cup sour cream
¾ teaspoon black pepper,
  freshly ground
½ teaspoon salt
⅛ teaspoon paprika

In 2-quart saucepan over high heat, bring potatoes and enough water to cover to boil. Reduce heat to low. Cook, covered 12 to 15 minutes until potatoes are just tender. Drain and cool to room temperature. In large bowl, combine potatoes, cucumbers, celery, green pepper, scallions and radishes. In a small bowl, stir mayonnaise, sour cream, pepper, salt, and paprika until blended well. Stir gently but thoroughly into vegetable mixture. Refrigerate up to 24 hours. Serve chilled or at room temperature.
Yield: 6 servings   *Flay MaCaskill Keys*

Greek Salad

½ head Iceberg lettuce, shredded
1 medium cucumber, sliced
3 scallions, chopped
1 small onion, sliced thin
½ green pepper, chopped
2 medium tomatoes
2 celery stalks, chopped
⅓ cup olive oil
3 tablespoons vinegar
1 teaspoon oregano
¼ pound feta cheese
Black olives
Garlic powder to taste
Salt and pepper to taste

Wash, drain and cut all vegetables. Toss together in a bowl. Mix olive oil, vinegar, oregano, garlic powder, salt and pepper in a jar. Shake dressing well and pour over vegetables. Toss and mix well. Top with feta cheese and black olives.
Yield: 4 servings

Phyllis Wallace Holley

Korean Salad And Dressing

Salad:
1 pound spinach, cut out veins
1 (3½-ounce) can bean sprouts, drained
1 (3½-ounce) can water chestnuts, drained, thinly sliced
5 strips of bacon, fried and crumbled
3 eggs, hard boiled and diced
1 cup fresh mushrooms, sliced

Dressing:
1 cup salad oil
¼ cup onion, diced
1 cup ketchup
¼ cup vinegar
¾ cup sugar
1 teaspoon Worcestershire sauce
Salt and pepper to taste

Mix all salad ingredients together in a large bowl. Combine all dressing ingredients in a jar; close and shake well to mix. Toss salad with dressing just prior to serving.
Yield: 6 to 8 servings

Donya Smith Rickman

Hot Salad

8 to 10 slices bacon
1 small onion
3 or 4 tomatoes
1 head of lettuce, chopped
or shredded

¼ cup vinegar
Salt and pepper to taste

Cook bacon, pour drippings out of pan, leaving enough to cover the bottom lightly. Dice the onion and cook in drippings. Cut tomatoes into eighths and add to onion pieces. Add lettuce; cook for a minute or two until slightly wilted. Turn heat down. Add vinegar, salt and pepper. Turn off heat. Crumble bacon into mix and stir. Serve immediately.
Yield: 4 to 6 servings

Susan Martin Riddle

Mandarin Salad
Shake and serve

¼ head lettuce, torn in
pieces
¼ head Romaine lettuce,
torn in pieces
2 medium stalks celery,
chopped

2 green onions, with tops,
thinly sliced
1 (11-ounce) can Mandarin
oranges, drained
¼ cup sliced almonds

Dressing:
¼ cup vegetable oil
2 tablespoons sugar
½ teaspoon salt
2 tablespoons vinegar

1 tablespoon snipped
parsley
Dash pepper
Dash red pepper sauce

Place lettuce pieces in a plastic bag. Add celery and onion. Refrigerate while making the dressing. Shake all dressing ingredients together in a tightly covered jar and refrigerate. This may be made well ahead of time and when serving time arrives, simply pour sweet and sour dressing into bag and add orange sections. Close bag tightly and shake until all is coated. Add almond slices, close bag again and shake. Salad is ready to serve!
Yield: 6 servings

Jeanne Powell Orman

Mediterranean Salad

2 (6-ounce) jars marinated
artichoke hearts,
chopped
½ cup pitted green olives,
sliced
3 stalks celery, chopped
½ cup pitted black olives,
chopped

1 green pepper, seeded
and cut into thin strips
1 red pepper, seeded and
cut into thin strips
¼ teaspoon oregano

Mix all ingredients, including oil from artichokes. Refrigerate at least one hour before serving.
Yield: 8 to 10 servings

Leckie Kern Stack

Marinated Asparagus
Uncomplicated but pleasing

1 (15-ounce) can extra
long asparagus
½ cup apple cider vinegar
½ cup sugar

1 scant teaspoon season
salt
Dash of black pepper
Juice of ½ lemon

Drain asparagus, reserving liquid. Mix remaining ingredients to make marinade. Place asparagus in dish and cover with marinade. If marinade doesn't cover asparagus, add some of the reserved liquid. In doubling the recipe, reduce slightly the amount of vinegar used and substitute the asparagus liquid.
Yield: 3 to 4 servings

Bebe Moor Meaders

Marinated Tomatoes

½ heaping teaspoon garlic
powder
¼ cup green onions and
tops, sliced
1 teaspoon salt
¼ teaspoon black pepper

¼ cup fresh parsley
½ teaspoon basil
6 fresh tomatoes, peeled
and sliced
⅔ cup olive oil
¼ cup vinegar

Combine first six ingredients and sprinkle over sliced tomatoes. Mix oil and vinegar and pour over tomatoes. Cover and chill several hours, spooning marinade over tomatoes several times while chilling.
Yield: 6 servings

Barbara Gully Allen

Marinated Vegetable Bowl
A great recipe to adjust according to likes and dislikes.

1 large green pepper in
bite size pieces
1 pint cherry tomatoes
1 pound fresh
mushrooms, sliced
1 can sliced water
chestnuts, drained
1 can artichoke hearts,
quartered
1 medium zucchini, sliced
1 can pitted black or green
olives

1 head cauliflower cut in
small pieces
1 bunch broccoli cut in
small pieces
For variations use:
Celery
Green onions
Sweet peppers
Chick peas
Snow peas
Kidney beans

Marinate any combination of these raw vegetables in a good Italian dressing for about 12 hours. Pour off excess dressing and arrange in a glass serving bowl.
Yield: 12 to 20 servings   *Claudia Mitchell Owens*

Pepperoni And Broccoli Salad
"A good year round salad"

1 package (0.75-ounce)
Italian salad dressing
mix
1 (1 pound) bunch
broccoli
½ pound fresh
mushrooms, sliced

1 cup (4-ounces) Swiss
cheese, diced
1 (3½-ounce) package
sliced pepperoni
1 green pepper, chopped

Prepare dressing mix according to package directions. Set aside. Wash broccoli. Break off florettes. Reserve stalks for other recipes. Combine florettes and next four ingredients in a large bowl. Pour dressing over salad. Toss gently. Cover and refrigerate eight hours or overnight.
Yield: 6 to 8 servings   *Donna Cates Robinson*

Romaine Salad
With Mustard Cream Dressing

½ cup whipping cream
1 tablespoon Dijon
  mustard
1 teaspoon dried chervil
  leaves
½ teaspoon salt

½ teaspoon pepper
1 head Romaine lettuce,
  torn in pieces
¾ cup walnut halves,
  toasted

Combine cream, mustard, chervil and salt in a small bowl. Add pepper. Refrigerate, covered for three hours. Arrange Romaine leaves in serving bowl. Add walnuts. Pour dressing over salad. Toss well.

Yield: 6 servings

Betty Parrott Barnett

Salad Nicoise

1 large can white potatoes,
  sliced
1 large can Blue Lake
  green beans
1 large can artichokes
1 large can black olives
1 red onion, sliced
Cherry tomatoes
Green pepper
Cucumber

Radishes
Zucchini or yellow squash
Optional:
  Anchovies
  Hard boiled eggs
  Tuna fish
  Lettuce
  Good Season Garlic
  Dressing Mix

Mix dressing and marinate in it potatoes, green beans, artichokes, black olives and onion for at least four hours. Line a salad bowl with lettuce leaves and pour marinated vegetables into center. Then add any other vegetables you are using and toss. Top with any optional items and serve.

Yield: 4 to 6 servings

Ann Hite Benson

Country Coleslaw

1 large cabbage, chopped
  coarsely
1½ cups carrots, shredded
1 cup green pepper,
  chopped
¼ cup green onion,
  chopped
1 cup mayonnaise
3 tablespoons sugar

3 tablespoons vinegar
½ teaspoon pepper
1½ teaspoons salt
¾ teaspoon dry mustard
¼ teaspoon celery seed
Garnish with:
Paprika
6 to 10 green olives
Green pepper ring

Combine cabbage, carrots, green pepper and green onion. Set
aside. Combine mayonnaise, sugar, vinegar, salt, pepper, mustard and celery seed to make dressing. Stir well. Pour dressing
over cabbage mixture and toss well. Chill. When ready to
serve, sprinkle with paprika and garnish with green olives and
green pepper ring.
Yield: 10 to 12 servings   *Lanier Scott Hoy*

Mrs. Mac's Slaw

1 medium head cabbage,
  chopped fine
1 (8¼-ounce) can
  pineapple tidbits
2 carrots, chopped fine
1 small green pepper,
  diced
1 large apple, unpeeled
  and chopped fine

½ cup flaked coconut
½ cup mini-marshmallows
7 tablespoons evaporated
  milk
7 tablespoons sugar
7 tablespoons vinegar
½ teaspoon celery salt
½ teaspoon onion salt

Combine first seven ingredients in large bowl. Put evaporated
milk, sugar, vinegar, celery and onion salts in a pint jar and
shake well to mix. Add to cabbage mix and toss. Cover bowl
and chill until ready to serve.
Yield: 8 to 10 servings   *Betty McCoy McPherson*

Peanut Crunch Slaw

My mother always served this at fish frys at the lake.

4 cups red cabbage, shredded
1 cup celery, finely chopped
½ cup sour cream
½ cup mayonnaise
1 teaspoon salt
¼ cup onion, chopped
¼ cup green pepper, chopped
½ cup cucumber, chopped
2 tablespoons butter
4 tablespoons Parmesan cheese
1 cup salted peanuts, chopped

Toss cabbage and celery together. Chill. Mix sour cream, mayonnaise, salt, onion, green pepper and cucumber to make dressing. In small skillet, melt butter; add peanuts and heat until lightly browned. Immediately stir in cheese. Just before serving, toss cabbage and celery with dressing. Sprinkle peanut mixture on top.

Yield: 10 to 12 servings

Betty Neel Cobb Lawton

24 Hour Slaw

1 large cabbage, shredded
1 large purple onion, diced
1 large green pepper, diced
¾ cup vinegar
¾ cup oil
1 cup sugar
1 teaspoon dry mustard
1 teaspoon celery seed
1 teaspoon salt

Put cabbage, onion and green pepper in large bowl. Boil vinegar, sugar, mustard, celery seed and salt until sugar dissolves. Add oil. Pour liquid mixture over dry ingredients, DO NOT STIR. Store in refrigerator at least 24 hours before serving. Stir gently before serving.

Yield: 10 servings

Meredith Webb Dykes

Sour Cream Potato Salad
Tastes similar to a "dressed up" baked potato.

8 medium potatoes
1½ cups mayonnaise
1 cup sour cream
1 tablespoon horseradish
½ teaspoon salt
1 cup fresh parsley, chopped
1 cup spring onions, (tops included), chopped

Peel and cube potatoes. Cook in boiling water until tender but not mushy. Combine mayonnaise, sour cream, horseradish and salt. When potatoes are cooled, toss with parsley and onions. Stir in dressing. The flavor develops best when chilled at least over night.
Yield: 8 to 10 servings   *Sydney Cobb Smith*

Spinach Salad
With Warm Bacon Dressing

2 bunches fresh spinach
4 hard cooked eggs, chopped
8 small mushroom caps, sliced
1 cup warm bacon dressing

Dressing:
½ pound bacon, chopped fine
1 cup sugar
1⅓ cups white vinegar
1⅔ cups water
5 teaspoons cornstarch

Wash spinach very well, then dry. Divide spinach equally on four plates. Top each with mushrooms and eggs. Pour four tablespoons of dressing over each and serve immediately.
Dressing: Sauté bacon in large fry pan. Add sugar and vinegar. Stir well. Add one cup water and bring to a boil. Mix cornstarch with remaining water and stir until dissolved. Pour cornstarch mixture into boiling dressing. Return to a boil and simmer for five minutes. Remove from heat and cool until slightly warm.
Yield: 4 servings   *Elizabeth deGaris Atherton*

Spaghetti Salad

1 pound thin spaghetti,
broken into quarters
1 onion, chopped
2 tomatoes, chopped
1 green pepper, chopped
3 celery stalks, diced

1 (16-ounce) bottle Italian
dressing
1 (2.75-ounce) jar Salad
Supreme Seasoning
Pepperoni slices or other
diced meat, optional

Cook spaghetti according to package directions; rinse and drain well. Add remaining ingredients and mix well. Refrigerate overnight. Toss well before serving.

Yield: 20 servings   *Becky Bridges Keenum*

Wilted Lettuce

5 slices bacon, cooked
and crumbled
1 medium head lettuce
2 green onions, thinly
sliced
½ cup sugar
½ cup cider vinegar

½ teaspoon season salt
½ garlic powder
¼ teaspoon dry mustard
Dash lemon pepper
¼ cup bacon drippings
2 hard boiled eggs,
chopped

Break up lettuce into bowl; add bacon, onion slices and eggs. Combine sugar, vinegar, salt, lemon pepper, garlic powder and mustard in sauce pan; cook until boiling. Add bacon drippings; pour over salad and toss. Serve immediately.

Yield: 6 to 8 servings   *Susan Thomas Burney*

Thomas Salad

Great in summer with any outdoor barbecue.

6 medium or 8 small ripe
tomatoes, chopped
1 small green pepper,
chopped
1 small onion, chopped

1 cup mayonnaise
1 stack saltine crackers,
crumbled
Salt and pepper to taste

In a large bowl, mix all vegetables. Add salt and pepper; refrigerate until ready to serve. Before serving, drain juice; add mayonnaise and crumbled crackers. Mix well. May be doubled easily.

Yield: 10 servings   *Virginia Clyde Thomas*

Tailgate Salad

⅔ cup vinegar
⅔ cup salad oil
¼ cup onion, chopped
2 cloves garlic, minced
1 teaspoon salt
1 teaspoon sugar
1 teaspoon basil leaves
1 teaspoon oregano leaves
¼ teaspoon pepper
1 cup fresh mushrooms, sliced

1 (16-ounce) can whole small carrots, drained
1 (14-ounce) can artichoke hearts, halved and drained
1 cup ripe olives, pitted and halved
1 cup celery, sliced
1 (2-ounce) jar sliced pimiento, drained and diced

Combine first nine ingredients in saucepan and bring to boil over medium heat, reduce and simmer uncovered for ten minutes. Combine remaining ingredients in a large bowl. Pour hot marinade over vegetables, stirring to coat. Cover and marinate in refrigerator for four hours or overnight.
Yield: 7 cups   *Carol Armbrust Fey*

Seven Layer Salad

1 head lettuce, bite size pieces
1 cup celery, thinly sliced
1 large red onion, thinly sliced
2 cups mayonnaise
2 tablespoons sugar
1½ teaspoons salt
12 slices bacon, cooked and crumbled

1 cup mozzarella cheese, grated
1 cup Cheddar cheese, grated
1 (10-ounce) package frozen chopped broccoli, thawed and uncooked

In three quart rectangular dish, layer the lettuce, celery, and onion. Mix together the mayonnaise, sugar and salt. Spread this over the lettuce. Top this with the bacon, broccoli and then the cheeses. Cover and refrigerate. Prepare one day ahead. Keeps two to three days.
Yield: 8 servings   *Cathy Colquitt*

Blender Thousand Island Dressing

1 cup mayonnaise
¼ cup chili sauce
1 teaspoon Worcestershire
8 stuffed green olives
1 slice onion ½ inch thick
1 dill pickle, cut in pieces
2 hard boiled eggs

Put mayonnaise, chili sauce, and Worcestershire sauce into blender and whip until well blended. Add remaining ingredients and blend just until grated. Chill.
Yield: 1½ cups
Anna Ferguson Tucker

Creamy Blue Cheese Dressing

½ cup blue cheese, crumbled
⅔ cup sour cream
½ teaspoon salt
1 teaspoon Worcestershire sauce
2 tablespoons lemon juice
½ cup mayonnaise

Mash blue cheese well with fork. Blend with sour cream, salt, Worcestershire and lemon juice. Add mayonnaise, mixing thoroughly. Chill. Serve over greens or as a chip dip. Make at least one day ahead of serving.
Yield: 1½ cups
Mary Roland Huggins

Cucumber Dressing

2 cucumbers, sliced paper thin
½ cup sour cream
2 tablespoons lemon juice
½ teaspoon salt
½ teaspoon sugar
Dash cayenne pepper
Fresh tomatoes, sliced

Combine first six ingredients and chill. Pour over tomatoes.
Yield: 4 to 6 servings
Betty Neel Cobb Lawton

Oriental Salad Dressing
Good on spinach!

¼ cup salad oil
3 tablespoons lemon juice
1 tablespoon honey
1½ teaspoons soy sauce
1 teaspoon toasted sesame seeds
½ teaspoon paprika

Mix all together and serve over spinach salad.
Lanier Scott Hoy

New Orleans French Salad Dressing
Keeps in refrigerator for one month if it lasts that long!!!

1 cup Wesson oil
½ cup red wine vinegar
4 bulbs garlic, crushed
1 teaspoon salt
½ teaspoon pepper
1 teaspoon dry mustard
½ teaspoon paprika

Place all ingredients in a jar and cover tightly. Shake well and refrigerate for at least one hour. Shake well before serving.
Yield: 1½ cups   *Judy Rogers Jervy*

Oil And Vinegar Salad Dressing

2 tablespoons white wine
⅓ cup vinegar
⅔ cup salad oil
1 teaspoon lemon pepper
1 teaspoon sugar
1 teaspoon Worcestershire
   sauce
¾ teaspoon salt

Mix all ingredients well and store in the refrigerator. This dressing is good on sliced tomatoes as well as mixed salad greens.
Yield: 1 cup   *Peggy Elder Little*

Sensational Salad Dressing

1½ cups vegetable oil
½ cup olive oil
¾ cup cider vinegar
⅓ cup lemon juice
½ cup fresh parsley,
   chopped
2 to 3 cloves garlic,
   minced
½ teaspoon salt
½ teaspoon pepper
8 ounces fresh Romano
   cheese, ground

Combine all ingredients except cheese in large jar. Cover tightly and shake; stir in cheese. Add dressing to mixed green salad.
Yield: 2 cups   *Marsha Brown Thomas*

Poppy Seed Dressing
Delicious on fruit salads.

⅓ cup vinegar
¾ cup sugar
1 teaspoon salt
1 teaspoon dry mustard

1 small onion, minced
2 tablespoons poppy
  seeds
1 cup oil

Mix all ingredients except oil in blender thoroughly. Add oil last as dressing thickens when this is added. Store in refrigerator.
Yield: 1 cup   *Dell Cochran James*

Alice's Shrimp Louis Sauce

1 cup sour cream
1 cup mayonnaise
2 tablespoons chili sauce
½ green pepper, chopped
Green tops of 3 spring
  onions, chopped finely

2 tablespoons parsley,
  chopped
Dash or two of
  Worcestershire sauce

Mix all ingredients and serve. Serving suggestion: Top lettuce with shrimp and garnish with chopped celery and tomatoes. Pour dressing over this. Sprinkle with chopped boiled egg.
Yield: 1 pint   *Marsha Brown Thomas*

Blueberry Dressing
Wonderful for fresh fruit

1 (15-ounce) can
  blueberries, drained or 1
  pint fresh
1 (8-ounce) carton sour
  cream

¼ cup brown sugar
1 tablespoon vanilla

Blend all together and pour over fresh fruit.
Yield: 1½ cups   *Nancy Suhr Hunter*

Blender Hollandaise

3 egg yolks
2 tablespoons lemon juice
Pinch of cayenne pepper
¼ teaspoon salt
½ cup butter

Put egg yolks, lemon juice, a pinch of cayenne pepper and salt in a blender. cover and blend on high about 3 seconds. Heat butter to bubbling stage. Pour butter into blender while blending on high. Serve at once or keep warm by immersing blender container in warm water.
Yield: 4 servings

Julie Beazel Flournoy

Bernaise Sauce

2 egg yolks
1 tablespoon lemon juice
¾ cup butter or margarine, melted
1½ teaspoons tarragon vinegar
½ teaspoon dried tarragon leaves

In top of double boiler, beat egg yolks with lemon juice using a wooden spoon until blended. Place over hot, not boiling water—do not allow water in the bottom pan to touch the top pan. Slowly add melted butter, a teaspoon at a time, stirring constantly with wooden spoon until mixture thickens. Remove from heat, add vinegar and tarragon. This may be prepared several hours before serving. Keep at room temperature.
Yield: 1 cup

Ann Bramblet Fowler

Champagne Mustard
A great hostess gift

1 (2-ounce) jar Colemans dry mustard
¾ cup apple cider vinegar
2 eggs
1 cup sugar
Dash salt

Put all ingredients in blender for 10 seconds. Put into saucepan and cook until it thickens. Perfect with pretzels.
Yield: 2 cups

Natalie Roy King

Fresh Fruit Sauce

1 (8-ounce) package cream
  cheese
1 (8-ounce) container sour
  cream
2 tablespoons cream
½ cup sugar
4 egg yolks
Amaretto, to taste

Blend all ingredients. Keep refrigerated until ready to use.
Spoon over fresh fruit. Strawberries may be marinated in a little
Amaretto overnight if desired.
Yield: 2 cups
Jeanne Powell Orman

Herb Butter

1 (1-pound) container soft
  butter
½ teaspoon fresh garlic
1 teaspoon fresh nutmeg,
  grated
1 to 2 teaspoons chives,
  fresh or frozen
2 teaspoons fresh parsley,
  minced
Salt and white pepper to
  taste

Soften butter for several hours. Use mixer and blend all ingredients. This is a good spread on French rolls with Parmesan
cheese sprinkled on top and toasted. Herb Butter is also
wonderful on fresh vegetables or fish.
Yield: 1 pound
Pamela Croy Newton

Hot Sauce For Avocados
A pretty first course for a Ladies Luncheon

4 tablespoons butter
2 tablespoons water
4 to 5 tablespoons
  ketchup
2 or 3 tablespoons vinegar
1 to 1½ tablespoons
  Worcestershire sauce
½ teaspoon salt
Few drops Tabasco

In a small saucpan heat all ingredients slowly until well blended. Serve in half an avocado, on a bed of lettuce surrounded
by grapefruit slices or hard boiled eggs.
Yield: 1 cup
Elleen Davis Wier

Mushroom Sauce

2 ounces butter
1 medium onion, chopped
1 pound fresh
  mushrooms, sliced
4 tablespoons ketchup

2 tablespoons red wine
1 teaspoon lemon pepper
1 teaspoon marjoram,
  dried
½ teaspoon salt

Sauté onion in butter, add sliced mushrooms and sauté until juice starts to form from the mushrooms. Turn off heat; add ketchup, wine, lemon pepper, marjoram and salt. Do not cook anymore. May be reheated to serve. Good especially on sliced tenderloin, but good even on hamburgers.
Yield: ¾ cup   *Peggy Elder Little*

Mustard Sauce

2 tablespoons flour
4 tablespoons dry mustard
1 cup sugar
1 teaspoon salt

2 eggs, slightly beaten
1 cup milk
¾ cup vinegar
¼ cup water

Mix all dry ingredients in top of double boiler. Add eggs and milk. Blend well. Heat. Add vinegar and water. Stir until thickened (this takes quite a while). *Great for a cocktail buffet with ham. Also doubles as a salad dressing on spinach.*
Yield: 2 cups   *Patty Hughes Eagar*

Raisin Sauce
It's good we heard it through the grape vine

1 cup raisins
2 cups water
2 tablespoons cornstarch
2 tablespoons sugar

2 tablespoons cold water
1 tablespoon butter
2 tablespoons lemon juice

Simmer raisins in water for 15 minutes. Make a paste of cornstarch, sugar, salt and 2 tablespoons cold water. Add to raisin mixture. Heat until thick; remove from heat. Add butter and lemon juice. Mix well. Serve with ham or pork roast.
Yield: 1½ cups   *Pamela Croy Newton*

Picante Sauce

1 quart cherry tomatoes
1 bell pepper
1 large onion
2 fresh jalapeno peppers
1 or 2 cloves garlic
½ cup vinegar

1 teaspoon salt
1 tablespoon sugar
½ teaspoon oregano
¼ teaspoon cayenne
  pepper
½ teaspoon cumin

Coarsley grind tomatoes in a food processor. Set aside. Grind the pepper, onion and garlic in processor. In a medium saucepan, simmer all ingredients, uncovered, for one hour. Put in sterilized jars. Process in a hot water bath for 15 minutes. Great served as an appetizer with corn chips, as a sauce on taco salads or on scrambled eggs.
Yield: 1 quart

Trisha McCutchen

Barbecue Sauce

4 cups ketchup
½ cup mustard
½ cup cider vinegar
½ cup Worcestershire
  sauce
¼ cup prepared
  horseradish
2 teaspoons salt

2 teaspoons ground sage
1 teaspoon pepper
2 tablespoons Tabasco
  sauce
1 tablespoon sugar
1 tablespoon garlic
  powder
1 tablespoon liquid smoke

Combine all ingredients in a large saucepan and simmer gently for 5 minutes. Use as you normally do in preparing barbecue chicken. If grilling on an outside grill, add to chicken as a baste when chicken is almost done (tomato base sauces burn easily). Leftover sauce keeps well in refrigerator.
Yield: 1 quart

Dianne Davison Isakson

Entrées

BEEF
Barbecue Beef, 93
Best Ever Beef Stew, 94
Castiglione Family
Meatballs, 95
Castiglione Family
Spaghetti Sauce, 95
Elegant Beef Tenderloin,
94
Father's Day Steak, 96
Ground Beef Stew, 98
Lasagna, 97
London Broil with
Onions, 96
Marinated London Broil,
97
Marinated Shish Kabob,
98
Saucy Meat Loaf, 99
Simply Elegant Steak, 99
Stroganoff Supreme, 100
Tenderloin, 93
CHICKEN
Capital Chicken, 102
Chicken and Shrimp
Supreme, 102
Chicken and Squash
Casserole, 101
Chicken Breasts
Brazilia, 103
Chicken Breasts
Champagne, 103
Chicken Breasts Oscar,
104
Chicken Kiwi, 105
Chicken Rockefeller, 106
Chicken Tarragon, 106
Cream Cheese Chicken,
107
Crescent Roll Chicken,
107
Crusty Parmesan
Chicken, 108
Galliano Cornish Hens,
109
Marinated Chicken Grill,
109
Oriental Chicken, 108
Russian Chicken, 105
Sherry's Chicken Curry,
101

Sour Cream Marinated
Chicken, 110
Stuffed Cornish Hens
with Mandarin Teriyaki
Sauce, 111
Turkey Enchilada
Casserole, 110
GAME
Baked Quail, 113
Christmas Quail, 111
Colorado Pheasant
Casserole, 112
Leg of Deer, 112
Venison Chili, 113
LAMB
Butterflied Grilled Leg of
Lamb, 114
Lamb Alexander, 114
PORK
Apricot Stuffed Chops,
115
Baked Country Ham, 116
Baked Ham, 115
Betsy's Grilled Marinated
Pork Chops, 116
Betty's Barbecue Pork,
117
Combo Gumbo, 122
Ercelens's Ham with
Blackberry Mustard
Sauce, 118
Frogmore Stew, 144
Ginny's Roast, 120
Ham and Broccoli,
Rollups, 117
Kielbasa and Cabbage,
118
Louisiana Jambalaya,
120
Louisiana Red Beans
and Rice, 121
Marinated Country Ribs,
121
Marinated Pork, 124
Pork Loin Roast with
Cherry Sauce, 124
Pork Tenderloin, 125
Roast Loin of Pork, 123
Stuffed Pork Roast, 119
SEAFOOD
Apricot Shrimp, 125

Bahama Grill, 135
Barbecue Shrimp, 128
Cheesy Scallops and
Rice, 128
Chinese Shrimp and
Peapods, 127
Coquilles St. Jacques a
lá Parisienne, 126
Crab Casserole, 129
Crab Royal, 129
Crab Stuffed Shrimp, 130
Crabmeat and
Asparagus Casserole,
130
Creole Seafood
Seasoning, 136
Delicious Fish, 131
Easy Crevette en
Croissant, 131
Flounder Florentine, 132
Flounder Supreme, 132
Garlic Shrimp, 133
Grilled Swordfish or
Salmon, 133
Grouper Gordon au
Gratin, 134
Paul's Island Grouper,
135
Poached Red Snapper,
134
Oysters Camille, 136
Oysters Supreme, 137
Shrimp and Artichoke
Casserole, 138
Shrimp and Fettuccine,
139
Shrimp and Vegetable
Tempura, 137
Shrimp and Wild Rice,
140
Shrimp Cabildo, 140
Shrimp Creole, 141
Shrimp Etouffee, 138
Shrimp in Cognac and
Cream, 141
Shrimp Mull, 142
Shrimp Stock, 139
Southern Scallops, 142
VEAL
Veal Forestier, 144
Veal Piccata, 143
Veal Vermouth, 143

Tenderloin
Simply Elegant

1 (7-pound) tenderloin,
trimmed of fat
1 tablespoon soy sauce

1 tablespoon brown sugar
½ cup Italian dressing
¼ cup lemon juice

Place tenderloin in a 9 x 13-inch baking pan or bottom of broiler pan. (Line pan with aluminum foil for quicker clean up.) Combine remainder of ingredients and pour over tenderloin. Marinate, in refrigerator, for several hours, turning once. When ready to cook, turn oven to broil. Place pan with tenderloin and marinade in oven on bottom shelf. Broil 20 minutes on each side. Cover and bake at 350° for 10 to 15 minutes. To serve, cut into 12 thick filets. *Wine Suggestion: California Petit Sirah*
Yield: 12 servings   *Dell Cochran James*

Barbecue Beef

1 (4 to 5-pound) beef
brisket (or pork if
desired)

Barbecue Sauce:
3 (8-ounce) cans tomato
sauce
½ cup water
½ cup onion, chopped
1 garlic clove, minced
¼ cup red wine vinegar
3 tablespoons
Worcestershire sauce
⅓ cup brown sugar, firmly
packed

2 tablespoons honey
2 teaspoons dry mustard
1 teaspoon chili powder
1 teaspoon salt
1 small lemon thinly sliced
(optional)
Dash liquid smoke, if
desired

Preheat oven 325°. Sprinkle meat with salt and pepper. Roast in covered roasting pan 3 to 4 hours until tender. While meat is cooking prepare sauce. Mix all ingredients in medium saucepan; bring to boil. Lower heat, simmer, uncovered 30 minutes; stir occasionally. Remove meat. Cut off excess fat. Slice meat into thin slices. Place meat in large casserole, cover with Barbecue Sauce. Bake 1 hour at 350° or put in microwave to heat meat and sauce until warm.
Yield: 10 to 12 servings   *Rebecca Edenfield Lingerfelt*

Best Ever Beef Stew

*This may be frozen to pull out and thaw on
the winter nights when there is no time to cook.*

2½ pounds rump roast or
   sirloin, cubed
1 quart tomatoes,
   undrained
2 cups carrots, cut in
   chunks
1½ cups celery, chopped
2 cups onions, diced
   coarsely
2 cups potatoes, cut in
   chunks
1 (10-ounce) package
   frozen peas, (optional)
1 (3-ounce) can sliced
   mushrooms, undrained

4 to 5 tablespoons quick
   cooking tapioca
2 beef bouillon cubes
2 teaspoons salt
1½ teaspoons sugar
1 teaspoon pepper
¼ teaspoon ground thyme
¼ teaspoon rosemary
   leaves
¼ teaspoon ground
   marjoram
¼ to ½ cup red wine
Several dashes of Maggi
   seasoning

Put all ingredients in order given in a small roaster with tight fitting lid and cook in a 275° oven for 5 hours. Stir after several hours.
Yield: 14 servings   *Pamela Croy Newton*

Elegant Beef Tenderloin

4 beef tenderloin steaks,
   cut ½ to 1 inch thick
1 tablespoon butter
¼ cup brandy
½ cup sour cream
2 tablespoons ketchup

¼ teaspoon salt
2 dashes Worcestershire
   sauce
4 drops bottled hot pepper
   sauce
Pinch of ground thyme

In a skillet, brown steaks in butter on both sides until desired doneness. Remove from heat. Pour half the brandy over the steaks. Transfer to warm platter and keep warm while preparing the sauce. Combine sour cream, ketchup, salt, Worcestershire, pepper sauce, thyme and remaining brandy. Add to same skillet. Heat, stirring constantly, until just heated through. Spoon some sauce over steaks when serving. Pass the remainder. *Wine Suggestion: Beaujolais Village*
Yield: 4 servings   *Susan Struzzieri Burns*

Castiglione Family Meatballs

1 pound sirloin or round
  steak, ground
2 slices bread, crumbled
⅓ cup milk
½ teaspoon garlic, finely
  chopped
1 tablespoon parsley
  flakes

¼ teaspoon oregano
2 tablespoons Romano or
  Parmesan cheese, grated
1 egg, slightly beaten
Black pepper
Cooking spray
Castiglione Family
  Spaghetti Sauce

Break up bread and add enough milk to wet it well. Add egg and mix well, then add remaining ingredients, except meat, mix well. Add the meat, blending well. Make one inch size meatballs and fry in a non-stick pan, sprayed with cooking spray. Add to Castiglione Family Spaghetti Sauce and simmer on low for thirty minutes before ready to serve. *Wine Suggestion: Barbaresco*
Yield: 8 servings
Linda Galt Best

Castiglione Family Spaghetti Sauce

¾ pound lean ground beef
¾ pound Italian sausage,
  link kind cut into chunks
¾ pound stew beef,
  chopped up
¾ pound pepperoni, link
  kind cut into chunks
2 (14½-ounce) cans Italian
  style tomatoes, crushed
1 (15-ounce) can tomato
  paste

2 large garlic cloves,
  chopped finely
1 teaspoon oregano
½ teaspoon basil leaves,
  crushed
3 to 4 large bay leaves
Pinch sugar
¼ teaspoon baking soda
Water
Castiglione Family
  Meatballs

Brown meat together, slowly. Drain on paper towels. In an 8 quart pot, put in all tomatoes, and tomato paste, add one full tomato paste can of water. In tomato cans rinse them with about ⅓ can of water and add to pot. Add remaining ingredients and simmer slowly, covered, for three to four hours until the sauce has thickened. If it is not quite thick enough leave cover ajar for the last half hour. Remove bay leaves and add meatballs. Simmer for thirty more minutes.
Yield: 8 servings
Linda Galt Best

Father's Day Steak
Grandfathers love it too.

3 to 4 pound London broil
or top round
½ cup sherry
½ cup soy sauce
¼ cup oil
¼ cup lemon juice
2 tablespoons brown
sugar
½ teaspoon ginger
1 garlic clove, minced
⅛ teaspoon hot pepper
sauce
4 teaspoons cornstarch
½ pound sliced
mushrooms
¼ cup sliced scallions

In a saucepan, mix sherry, soy sauce, oil, lemon juice, brown sugar, ginger, garlic and hot sauce. Cook ten minutes and cool. Place the steak in a plastic bag and pour cooled marinade over steak. Tie bag. Refrigerate for 24 hours. Remove steak, reserving marinade to make steak sauce. Place steak over hot coals or on a broiling rack 4 to 5 inches from heat. Broil 25 to 40 minutes for a rare to medium steak. Brush with marinade; turn occasionally. Carve thin slices diagonally across grain. To make sauce, stir cornstarch into remaining marinade. Bring to a boil. Add sliced mushrooms and scallions. Cook about 2 minutes until thickened. Spoon sauce over steak and serve.
Yield: 6 to 8 servings   *Jeanne Powell Orman*

London Broil With Onions

1½ pound flank steak or
London broil
⅓ cup vinegar
⅓ cup salad oil
3 tablespoons brown
sugar
3 tablespoons soy sauce
2 medium onions, sliced
and separated
1 garlic clove, crushed
½ teaspoon ground
pepper

Place steak in shallow glass dish. Mix all ingredients and pour over meat. Cover with plastic wrap and refrigerate 8 hours or more; turn occasionally. Remove meat, place on medium coals for 5 to 10 minutes on each side until medium rare. Place sauce and onions in saucepan and heat until onions are clear. Cut meat on diagonal and serve with the onions and sauce. Easy to double. Try the leftover sauce on baked potatoes! *Wine Suggestion: California Pinot Noir*
Yield: 4 to 6 servings   *Ginger Byrd McPherson*

Marinated London Broil

¼ cup soy sauce
2 tablespoons vinegar
3 tablespoons honey
1½ teaspoons garlic chips
1½ teaspoons ground
 ginger

¾ cup vegetable oil
1½ to 2 pound London
 broil

Mix all ingredients and pour over meat. Refrigerate at least overnight. Grill over very hot coals 5 minutes on each side. It is best served rare. This meat is wonderful chilled after grilling and then sliced and served for picnics.
Yield: 6 servings   *Barbara Gully Allen*

Lasagna
Mama Mia!

1 pound Italian sausage
1 pound ground beef
1 garlic clove, minced
1 tablespoon dried basil,
 crushed
1½ teaspoons salt
1 (1-pound) can tomatoes
2 (6-ounce) cans tomato
 paste
10 ounces lasagna
 noodles

3 cups fresh cream style
 cottage cheese
2 tablespoons dried
 parsley flakes
2 eggs, beaten
1 teaspoon salt
½ teaspoon pepper
1 pound mozzarella
 cheese, thinly sliced

Preheat oven to 375°. Brown meat slowly; drain. Add garlic, basil, 1½ teaspoons salt, tomatoes and tomato paste. Simmer uncovered for thirty minutes, stirring occasionally. Cook noodles in a large amount of boiling water until tender; drain and rinse. Combine remaining ingredients, except mozzarella. Place half the noodles in a 13 x 9 x 2-inch dish. Spread with half the mozzarella cheese and half the meat sauce. Repeat layers. Bake at 375° for 30 minutes. Let stand ten minutes before cutting into squares.
Yield: 10 to 12 servings   *Jennie Inglesby Adams*

Ground Beef Stew
A "suit yourself" recipe.

1 pound ground beef
2 medium potatoes, cut in
½ inch cubes
1 onion, chopped
2 carrots, sliced
1 (16-ounce) can stewed
tomatoes
1 (8-ounce) can tomato
sauce
1 cup frozen yellow corn
1 cup frozen lima beans
1 cup frozen blackeyed
peas

½ cup English peas
4 okra pods, sliced
½ tablespoon salt
2 teaspoons pepper
½ teaspoon Italian
seasoning
1 bay leaf
½ teaspoon garlic powder
1 teaspoon chili powder
6 cups water

In a large Dutch oven, brown and drain meat. Add all the other ingredients and bring the stew to a boil. Reduce heat and cover; simmer for one hour, stirring occasionally. *This recipe may be varied to suit your family's tastes, using many kinds of vegetables. It is a fantastic way to clean the refrigerator.*
Yield: 8 to 10 servings   *Connie Heidt Kirk*

Marinated Shish Kabob
Summer night special

2 pounds sirloin, cut into
1½-inch cubes
½ cup Burgundy wine
1 teaspoon Worcestershire
sauce
½ teaspoon monosodium
glutamate
1 clove garlic, minced

½ cup vegetable oil
½ teaspoon salt
2 tablespoons ketchup
1 teaspoon sugar
1 tablespoon vinegar
½ teaspoon marjoram
½ teaspoon rosemary
Cooked rice

Place steak in large bowl. Combine remaining ingredients and pour over steak. Marinate steak, in refrigerator, for 2 hours. When ready to cook, alternate marinated pieces of steak on skewers with potatoes, fresh mushrooms, bell peppers, onions, tomatoes, etc. Cook on grill, basting with marinade until cooked as desired. Serve over rice.
Yield: 6 to 8 servings   *Rebecca Hardison Ferguson*

Saucy Meat Loaf
Why be ordinary?

2 pounds ground beef
1 large onion, chopped
2 eggs, beaten
1 (8-ounce) can tomato
  sauce

1 cup crackers, crushed
2 teaspoons
  Worcestershire sauce
1 to 1½ teaspoons salt
Pepper

Sauce:
¾ cup brown sugar
⅔ cup ketchup

2 teaspoons mustard

Preheat oven to 325°. Mix together beef, onion, egg, tomato sauce, crackers, Worcestershire, salt and pepper and shape into loaf. Place in loaf pan or casserole. Bake 1 to 1½ hours at 325°. Drain grease twice during cooking. While baking, prepare sauce by mixing all ingredients. While meat loaf is still warm, top with sauce.
Yield: 6 servings   *Cindy Clotfelter Rozen*

Simply Elegant Steak

1½ pounds tenderized
  boneless beef round
  steak
1½ tablespoons vegetable
  oil
2 large onions, cut in ½
  inch slices and
  separated into rings
1 (4-ounce) can sliced
  mushrooms (drained and
  reserve liquid)

1 (10¾-ounce) can
  condensed cream of
  mushroom soup
½ cup cooking sherry
1½ teaspoons garlic salt
3 cups hot cooked rice

Cut steak into thin strips. In a large skillet (oven-proof if desired), brown steak in oil, using high heat. Add onions and sauté until tender crisp. In a small bowl, blend soup, sherry, liquid from mushrooms, and garlic salt. Pour over steak and add mushrooms. Reduce heat, cover and simmer for one hour or until steak is tender. (Or, cover and bake at 350°). Serve over the 3 cups of cooked rice.
Yield: 6 servings   *Charlotte Cox Smithwick*

Stroganoff Supreme

1½ pounds beef (thinly
sliced or cubed)
4 tablespoons flour
1½ teaspoons salt
1 teaspoon garlic powder
¼ teaspoon paprika
5 tablespoons solid
shortening
1 medium onion, thinly
sliced
2 cups sliced mushrooms,
sautéed
1 (10-ounce) can cream of
mushroom soup

½ (11-ounce) can beef
consommé
¼ cup water
1 cup sour cream
Dash Worcestershire
sauce
Dash (slight) Tabasco
½ cup dry sherry
3 tablespoons chopped
chives, fresh or frozen
Parsley for garnish
Cooked rice or noodles

Mix flour, salt, pepper, garlic powder, and paprika; add steak strips and toss until coated. Reserve remaining flour mixture. Heat shortening in heavy skillet and add meat. Brown meat; add onions and cook until transparent. Add sautéed mushrooms and the reserved flour; mix well. Add both soups, water, Worcestershire, Tabasco and sherry; cover. Cook slowly, stirring occasionally for 45 minutes to one hour, until meat is tender. Remove cover, continue cooking until mixture is slightly thickened. If too thick, add a little extra consommé. Stir in sour cream and chives, heat thoroughly. Serve over rice or noodles.
Yield: 6 to 8 servings   *Pamela Croy Newton*

Sherry's Chicken Curry
An entertaining meal

½ cup butter
2 cloves garlic
1 teaspoon ground ginger
1 tablespoon curry powder
½ cup flour
1 cup milk

1½ cups chicken broth
5 pounds chicken, cooked
   and diced
Cooked rice for 6 to 8
   servings

Condiments:
Shredded coconut
Bacon crumbs
Chopped celery
Diced hard cooked eggs
Chopped black olives

Chopped peanuts
Chopped onions
Chopped tomatoes
Chutney

Melt butter and brown garlic. Add ginger, curry, flour, milk and broth. Cook until thickened, stirring constantly. Add diced chicken. Heat thoroughly. Serve chicken mixture over rice. Top with *all* of the condiments for best results.
Yield: 6 to 8 servings   *Jean Jones Warren*

Chicken And Squash Casserole
Perfect for a ladies' luncheon

3 cups cooked chicken,
   cut into bite size pieces
2 cups cooked squash,
   seasoned while cooking
   with onions, salt and
   pepper
1½ cups Pepperidge Farm
   Herb dressing mix

1 (10¾-ounce) can cream
   of chicken soup
1 pint sour cream
1 (8-ounce) can sliced
   water chestnuts
3 to 4 tablespoons butter

Preheat oven to 350°. Sprinkle bottom of buttered 9 x 13-inch casserole with ¾ cup dressing mix. Place squash on top of dressing. Make a sauce combining soup, sour cream, and water chestnuts. Add chicken to sauce and place on top of squash. Sprinkle top with remainder of dressing mix and dot with butter. Bake for 30 to 45 minutes until hot and bubbly.
Yield: 8 to 10 servings   *Dell Cochran James*

Capital Chicken
Good enough for the governor

4 tablespoons butter
1 tablespoon cooking oil
4 chicken breasts
1 (8-ounce) package fresh
mushrooms, sliced
1 tablespoon flour
1 (10¾-ounce) can cream
of chicken soup
1 cup dry white wine
1 cup water
½ cup whipping cream

1 teaspoon salt
½ teaspoon tarragon
leaves
¼ teaspoon pepper
1 (15-ounce) can artichoke
hearts, drained and
quartered
6 green onions, chopped
2 tablespoons chopped
parsley

Preheat oven to 350°. Combine butter and oil in a large frying pan; heat until butter is melted. Add chicken and cook until brown on all sides, about 10 minutes. Remove chicken and place in a 3 quart casserole dish. In same frypan, sauté mushrooms until tender. Stir in flour, then add soup, wine and water; simmer, stirring constantly, until sauce thickens. Stir in cream, salt, tarragon and pepper. Pour sauce over chicken and bake, uncovered, for 45 minutes. Remove casserole from oven and add artichoke hearts, green onions and parsley; mix gently. Return to oven and bake for an additional 30 minutes.
Yield: 4 servings   *Ginger Colquitt Autry*

Chicken And Shrimp Supreme

¼ cup butter
1 onion, chopped
½ pound fresh
mushrooms, sliced
2 (10¾-ounce) cans cream
of mushroom soup
½ cup sherry

½ cup light cream
1 cup Cheddar cheese,
shredded
2 cups chicken, cooked
2 cups shrimp, cooked
1 tablespoon parsley
Cooked rice or noodles

In a three quart saucepan, melt butter; add onion and mushrooms; sauté 5 minutes. Add soup, gradually stir in sherry and cream. Add cheese; stir over low heat until melted. Add chicken and shrimp, heat to serving temperature (do not boil). Just before serving stir in parsley. Serve over rice or noodles.
Yield: 6 to 8 servings   *Susan Drew Blunk*

Chicken Breasts Brazilia

4 boneless whole chicken
breasts (about 6 or 7
ounces each)
1 (14-ounce) can hearts of
palm

Melted butter
Salt
White pepper
Hollandaise sauce
Chives, chopped

Preheat oven to 400°. Wrap chicken breasts around stalks of palm hearts and attach with a toothpick. Place open seam side down in a buttered pan. Cover breasts generously with melted butter. Season to taste with salt and white pepper. Bake for 25 minutes. Remove from oven and top with Hollandaise sauce and chopped chives. *Note:* Hollandaise sauce recipe on page 87. *Wine Suggestion: Pouilly Fumé*
Yield: 4 servings   *Leckie Kern Stack*

Chicken Breasts Champagne

3 skinless, boneless whole
chicken breasts (about
2½ pounds), halved
lengthwise
1 teaspoon lemon juice
Salt and pepper
2 tablespoons butter

2 tablespoons green
onion, chopped
1 cup champagne
½ cup whipping cream
2 egg yolks, beaten
2 tablespoons snipped
parsley

Place each chicken breast between two pieces of clear plastic wrap and pound with meat mallet to flatten slightly. Rub each chicken breast with lemon juice and season with salt and pepper. Melt butter in large, heavy frying pan. Add onions and cook until tender, but not brown. Add chicken and cook 3 minutes per side, or until done. Remove chicken to serving platter and keep warm. Add champagne to frying pan and boil vigorously until liquid is reduced to ½ cup. Stir in whipping cream. Place egg yolks in separate bowl and beat. Add ½ champagne mixture to egg yolks and stir. Return egg yolk mixture to frying pan and cook with remainder of champagne mixture until slightly thickened and bubbling. Spoon sauce over chicken and sprinkle with parsley. *Wine Suggestion: Saint Veran*
Yield: 6 servings   *Leigh Ellen Carlson*

Chicken Breasts Oscar
Impress your guests

4 to 6 whole chicken breasts (allow ½ breast per person)

4 tablespoons dried soup greens

2 tablespoons dry onions or 2 fresh onions, chopped

6 to 8 cups water

Stuffing:

6 to 8 ounces frozen baby shrimp, cooked and well-drained

1 (12-ounce) can crabmeat

1 cup seasoned stuffing

4 ounces cream cheese, room temperature

1 egg

2 teaspoons lemon pepper

½ teaspoon herb pepper

2 teaspoons horseradish

2 teaspoons pickled capers

1 teaspoon Worcestershire sauce

1 tablespoon lemon juice

Sauce:

1 (10¾-ounce) can cream of shrimp soup

1 teaspoon horseradish

1 envelope hollandaise sauce mix

2 ounces butter, melted

Parmesan cheese

Bring water to a boil. Add soup greens, onions, salt and chicken breasts (put skin down into water). Cook 12 to 18 minutes, depending on number of chicken breasts. Turn heat off and let sit in pot 30 minutes more. Remove chicken from pot; skin and debone. Split whole breasts in half and place in a 9 x 13-inch baking dish. Preheat oven to 350°. Combine all stuffing ingredients and mix well. Shape stuffing into oval patties and place on top of chicken breasts. Combine soup, horseradish, hollandaise mix and butter. Mix well and pour over stuffing and chicken. Sprinkle with Parmesan cheese bake for 40 minutes. *Note:* Stuffing mixture is good on top of toast points for luncheons. *Wine Suggestion: California Sylvaner*
Yield: 8 to 12 servings   *Jane Smith Williams*

Chicken Kiwi
Unusual

1 pound chicken breasts;
skinned, boned and
sliced into strips
3 tablespoons oil (divided
1 tablespoon and 2
tablespoons)
1 medium onion, chopped
or 1 bunch spring
onions, chopped
1 cup carrots, thinly sliced
1 cup fresh mushrooms,
sliced
1 cup celery, sliced
diagonally

1 (13¾-ounce) can chicken
broth
4 teaspoons cornstarch
½ teaspoon salt
½ teaspoon grated lemon
or lime peel
1 tablespoon soy sauce
1 teaspoon hot sauce
Dash of pepper
2 to 3 Kiwi fruit, sliced
Cooked rice

Sauté chicken in 1 tablespoon oil until cooked, approximately 10 to 15 minutes. Remove chicken and keep warm. Sauté onions, carrots, mushrooms and celery in 2 tablespoons oil until tender but still crisp. Return chicken to skillet with vegetables. Combine broth, cornstarch and seasonings. Add to chicken mixture and cook until thickened. Gently stir in Kiwi fruit. Serve over cooked rice. *Wine Suggestion: Montrachet*
Yield: 4 to 6 servings   *Betsy Lee McNair Holladay*

Russian Chicken
When you are too busy to cook

1 (8-ounce) bottle of
Russian salad dressing
5 ounces apricot
preserves
¼ cup water

1 package dry onion soup
mix
6 chicken breast halves,
skin removed

Preheat oven to 350°. In a saucepan, combine the first 4 ingredients; bring to a slow boil, then remove from heat. Place chicken breasts in a shallow baking dish; pour sauce over breasts. Cover dish with aluminum foil and bake for 60 minutes. Uncover, baste with sauce, and bake uncovered for 30 minutes more.
Yield: 6 servings   *Phyllis Wallace Holley*

Chicken Rockefeller
Don't have to be rich to enjoy this one.

4 chicken breasts, skinned
and boned
1 tablespoon butter or
margarine
1 tablespoon olive oil
1 (10-ounce) package
frozen chopped spinach,
cooked and drained
1 (10¾-ounce) can cream
of chicken soup

½ cup mayonnaise
½ cup sour cream or plain
yogurt
1 tablespoon lemon juice
¼ cup sherry
½ cup grated yellow
cheese
Paprika (optional)

Preheat oven to 350°. Combine butter and oil in skillet and brown chicken. Place cooked spinach in bottom of 2 quart casserole; top with chicken. Mix remaining ingredients together. Spoon sauce over chicken. Sprinkle with paprika (if desired). Bake for 30 minutes.
Yield: 4 servings   *Kathy Chiles Pilcher*

Chicken Tarragon
Tarragon makes the difference

2 cups uncooked egg
noodles
2 cups water
1 cup dry white wine
1 teaspoon dried tarragon
leaves

1 (1.4-ounce) package dry
vegetable soup mix
4 chicken breast halves,
skinned and boned
1 cup sour cream

Cook egg noodles per package directions and drain. In 10-inch skillet, over medium heat, bring water, wine and tarragon leaves to boil. Stir in dry soup mix and boil 5 minutes. Add chicken; reduce heat. Cover and simmer for 10 to 12 minutes or until chicken is tender. Arrange noodles in buttered, heated casserole. With slotted spoon, remove chicken and vegetables from skillet (reserving liquid) and arrange over noodles. Cover to keep warm. Boil liquid in skillet over high heat 10 minutes or until reduced to ½ cup. Reduce heat to low. Stir in sour cream, stirring constantly, cook 3 to 4 minutes (do not boil). Spoon over chicken and noodles.
Yield: 4 servings   *Cheryl Tilly Briscoe*

Cream Cheese Chicken

3 pounds chicken
breasts-cooked, skinned,
boned
2 (10-ounce) packages
frozen broccoli, cooked
and drained
2 (8-ounce) packages
cream cheese

2 cups milk
¾ teaspoon garlic salt
1 teaspoon salt
Sherry to taste
1 cup Parmesan cheese
1 small can onion rings

Preheat oven to 350°. Combine cream cheese, milk, salts and sherry in blender. Blend until well mixed. Butter a 3 quart casserole dish and place broccoli on bottom. Pour half of cheese mixture over broccoli. Place chicken on top and pour rest of cheese mixture over chicken. Cover with Parmesan cheese. Bake for 45 minutes. Place onion rings on top during last 5 minutes of baking.
Yield: 8 servings

Cathy Colquitt

Crescent Roll Chicken

4 ounces cream cheese,
softened
2 tablespoons milk
2 cups cooked chicken,
finely chopped
½ teaspoon salt
½ teaspoon pepper

2 (8-ounce) cans
refrigerated crescent
dinner rolls
¼ cup plus 2 tablespoons
butter, melted
1½ cups crushed croutons

Preheat oven to 350°. Combine cream cheese with milk; beat or mix well until smooth. Stir in chicken, salt and pepper. Separate crescent roll dough into triangles. Place 2 to 3 tablespoons of chicken mixture on each of 8 triangles, spreading to within ½ inch of edges; moisten edges of dough with water. Place the remaining eight triangles of dough on top; press edges to seal. Dip each sandwich in butter; roll in crushed croutons. Place on lightly greased baking sheets. Bake for 20 to 25 minutes or until lightly browned.
Yield: 8 servings

Yvonne Miller Newman

Crusty Parmesan Chicken
Serve as a main dish or cut chicken into strips for an appetizer

2 cups dry bread crumbs
¾ cup grated Parmesan
  cheese
1 teaspoon paprika
1 teaspoon garlic salt
1 teaspoon pepper
4 tablespoons chopped
  parsley

½ cup unsalted butter
1 teaspoon Worcestershire
  sauce
1 teaspoon dry mustard
4 whole chicken breasts -
  halved, boned, skinned

Preheat oven to 350°. Line 9 x 13-inch baking dish with foil. Combine first 6 ingredients in a bowl and mix thoroughly. Melt butter in a saucepan. Add Worcestershire and mustard. Dip chicken in butter mixture, then in crumb mixture, coating well. Arrange chicken in baking dish. Pour remaining butter mixture over chicken. Bake 50 to 60 minutes. *Wine Suggestion: California Sauvignon Blanc*
Yield: 8 to 10 servings   *Betty Parrott Barnett*

Oriental Chicken
Serve with cheese soufflé

½ cup butter
½ cup flour
1 tablespoon salt
1 cup cream
3 cups milk
2 cups chicken stock
4 cups cooked chicken,
  diced

½ cup sautéed
  mushrooms
½ cup almonds, sliced
1 cup water chestnuts,
  sliced
¼ cup pimento strips
¼ cup sherry
Cheese Soufflé -page 223

Melt butter in top of double boiler. Add flour and salt; cook until well mixed. Add cream, milk and stock. Cook over water for 30 minutes, stirring constantly. Just before serving, add the next six ingredients and heat. Serve over cheese soufflé.
Yield: 4 to 6 servings   *Sybil Kendall Little*

Galliano Cornish Hens
Elegant for any entertaining

Stuffing:
1 (6-ounce) package wild rice
1 medium onion

1 tablespoon butter
1 (2½-ounce) jar sliced mushrooms, drained

Basting Sauce:
Juice of one lemon
¼ pound butter

2 ounces Galliano liqueur

Hens:
4 Cornish hens
Salt

Pepper
Garlic salt

Stuffing: Cook rice according to package directions. Sauté onion in butter; add onion and mushrooms to cooked rice. Set aside.

Basting Sauce: Melt butter; add lemon juice and Galliano. Heat just to boiling.

Hens: Preheat oven to 325°. Wash hens and season inside and out to taste with salt, pepper, and garlic salt. Stuff with rice mixture; baste with sauce and transfer to baking pan. Cover with remaining sauce. Bake, covered, for 30 minutes. Uncover, bake an additional 30 minutes or until brown. Baste and turn birds 2 or 3 times during last 30 minutes. Serve whole or split.

Wine Suggestion: Pinot Blanc
Yield: 4 servings

Ansley Little Meaders

Marinated Chicken Grill
Prepare in advance

10 to 12 chicken breast halves, boned
1 cup soy sauce
1¾ cups pineapple juice

1 cup wine vinegar
½ cup sugar
1½ teaspoons garlic powder

Place chicken in plastic bag or a container with cover. Mix remainder of ingredients and pour over chicken. Marinate for 24 to 48 hours. Grill.

Yield: 10 to 12 servings

Barbara Gully Allen

Sour Cream Marinated Chicken
A good do ahead company dish!

1 cup sour cream
2 tablespoons lemon juice
2 teaspoons
   Worcestershire sauce
1½ teaspoons celery salt
1 teaspoon paprika
¼ teaspoon garlic powder

1½ teaspoons salt
½ teaspoon pepper
2 cups dry bread crumbs
½ cup margarine
6 chicken breast halves,
   skinned and boned

Combine all ingredients, except bread crumbs, margarine and chicken. Marinate chicken in mixture overnight, turning once or twice. Preheat oven to 350°. Roll chicken in bread crumbs to coat. Roll chicken jelly roll style and secure with a toothpick. Melt margarine in a 8-inch square baking dish. Roll chicken in melted margarine to coat. Bake, uncovered, for one hour. Do not turn while baking. Remove from oven and drain chicken on heavy brown paper. * *Recipe may be doubled and baked in 9 x 13-inch dish for one hour.*
Yield: 4 to 6 servings   *Angel Layne Daniels*

Turkey Enchilada Casserole
Spice up your leftover turkey

2 (10¾-ounce) cans cream
   of chicken soup
4 cups chopped cooked
   turkey
1 (4-ounce) can chopped
   green chilies, drained
1 pint sour cream
1 clove garlic, pressed

1 tablespoon chili powder
1 tablespoon cumin
1 tablespoon coriander
½ soup can of milk
1 (8-ounce) bag of corn
   chips, crushed
8 ounces Monterey Jack
   cheese, shredded

Preheat oven to 350°. Combine all ingredients, except corn chips and cheese. Mix well. Grease a 3 quart casserole dish. Alternate layers of turkey mixture with corn chips, beginning and ending with turkey mixture. Top with cheese and cover with foil. Bake for 30 to 45 minutes. Remove foil last five minutes of cooking time to brown.
Yield: 8 to 10 servings   *Leigh Ellen Carlson*

Stuffed Cornish Hens With Mandarin Teriyaki Sauce

"Grand Prize Winner...Marietta Daily Journal Cookbook Contest"

1 (10½-ounce) can
condensed chicken broth
1 cup water
½ teaspoon salt
1½ cups rice
½ cup chopped onion
½ cup chopped celery
5 tablespoons butter
1 cup pitted ripe olives
1 (11-ounce) can mandarin
oranges

¾ teaspoon basil leaves
¾ teaspoon savory leaves
¼ teaspoon white pepper
6 cornish game hens
¼ cup canned syrup from
oranges
¼ cup teriyaki sauce
1 teaspoon cornstarch

Mix together broth, water and salt and heat to boiling. Stir in rice. Cook over low heat, covered for 15 minutes. Melt 4 tablespoons butter. Add onion and celery; cook till soft. Cut olives in half. Drain oranges; save syrup. Cut oranges in half. Mix cooked rice, onion-celery mix, ripe olives, orange halves and seasoning. Preheat oven to 350°. Stuff each cornish hen with about 1 cup of mixture. Cover stuffing with aluminum foil to prevent drying. Roast about 1 hour. In sauce pan, combine ½ cup orange syrup, teriyaki sauce, cornstarch and 1 tablespoon butter. Cook until clear and slightly thickened. Brush over hens after 1 hour, then roast 15 minutes longer until hens are glazed and well browned. *Wine Suggestion: Corton- Charlemagne*
Yield: 6 servings   *Malinda Jolley Mortin*

Christmas Quail

12 strips of bacon
12 quail, oven-ready

¾ cup butter
2 cups champagne

Wrap bacon around quail; secure with toothpicks. Melt butter in ovenproof casserole on stove top. Add quail; sauté until delicately browned on all sides, about 15 minutes. Add champagne; season with salt and pepper. Cover casserole and simmer gently for 12 to 15 minutes.
Yield: 6 servings   *Cheryl Tilley Briscoe*

Colorado Pheasant Casserole

12 ounces mild pork
  sausage
1 large onion, chopped
½ pound mushrooms,
  sliced
1 (8-ounce) can water
  chestnuts, sliced
2 cups cooked pheasant,
  (turkey or chicken may
  be substituted)
Juice of ½ lemon
1 (6-ounce) box wild rice
¼ cup butter
¼ cup flour
¼ cup milk
1¾ cups chicken broth
1 teaspoon salt
⅛ teaspoon pepper
½ cup slivered almonds,
  toasted

Brown sausage; remove sausage from pan. Sauté onion and mushrooms in remaining sausage grease. Add sliced water chestnuts and return sausage to the pan. Lightly toss pheasant with this mixture; squeeze lemon juice over mixture. Cook rice according to package directions; stir into the sausage mixture. In a separate saucepan, make a white sauce using the butter, flour and milk. Add chicken broth, salt, and pepper to the white sauce. Mix white sauce and pheasant mixture; pour into casserole and bake one hour at 350°. Remove from oven and sprinkle with almonds before serving.
Yield: 8 to 10 servings   *Sally Bailey Dete*

Leg of Deer

1 to 5 pounds leg of deer *
1 (10½-ounce) can cream
  of mushroom soup
½ cup butter or margarine
Dash of Worcestershire
  sauce
1 medium onion, chopped

If roast is over 5 pounds double recipe!
Place deer in large roasting pan, cover with mushroom soup and dot with butter and dash with Worcestershire sauce and onion. Cover with foil. Bake at 400° until steam comes out of foil. Turn down to 200° and cook all day or all night (about 6 to 8 hours). Take out of oven and remove any bones, chop meat and return it to the gravy and return to oven for one more hour.
Yield: 8 servings   *Linda Galt Best*

Baked Quail
A family favorite for the holidays

12 quail, ready to cook
1 stick butter, softened
1 cup flour
1 teaspoon marjoram
½ teaspoon ground thyme
1 teaspoon paprika
2 teaspoons salt
¼ teaspoon pepper

1 (11-ounce) can cream of
  chicken soup
½ cup cream of celery
  soup
1 tablespoon
  Worcestershire sauce
1½ cups water
½ cup dry white wine

Rub softened butter over quail. Combine flour and spices in a bag. Place quail, a few at a time, in the bag and shake well to coat. Heat about ¼ inch of oil in a skillet and brown quail quickly. Place quail in a shallow baking pan. Combine remaining ingredients and pour over quail. Bake at 375°, covered, for one hour. Uncover for last ten minutes of baking. *Wine Suggestion: Gevery-Chambertin.*
Yield: 6 servings   *Lynn Stiles Foster*

Venison Chili
A hunter's delight

2 pounds ground venison
  (may use ground sirloin
  or ground round)
1 medium onion, chopped
1 cup celery, chopped
1 green pepper, chopped
  (optional)
Salt and pepper to taste
1 (8-ounce) can tomato
  sauce

1 (8-ounce) can tomatoes
1 (15-ounce) can chili con
  carne
1 (16-ounce) can red
  kidney beans
¼ teaspoon garlic powder
1 teaspoon chili powder
½ cup red wine

Brown meat, onion, celery, and green pepper; season with salt and pepper. Drain off all fat. Add remaining ingredients, cook covered for 30 minutes and simmer uncovered for several hours. This freezes well.
Yield: 6 to 8 servings   *Sybil Kendall Little*

Lamb Alexander
Exceptional!

8 dried apricots
1½ cups Courvoisier
8 1 inch thick lamb chops
1 tablespoon paprika
2 tablespoons butter

2 tablespoons soy sauce
½ cup Madeira
½ pint whipping cream
8 teaspoons apricot jam

Simmer dried apricots with ½ cup Courvoisier in a small saucepan until Courvoisier is absorbed (approximately 10 minutes). Set aside. Trim excess fat from lamb chops and coat with paprika. Melt butter in large skillet and brown lamb chops on both sides. Pour off any excess fat. Sprinkle soy sauce over the tops of chops. Add Madeira and simmer for 5 minutes, until Madeira begins to reduce. Warm the remaining 1 cup of Courvoisier, pour over the chops, and ignite. When the flames have died down, remove the chops and add whipping cream. Boil to reduce sauce to 1 cup. Return the chops to the sauce and top each with 1 teaspoon of apricot jam. Heat. To serve, place the chops on a platter, pour the sauce over each; top with the dried apricots. *Wine Suggestion: Chateau Leóville-Barton*
Yield: 4 servings   *Leckie Kern Stack*

Butterflied Grilled Leg Of Lamb

1 leg of lamb, butterflied
  by butcher
1 (12-ounce) bottle oil and
  vinegar salad dressing
½ cup butter

Juice of 3 lemons
1½ teaspoons onion salt
1½ tablespoons lemon
  pepper seasoning

Place lamb in a pan; cover with dressing; marinate in refrigerator 6 to 8 hours or overnight, turning occasionally. Start grill and allow coals to burn until medium heat. Melt butter and stir in lemon juice, onion salt, and lemon pepper. Baste meat while cooking. Grill approximately 20 minutes per side. Lamb should be pink in the middle. *Wine Suggestion: California Cabernet Sauvignon*
Yield: 8 to 10 servings   *Ellen Fox Hammond*

Apricot Stuffed Chops

This sauce freezes well, so when cooking double sauce and freeze. You can use later to baste pork chops or pork roast.

**6 rib pork chops, 1 inch
thick
2 (17-ounce) cans apricot
halves
½ cup ketchup**

**4 tablespoons oil
2 tablespoons lemon juice
1 teaspoon dry mustard
4 tablespoons onion,
chopped**

Cut pocket into chops. Season inside with salt and pepper. Drain apricots reserving 1 cup liquid. Place 2 apricot halves in pockets of chops. Dice remaining fruit and set aside. Grill chops over medium coals for 35 minutes, turning once. In saucepan combine ketchup, oil, lemon juice, dry mustard, onions, diced apricots and reserved juice. Heat to boiling, reduce heat and simmer for 15 minutes. Cook chops 5 more minutes brushing with sauce. Serve apricot sauce on the side. *Wine Suggestion: Sancerre*
Yield: 6 servings

Baked Ham

Old family recipe which cooks the ham in a dough basket

**Country ham or frozen
ham 8 to 15 pounds
4 cups flour
2 tablespoons ground
cloves
2 tablespoons cinnamon**

**2 tablespoons dry mustard
1 teaspoon black pepper
Peach pickle juice or apple
cider
1 cup brown sugar**

Remove rind from ham. Combine flour, cloves, cinnamon, mustard, pepper and enough juice to make a dough which can be rolled. Cover fat portion of ham with dough. Place in a large baking pan. Put in a cold oven and bake at 325° for about 20 to 25 minutes per pound. Baste ham every thirty minutes. Take dough off of ham and brown with brown sugar.
Yield: 8 to 10 servings   *Elizabeth Sherwood*

Baked Country Ham
"A truly Southern meal"

1 uncooked country ham

Saw off the hock end of the ham so that it will fit into a covered roasting pan. Save the hock to use for seasoning vegetables. Place the ham in the roasting pan and cover with water. Bring to a boil, cover, remove from heat, and let stand for several hours. If you do not like the salty taste of country ham, this procedure can be repeated with fresh water. After soaking, pour off the water and add 4 cups of cold water. Place the ham, in its covered roaster, in a cold oven and turn the heat to 500°. DO NOT OPEN THE OVEN DOOR UNTIL THE ENTIRE PROCESS IS COMPLETED! When the oven reaches 500°, about 10 minutes, cook the ham for 1 minute per pound, and then turn the oven off. Without ever opening the door, repeat the cooking instructions in 3 hours. Turn off the oven again and leave the ham inside the oven overnight. In the morning, remove the roaster from the oven, and pour out the water. Slice off the skin and all but ¼ inch of fat. Score the fat in a diamond pattern and brown the ham under the broiler. *This recipe is guaranteed to produce a delicious, moist ham everytime!*
Yield: 1 ham   *Sydney Cobb Smith*

Betsy's Grilled Marinated Pork Chops

1½ cups salad oil
¾ cup soy sauce
¼ cup Worcestershire
   sauce
2 tablespoons dry mustard
2¼ teaspoons salt
1 tablespoon pepper

½ cup red wine vinegar
1½ teaspoons parsley
   flakes
2 garlic cloves, crushed
⅓ cup fresh lemon juice
8 pork chops, one inch
   thick

Combine all ingredients except chops and mix well. Pour marinade over pork chops and marinate at least 3 hours. Grill over medium coals, basting with remaining marinade. Unused marinade will keep in refrigerator for two weeks. *One of my first recipes and still a favorite.*
Yield: 6 to 8 servings   *Anna Ferguson Tucker*

Betty's Barbecue Pork
(for sandwiches)

4 to 6 pound pork loin
  roast
3 tablespoons brown
  sugar
1 cup vinegar
½ cup Worcestershire
  sauce

1 large onion, chopped
3 tablespoons prepared
  mustard
¼ teaspoon pepper
1½ cups ketchup

Pour all ingredients over pork roast in a Dutch oven and cook covered over low heat for 4 to 5 hours. Break up large pieces and remove bones if any. Serve in sandwich buns.
Yield: 25 to 30 sandwiches   *Donya Smith Rickman*

Ham and Broccoli Rollups

8 rectangular slices boiled
  ham
8 slices Swiss cheese
2 (10-ounce) packages
  broccoli spears, cooked
  and drained
1 tablespoon butter or
  margarine
1 tablespoon flour
¼ teaspoon salt

1 tablespoon prepared
  horseradish
2 teaspoons prepared
  mustard
½ teaspoon
  Worcestershire sauce
½ teaspoon grated onion
2 egg yolks, beaten
1 cup pineapple juice
½ cup milk

Preheat oven to 350°. Place one slice of cheese on each slice of ham; top with 1 to 2 spears of broccoli. In medium sauce pan melt butter; blend in flour, salt, horseradish, mustard, Worcestershire and onion. Combine egg yolks and pineapple juice; gently stir into butter mixture. Stir in milk; cook over low heat, stirring constantly until thick and bubbling. Spoon one tablespoon of sauce over broccoli; roll ham and cheese around broccoli and secure with a toothpick. Place roll-ups in baking dish; cover and cook at 350° for 25 to 30 minutes. Spoon any remaining hot mustard sauce over ham rolls just before serving.
Yield: 6 to 8 servings   *Anna Ferguson Tucker*

Ercelene's Ham With Blackberry Mustard Sauce

Serve with Ercelene's Spoon Bread

1 (2½ to 3 inch) slice of center cut ham (any butcher will be glad to cut this for you)

2 (18-ounce) jars blackberry jam
1 (16-ounce) jar mustard
Butter for browning ham

Brown ham in skillet with butter on each side. Place in a large glass dish with ½ inch of water. Cover with foil. Bake in a 300° oven for 1½ hours or until tender. Drain and discard juices. Make blackberry mustard sauce by heating mustard and blackberry jam in a saucepan until bubbly and smooth. The precooked ham may be warmed on the grill for a short time and basted with half the blackberry mustard sauce, or cooked a little longer in the oven and basted with half blackberry mustard sauce. Reserve half blackberry mustard sauce to serve with ham, or to use as a gravy.

Yield: 6 servings

Adrian Winship Pressley

Kielbasa And Cabbage

Perfect for an autumn evening

6 slices of bacon
1 medium head of cabbage, cut into thin wedges
1 medium onion, chopped
½ cup water
2 tablespoons brown sugar

1 clove of garlic, minced
1 teaspoon seasoned salt
1 pound kielbasa or Polish sausage, cut into 1 inch cubes

Cook bacon in large skillet or Dutch oven until crisp; remove and crumble; set aside. To the bacon drippings add cabbage, onion, water, sugar, garlic, and salt; cover and simmer 8 minutes over medium heat, turning cabbage once. Add sausage; cover and cook 5 minutes or until sausage is heated. Transfer to serving dish with slotted spoon; sprinkle with bacon.

Yield: 6 servings

Linda Allen Milligan

Stuffed Pork Roast

1 (4 to 5 pounds) center
  loin pork roast
12 to 15 premium pitted
  prunes
10 black peppercorns
5 whole allspice
5 whole cloves

5 juniper berries
3 bay leaves
Lemon pepper
Salt
1 carrot, sliced
1 onion, sliced
1 cup boiling water
Heavy duty foil

Using a paring knife, make pockets in back of roast and insert prunes. Line a baking pan with foil. Place roast, rib side down in pan. Add peppercorns, allspice, cloves, juniper berries, and bay leaves to the side of the roast. Sprinkle roast with lemon pepper; add carrots and onions. Roast may be prepared ahead to this point and refrigerated for several hours. Preheat oven to 400°. Add 1 cup boiling water; seal roast by topping with additional foil and form a tent over the roast. Foil should be secure with no holes. Bake 45 minutes for 3½ to 4 pounds or 1 hour for 5 pounds. Remove from oven, cut foil; fold down to sides and continue cooking for 1 hour. Serve roast on platter; cutting roast from rib bones and slicing. *Wine Suggestion: Pouilly Fumé*

Yield: 8 servings   *Marcelle Black David*

Ginny's Roast
You must try this to believe it!!

1 (2 to 3 pound) pork roast | 1 large onion, thinly sliced
1 (8-ounce) jar mustard | 1 tablespoon vinegar

Preheat oven to 275°. Place roast in large dish. Cover top and sides of roast with mustard. Next cover with sliced onions. Add one inch of water to bottom of pan; add vinegar. Bake at least six hours at 275°. Roast will become black, crusty and delicious.
Yield: 6 servings   *Martina Goscha*

Louisiana Jambalaya

2 tablespoons bacon grease
1 cup onion, finely chopped
1 cup green pepper, finely chopped
2 cloves garlic, finely minced
1 cup cooked chicken, diced
1 cup cooked ham, diced
12 tiny pork sausages, cut in pieces
2½ cups canned tomatoes, undrained

1 cup brown rice, cooked in chicken broth
2 tablespoons butter
1½ cups chicken broth
½ teaspoon thyme
1 tablespoon parsley
¼ teaspoon chili powder
1½ teaspoons salt
¼ teaspoon freshly ground black pepper
Tabasco sauce to taste
1 to 2 cans beer

Heat bacon grease and add onion, green pepper and garlic. Cook slowly until onion and pepper are tender. Add chicken, ham, sausage and cook five minutes. Cook rice in 1½ cups chicken broth with butter. Bring broth and butter to a boil, add rice, cover and simmer for twenty minutes. Remove from heat and fluff with a fork. Combine all ingredients and put in a 9 x 11-inch casserole. Bake covered at 350° for 30 to 45 minutes, until heated throughly. If too soupy, remove cover and let liquid evaporate for the last five minutes of cooking.
Yield: 8 servings   *Louise Hetherwick Hunter*

Louisiana Red Beans And Rice

1 pound dried red beans
½ pound salt pork
2 quarts water
3 cups white onions, chopped
1 cup parsley, chopped
1 cup bell pepper, chopped
2 large pods garlic, crushed
1 tablespoon salt
¼ to ½ teaspoon red pepper, depending on taste
3 generous dashes Tabasco
1 tablespoon Worcestershire sauce
1 (4-ounce) can tomato sauce
¼ teaspoon oregano
¼ teaspoon thyme
1 pound smoked sausage, sliced into bite size pieces
Rice, cooked

Soak beans overnight in water. Cook beans and pork in salted water 45 minutes. Add all remaining ingredients except for sausage. Cook slowly another hour. Stir occasionally. Add sausage and cook 45 minutes. Cool. Reheat and bring to a boil. Serve over rice. If desired, top with chopped tomatoes, chopped green onions, oil, vinegar, salt and pepper, or tomato relish.
Yield: 8 servings   *Louise Hetherwick Hunter*

Marinated Country Ribs
Easy and flavorful

3 (3 pounds each) packages country style ribs
⅓ cup soy sauce
3 tablespoons salad oil
1 teaspoon ground ginger
¼ teaspoon pepper
1 clove garlic, crushed
1 teaspoon dry mustard

Parboil ribs until tender; drain well. Mix remaining ingredients together and pour over ribs; marinate 24 hours, rotating several times. Prepare grill and cook ribs until done, basting with remaining marinade. This is a wonderful summer time meal.
Yield: 6 servings   *Carol Armbrust Fey*

Combo Gumbo
*Don't let the number of ingredients keep
you from trying this wonderful Gumbo.*

1 (3-pound) broiler or fryer
2 quarts of water
½ cup of bacon drippings
½ cup all-purpose flour
4 stalks of celery, chopped
2 medium onions,
   chopped
1 large green pepper,
   chopped
2 cloves garlic, minced
½ cup fresh parsley,
   chopped
3 pounds shrimp
1 pound okra, sliced
2 tablespoons bacon
   drippings
3 (15-ounce) cans whole
   tomatoes, drained
2 tablespoons
   Worcestershire sauce
¼ teaspoon hot sauce

1 large bay leaf
2 teaspoons dried whole
   thyme
½ teaspoon dried whole
   rosemary
1 teaspoon salt
½ teaspoon pepper
1 teaspoon paprika
1 ham hock
2 cups cubed cooked ham
1½ pints fresh crab meat
1½ pints raw fresh
   oysters, cut in half
2 teaspoons molasses
Juice of 1 large lemon
Hot cooked rice
Gumbo filé (optional)
Hot sauce (optional - to be
   added at the table for
   those who like it hot)

Combine chicken and water in a Dutch oven. Bring to a boil;
cover and simmer 1½ hours or until chicken is tender. Remove
chicken from broth; cut into 1 inch cubes. Strain broth, reserving 6 cups. Heat ½ cup bacon drippings in an 8 quart Dutch
oven; stir in flour. Cook over low heat, stirring occasionally, until
roux is the color of a copper penny (30 minutes or maybe and
hour). Add celery, onion, green pepper, garlic and parsley; cook
over low heat for 45 minutes. (Mixture will be dry). Peel shrimp,
reserving shells; refrigerate shrimp until needed. Combine
shells and enough water to cover in a saucepan. Bring to a boil
and boil for 20 minutes. Strain shell stock, reserving 2 cups.
* Cook okra in 2 tablespoons bacon drippings until tender, stirring occasionally. Add okra, reserved chicken stock, shrimp
stock and next 9 ingredients to roux. Bring to a boil; then reduce
heat and simmer 2½ hours, stirring mixture occasionally. Add

(Cont.)

cooked chicken, ham hock, cubed ham, crab meat, oysters and molasses; simmer 30 more minutes. Add shrimp and simmer 10 more minutes. Stir in lemon juice. Serve over rice. A small amount of filé and/or hot sauce can be added to each serving, if desired.

Yield: 3½ quarts   Linda Allen Milligan

* This recipe can be done ahead of time, up to this point. The day you plan to serve the Gumbo finish the recipe by cooking the okra and continuing from there.

Roast Loin Of Pork

5 to 6 pound center cut
  pork loin
1 cup brown sugar
2 tablespoons dark rum
2 teaspoons garlic, finely
  chopped
2 teaspoons ground
  ginger
2 teaspoons ground
  cloves

1 bay leaf, crumbled
1 teaspoon salt
¼ teaspoon black pepper
2 chicken bouillon cubes
2 cups hot water
2 teaspoons corn starch
2 tablespoons cold water

Preheat oven to 350°. Score fatty side of roast diagonally in one inch squares. Place in roasting pan, bone side down. Roast one hour at 350°. While roasting, mix, in a blender, brown sugar, rum, garlic, ginger, cloves, bay leaf, salt and pepper until smooth. Remove roast from oven; drain juices and reserve. Spread paste mixture over fatty side of roast. Bake an additional 30 minutes until crusty and brown. Skim fat from reserved juices and place in saucepan. Add boullion cubes and hot water; boil. Dissolve cornstarch in cold water and add to juice, stirring briskly. Serve roast with sauce on the side. Roast may be prepared on grill by spreading ½ of the paste mixture on the roast and grill covered 2½ to 3 hours. Baste every 30 minutes with remaining paste.

Yield: 6 to 8 servings   Paulette Riley Gebhardt

Marinated Pork
Great for dinner at Chastain Park!

3 pounds pork tenderloin
⅔ cup soy sauce
⅔ cup brown sugar
2 tablespoons cornstarch
3 cloves minced garlic
2 tablespoons vinegar
2 teaspoons ground ginger
⅓ cup finely chopped candied or crystalized ginger

Trim tenderloins, place in a large enameled or glass baking dish. Combine all ingredients and pour over meat. Marinate six to eight hours or overnight. Remove from marinade, boil marinade and simmer three to five minutes. Bake meat in a pre-heated 350° oven, 30 to 45 minutes. Remove meat from pan and let cool. Slice meat into ¼-inch slices and arrange in a small baking dish. Pour marinade over and refrigerate four to six hours before serving. *Wine Suggestion: Zeller Schwarze Katz*
Yield: 6 to 8 servings   *Paula Finley Grayson*

Pork Loin Roast With Cherry Sauce

4 to 5 pound boneless pork loin roast
1 (12-ounce) jar cherry preserves
2 tablespoons light corn syrup
¼ cup red wine vinegar
½ teaspoon salt
½ teaspoon cinnamon
½ teaspoon ground cloves
½ teaspoon nutmeg
¼ to ½ cups slivered almonds, toasted

Preheat oven to 325°. Rub roast with salt and pepper. Place on rack in shallow baking pan. Roast uncovered for 2 to 2½ hours. Combine preserves, syrup, vinegar, salt, cinnamon, cloves, and nutmeg in saucepan. Heat to boiling, stirring frequently. Reduce heat and simmer two minutes. Add almonds; keep sauce warm. After roast has cooked 2 to 2½ hours, spoon enough sauce over roast to glaze. Return to oven for 30 additional minutes. Baste several times with cherry sauce during last 30 minutes. Let roast stand about 20 minutes before slicing. Serve with remaining cherry sauce. *Wine Suggestion: Macon Blanc*
Yield 8 servings   *Esther Barnes Mulling*

Pork Tenderloin

2 pound pork tenderloin
Salt and pepper to taste
4 tablespoons butter,
  softened

1 to 2 teaspoons dried
  thyme

Apricot Sauce:
9 ounces apricot
  preserves
1 to 2 tablespoons honey
1 tablespoon dry mustard

Garlic powder to taste
1 to 2 tablespoons dry
  sherry or madeira

Preheat oven to 350°. Spread butter on meat; sprinkle with salt, pepper, and thyme. Bake 30 to 40 minutes. While meat is baking mix all ingredients for apricot sauce. Remove meat from oven and brush with apricot sauce. Return to oven and continue baking for 15 minutes more, basting with the remaining apricot sauce. Do not overcook. *Wine Suggestion: Meursault*
Yield: 6 to 8 servings   *Pamela Croy Newton*

Apricot Shrimp
Tangy blend of flavors

½ cup chopped dried
  apricots
⅓ cup apricot brandy
2 tablespoons butter
1 tablespoon peanut oil
1 bell pepper, cut in strips
½ cup sliced green onions
1 clove garlic, chopped
1 pound small shrimp,
  peeled

1 tablespoon lemon juice
1 tablespoon soy sauce
2 teaspoons corn starch
⅛ teaspoon pepper
¼ cup slivered almonds,
  toasted
Cooked rice

Combine apricots and brandy, let soak for 15 minutes. Heat butter and oil. Add peppers, onions and garlic, stir for three minutes. Add shrimp for two minutes. Add apricot mixture stirring for two more minutes. Mix lemon juice, soy sauce, corn starch and pepper and blend until thick, about two minutes. Serves over rice and top with toasted almonds. *Wine Suggestion: Saint Véran*
Yield: 4 servings   *Leckie Kern Stack*

Coquilles St. Jacques a la Parisienne
(Scallops and Mushrooms in White Wine Sauce)

Cooking the Scallops:

1 cup dry white wine or
¾ cup dry white vermouth
½ teaspoon salt
Pinch of pepper
½ bay leaf
2 tablespoons minced
  shallots

1 pound sea scallops,
  cleaned
½ pound fresh
  mushrooms, sliced

Simmer wine, salt, pepper, bay leaf and shallots in a 2 quart saucepan. Add scallops and mushrooms to wine; add enough water to barely cover the ingredients. Bring to a simmer and simmer slowly for 5 minutes. Remove scallops and mushrooms with a slotted spoon, set aside. Rapidly boil down the above cooking liquid until it is reduced to one cup.

Cooking the Sauce:

3 tablespoons butter
4 tablespoons flour
¾ cup milk
2 egg yolks

½ cup whipping cream
  (more if needed)
Salt and pepper
Drops of lemon juice

Melt the butter, blend in the flour, cook, stirring slowly, for two minutes. Remove from heat. Blend in reduced liquid, then the milk. Return to heat and boil for one minute. Blend the egg yolks and cream in a bowl, then beat the hot sauce into them by driblets. Return the sauce to the pan and boil, stirring for one minute. Thin out with more cream if necessary. Season to taste with salt, pepper and lemon juice.

Final Assembly:

6 scallop shells or a 9 x
  11-inch baking dish

Cut scallops into
crosswise pieces (about ⅛
  inch thick)
½ tablespoon butter
6 tablespoons grated
  Swiss cheese

1½ tablespoons butter, cut
  into pieces

Blend ⅔ of the sauce with the scallops and mushrooms. Butter the shells (or baking dish) with ½ tablespoon butter. Spoon scallops and mushrooms into shells, cover with the rest of the sauce. Sprinkle with the cut up butter and cheese. Fifteen minutes before serving, broil scallops until cheese melts and turns golden brown. Serve immediately. *Wine Suggestion: Pouilly Fuissé*
Yield: 6 servings   *Thalia V. Eden*

Chinese Shrimp And Peapods
"Light and easy"

1½ pounds shrimp, peeled
  and cleaned
2 tablespoons butter
1 bunch green onions,
  chopped
⅓ cup soy sauce
1 tablespoon
  Worcestershire sauce

Juice of 1 medium lemon
2 tablespoons parsley
1 package frozen peapods
  (thaw 10 minutes)
Chinese noodles

Sauté onions and shrimp in butter. Cook for three minutes (five if shrimp are large). Add remaining ingredients, except peapods, blending well. Add peapods and sauté for two minutes or until tender and hot. Don't overcook! Serve over rice and top with Chinese noodles. *Wine Suggestion: California Pinot Chardonnay*
Yield: 4 servings   *Barbara Gully Allen*

Barbecue Shrimp
This is a snap!

4 pounds shrimp in shells
2 cups margarine or butter
½ teaspoon cayenne
  pepper
2 teaspoons garlic salt
2 teaspoons barbecue
  spice
1 tablespoon black pepper
3 tablespoons
  Worcestershire sauce
2 tablespoons paprika

Preheat oven to 300°. Wash and drain shrimp (do not peel). Place the shrimp in a shallow baking pan. Melt the butter and add all the seasonings; pour over the shrimp. Bake in a 300° oven for thirty minutes, turning once halfway through cooking. Scoop shrimp out into a serving bowl with a side bowl of sauce for dipping French bread.
Yield: 6 to 8 servings
Martha Williams Moore

Cheesy Scallops And Rice

1½ pounds scallops, fresh
  or frozen
1 medium onion, chopped
2 stalks celery, chopped
1 green pepper, chopped
¼ cup butter or margarine,
  melted
¼ cup all-purpose flour
1 teaspoon salt
⅛ teaspoon pepper
1 cup milk
4 cups cooked rice
1½ cups shredded sharp
  Cheddar cheese
½ teaspoon Italian
  seasoning (if desired)

Thaw scallops, if frozen. Cut large scallops into quarters. Cook onion, celery, and bell pepper in butter until tender. Blend in flour and seasonings. Add milk gradually and cook until thick, stirring constantly. Add scallops. Grease a 2 quart casserole, cover bottom with half the rice, then with half the scallop mix, and then half the cheese; repeat layers. Bake at 350° for 25 minutes or until golden brown. *Variation:* May substitute 2 pounds shrimp, peeled and cleaned, for scallops.
Yield: 6 to 8 servings
Donna Cates Robinson

Crab Casserole
A nice company dish for a small group

2 eggs, well beaten
1 cup milk
1 pound fresh crabmeat
½ cup butter, melted
2 tablespoons mayonnaise
½ teaspoon salt
½ teaspoon pepper
½ teaspoon paprika

1 teaspoon mustard
1 teaspoon lemon juice
1 tablespoon
 Worcestershire sauce
1 tablespoon finely
 chopped onion
¼ pound Ritz Crackers,
 crushed

Add milk to well beaten eggs. Combine all other ingredients, except crackers and mix well. Pour into a buttered casserole dish and top with crackers. Bake at 350° for 30 to 40 minutes or until heated throughout and bubbly.
Yield: 6 servings

Sybil Kendall Little

Crab Royal

3 tablespoons butter
1½ tablespoons minced
 onion
2 tablespoons minced
 green pepper
½ cup sliced mushrooms
2 tablespoons flour

1 teaspoon salt
¼ teaspoon dry mustard
2 (5-ounce) cans
 evaporated milk
2 egg yolks, well beaten
3 cups lump crabmeat
Grated cheese

Melt butter, sauté onions and pepper. Blend in flour, salt and mustard. Gradually add milk, stirring until smooth. Stir in egg yolks. Fold in drained mushrooms and crabmeat. Divide into four ramekins or baking shells. Top with grated cheese and bake at 350° until cheese melts. *Wine Suggestion: California Fume Blanc*
Yield: 4 servings

Joann Carrington Walker

Crab Stuffed Shrimp

10 to 12 jumbo shrimp	Flour for dipping
2 tablespoons butter	Egg batter (thoroughly mix
2 tablespoons flour	1 cup milk and 1 egg)
½ cup milk	Bread crumbs
1¼ cups lump crabmeat	Oil for frying

Shell and clean shrimp. Split down the back without cutting through to the other side. Melt butter and add flour stirring until smooth. Add milk and stir until thick. Add crabmeat. Mold equal portions of crab mixture into each shrimp, pressing firmly with your hand. Dip stuffed shrimp into flour, then batter, then crumbs. Fry in deep oil at 375° until brown (approximately 8 to 10 minutes).
Yield: 4 servings   *Leckie Kern Stack*

Crabmeat And Asparagus Casserole
A holiday brunch dish

1 (15-ounce) can	1 teaspoon Worcestershire
asparagus	sauce
1 pound crabmeat *	¼ cup medium - dry
¾ pound sliced fresh	sherry
mushrooms, sautéed	Paprika
4 tablespoons butter	Pepper
2½ tablespoons flour	¼ cup grated Parmesan
1 cup cream	cheese
½ teaspoon salt	

Place asparagus in the bottom of a lightly greased casserole. Sprinkle with crabmeat; top with sautéed mushrooms. Melt butter in a saucepan; add remaining ingredients, except cheese. Cook stirring well to form a smooth sauce. Pour over the asparagus and crab, sprinkle with the cheese. Bake at 375° for 20 minutes.
Yield: 6 to 8 servings   *Claudia Mitchell Owens*

* *May substitute with canned crabmeat or the less expensive crab sticks.*

Delicious Fish

¾ cup Parmesan cheese
½ cup butter, softened
3 tablespoons green
  onions, chopped
3 tablespoons mayonnaise
2 teaspoons chives

6 fresh fish filets (scrod,
  orange roughy or
  grouper)
3 tablespoons lemon juice
¼ teaspoon pepper

Mix first five ingredients together in a small bowl, set aside. Place fish fillets in a single layer in a lightly greased 13 x 9 x 2-inch baking dish. Pour lemon juice over fish; sprinkle with pepper. Broil fillets six to ten minutes or until fish flakes easily when tested with a fork. Remove dish from oven, spread top of fillets with cheese mixture. Broil an additional two to three minutes or until cheese is lightly browned and bubbly. *Wine Suggestion: Verdicchio*
Yield: 6 servings   *Georgia Grimland Rambo*

Easy Crevette En Croissant
(Shrimp in Cresent Rolls)

1 (3-ounce) package cream
  cheese
2 cups cooked shrimp
3 tablespoons butter
2 tablespoons milk
¼ teaspoon salt
⅛ teaspoon pepper
1 tablespoon chopped
  chives

1 (8-ounce) can of
  refrigerated crescent
  rolls
1 tablespoon butter,
  melted
¾ cup herb seasoned
  croutons, crushed

Preheat oven to 350°. Cut cooked shrimp into bite-sized pieces. Blend cream cheese and butter. Add milk, salt, pepper, and chives to cream cheese and butter. Mix well. Add cut up shrimp to cheese mixture. Separate dinner rolls into four rectangles and seal perforations. Spoon one-half cup shrimp mixture onto center of mixture and seal completely. Brush tops of dough packages with melted butter. Roll packages into crushed croutons. Bake 20 to 30 minutes at 350.° until lightly browned.
Yield: 4 servings   *Joellen Shaw Page*

Flounder Florentine

1 (2-pound) box frozen or
fresh flounder fillets
1 (10-ounce) box frozen,
chopped spinach,
thawed and drained
1 cup Pepperidge Farm
Herb stuffing mix

2 teaspoon minced onion
⅛ teaspoon thyme
Milk to moisten
Salt

Sauce:
⅔ cup mayonnaise
½ cup water
1 cup Swiss cheese,
grated

Paprika

Place thawed fish in a greased baking dish in one layer.
Sprinkle with a little salt. Combine spinach, stuffing, onion,
thyme and enough milk to make a very soft mixture. Spread
over fish and dot with butter. Bake at 350° uncovered for about
30 minutes, or until fish flakes easily.
Sauce: Combine the mayonnaise and water and pour over the
fish and spinach. Sprinkle with grated cheese and paprika.
Broil until the cheese is melted.
Yield: 4 to 6 servings   *Linda Marett Disosway*

Flounder Supreme
Very rich

¼ cup butter
2 medium onions, sliced
1 pound flounder or sole
fillets
¾ cup mayonnaise
1 teaspoon parsley,
chopped

Juice of 1 lemon
¼ cup grated Parmesan
cheese
Toasted almonds
(optional)

Melt butter in a baking dish at 350°. Slice onions over bottom.
Place fish over onions. Mix together mayonnaise, parsley,
lemon juice and cheese. Spread over fish. Bake at 350° for 25
minutes. Sprinkle with toasted almonds if desired. *Wine
Suggestion: Gewürztraminer*
Yield: 4 servings   *Karen Coleman Hirons*

Garlic Shrimp

2 pounds shrimp, cooked
and cleaned
½ cup butter, softened
½ cup seasoned bread
crumbs
2 tablespoons sour cream
2 tablespoons parsley,
chopped

1 clove garlic, chopped
1 teaspoon salt
½ teaspoon
Worcestershire sauce
Pepper
2 teaspoons lemon juice

Preheat oven to 450°. Layer shrimp in a one quart casserole.
Combine remaining ingredients and mix until smooth. Spread
mixture evenly over shrimp and pat with a spatula. Bake for 10
minutes until bubbly and lightly browned.
Yield: 4 servings   *Dell Cochran James*

Grilled Swordfish Or Salmon

½ cup fresh dill sprigs (or
dillweed)
2 pounds fresh swordfish
or salmon steaks
⅓ cup oil
Peel of 1 lemon, cut into
strips

3 tablespoons lemon juice
1 tablespoon soy sauce
¼ teaspoon black pepper
(freshly cracked)
¼ teaspoon salt

Place dill in a casserole dish, put fish steaks on top. Combine
oil, lemon peel, lemon juice, soy sauce, salt and pepper and
pour over the fish. Refrigerate, turning occasionally. Place fish
on a grill over hot coals. Grill until fish flakes, turning only once.
May brush with reserved marinade. Garnish with dill. *Wine
Suggestion: Puligny-Montrachet*
Yield: 6 servings   *Pamela Croy Newton*

Grouper Gordon au Gratin

2 to 3 grouper fillets (4 ounces per person)
1 cup white wine
1 bay leaf

1 teaspoon peppercorns
Salt to taste
½ teaspoon tarragon

Cheese Sauce:
3 tablespoons butter
3 tablespoons all-purpose flour
1 cup milk

Salt and pepper to taste
¼ teaspoon dry mustard
6 ounces Velveeta or Cheddar cheese, cubed

Topping:
½ cup bread crumbs
1 cup grated Cheddar cheese

Poach fillets in wine with bay leaf, peppercorns, salt, tarragon and enough water to barely cover fish. Poach until flakey (no more than 10 minutes depending on the size of the fillets). Set aside. Melt butter in a saucepan, stir in flour and milk until well blended and smooth. Add salt, pepper and mustard. Add cheese stirring until melted and the sauce is smooth. Drain fish, remove peppercorns and flake fish (in bite size pieces) into cheese sauce. Blend evenly and divide into four or six ramekins. Top with bread crumbs, a dot of butter and the cheese. Bake at 400° until brown and bubbly.
Yield: 4 to 6 servings   *Sharon McPherson Gordon*

Poached Red Snapper

4 (8-ounce) portions of red snapper
1 cup water
1 cup dry white wine
1 lemon, sliced

1 onion, sliced
4 whole peppercorns
2 bay leaves
4 sprigs fresh parsley
2 cloves garlic

Put fish in a large skillet. Add remaining ingredients. Cover and simmer for eight minutes or until fish is flakey.
Yield: 4 servings   *Jeanne Tonkin*

Bahama Grill

The island's in your own back yard

1½ pounds fresh fish
(Grouper is best)
2 medium tomatoes, cut
into chunks

½ green pepper, sliced
½ medium onion, sliced
Lemon pepper
Butter

Season vegetables with lemon pepper. Place tomatoes, green pepper and onions on top of fish. Place two pats of butter on top. Double wrap in foil. Place on medium hot grill. Cook 45 minutes to one hour.

Yield: 4 servings   *Susan Thomas Burney*

Paul's Island Grouper

1 clove garlic, minced
1 small onion, chopped
3 tablespoons olive oil
1 small green pepper, cut
in thin strips
1 (8-ounce) can tomato
sauce
1 cup chopped tomatoes

1 bay leaf
3 to 5 dashes Tabasco
sauce
2 (1-pound) fillets of fresh
grouper
Stuffed green olives
8 lemon wedges
Salt and pepper to taste

Sauté garlic, onion and green pepper in a large iron skillet until tender. Add tomato sauce, tomatoes, bay leaf and Tabasco sauce. Stir and heat thoroughly over medium heat. Add fish and cook two or three minutes on each side, turning only once. Test fish for doneness (it should flake easily, do not overcook!). Remove skillet from heat and place under broiler to brown. (About one minute, watch it constantly.) To serve, place fish on a large platter and cover fish with sauce. Salt and pepper to taste. Garnish with whole olives on top and surround with lemon wedges. Serve with crusty french bread. The extra sauce makes a nice dip for the bread. *Wine Suggestion: California White Zinfandel*

Yield: 4 servings   *Joanna Owens Conyngham*

Oysters Camille

2 pints fresh oysters, well drained
1 bunch green onions, chopped
3 medium cloves garlic, minced
¾ pound bacon, fried and crumbled
1 cup Havarti cheese, thinly sliced
Cajun spice
½ teaspoon sweet basil
½ teaspoon Italian seasoning
4 crushed bay leaves
½ teaspoon thyme
Juice of one lime
¾ cup Italian bread crumbs
½ stick of margarine
10 drops Tabasco sauce
Olive oil
½ cup fresh Parmesan cheese, grated

Preheat oven to 325°. Cover the bottom of 10 x 14-inch oval baking dish with olive oil. Lay oysters flat in bottom of dish. Sprinkle with cajun spice to taste. Sprinkle evenly over the oysters the basil, Italian seasoning, bay leaves, thyme, lime juice, green onions, garlic and ½ cup Italian bread crumbs. Dot with butter, then the Tabasco sauce, half the bacon, Havarti cheese, and the remaining bacon. Top with ¼ cup bread crumbs and Parmesan cheese. Bake uncovered at 325° for 45 to 50 minutes. *Wine Suggestion: Frascati*
Yield: 6 servings
Melanie Buzbee

Creole Seafood Seasoning

⅓ cup salt
¼ cup granulated or powdered garlic
¼ cup freshly ground black pepper
2 tablespoons cayenne pepper
2 tablespoons thyme
2 tablespoons oregano
⅓ cup paprika
3 tablespoons granulated or powdered onion

Combine all ingredients and mix thoroughly. Pour into a large glass jar and seal airtight. Keeps indefinitely. Use this in place of commercial crab or seafood boils.
Janice Gamel Tucker

Oyster Supreme

3 cups hot wild rice, drained
½ cup onions, chopped
2 cups celery, chopped
½ stick butter or margarine
1½ cups milk
3 tablespoons flour
½ teaspoon salt
¼ teaspoon sage
¼ teaspoon thyme
⅛ teaspoon black pepper
2 (8-ounce) cans fresh oysters, drained
½ cup butter, melted
Ritz cracker crumbs

While rice is cooking according to package directions, brown onions and celery in butter. Remove form heat and add milk, flour, salt, sage, thyme and black pepper. Add well drained rice and pour into a 2 quart casserole. Drain oysters and let soak in lukewarm melted butter for 5 to 10 minutes. Pour oysters and butter over rice mixture and spread evenly. Top with Ritz cracker crumbs. Bake at 350° for 45 minutes or until oysters curl.
Yield: 8 servings   *Lillian Budd Darden*

Shrimp And Vegetable Tempura

4 eggs
4 tablespoons milk
1 cup sifted flour
2 teaspoons melted butter
½ teaspoon salt
2 teaspoons baking soda
Carrot sticks
Mushrooms
Potato cubes
Fresh green beans
Shrimp, peeled and cleaned
Broccoli florettes
Cauliflower florettes

Combine the flour with 2 eggs and 2 egg yolks. Stir in ½ of the milk and all of the melted butter and salt. Beat mixture until smooth. Add the remaining milk, baking soda and mix thoroughly. Fold in 1 stiffly beaten egg white. Chill batter for 30 minutes. Beat batter before using. Dip each vegetable individually into batter and fry in fondue pot in hot oil (370°) until brown. Fun to do around a table with fondue forks.
Yield: 6 to 8 servings   *Debbie Lewis Mitchell*

Shrimp And Artichoke Casserole
A company pleaser

6½ tablespoons butter
4½ tablespoons flour
1 cup whipping cream
½ cup half and half
Salt and pepper to taste
1 (14-ounce) can artichoke
  hearts, drained and
  quartered
2 to 3 pounds shrimp,
  cooked and cleaned

¾ pound fresh
  mushrooms
¼ teaspoon flour
¼ cup dry sherry
1 tablespoon
  Worcestershire sauce
¼ to ½ cup Parmesan
  cheese, grated
Paprika

Preheat oven to 375°. In a skillet melt 4½ tablespoons of butter; stir in flour, add creams, stirring constantly. When thick add salt and pepper. Place artichokes in bottom of 3 quart casserole. Sauté mushrooms in remaining butter. Sprinkle ¼ teaspoon flour over mushrooms. Stir. Scatter mushrooms over artichokes. Place shrimp over mushrooms. Add sherry and Worcestershire to cream sauce. Pour over casserole. Top with cheese and paprika. Bake at 375° for 20 minutes or until bubbly and cheese has melted.
Yield: 8 servings

Roddy Thomas Hiser

Shrimp Etouffee

¾ cup butter
24 large shrimp, peeled
  and deveined
1 green pepper, chopped
⅓ cup flour
2 cups heavy cream
½ teaspoon cayenne
  pepper

¼ teaspoon paprika
2 tomatoes, seeded and
  diced
Salt and pepper
Cooked rice

Melt ½ cup butter in a fry pan. Add shrimp and cook a few minutes but not all the way. Remove shrimp and add peppers. Sauté about three minutes. Add the flour and stir until smooth, then add cream. Use a whisk and cook over low heat. Add cayenne pepper and paprika. Add shrimp and tomatoes. Cook a few minutes then add remaining butter. Serve over rice.
Yield: 6 servings

Judy Gorrell Harper

Shrimp And Fettuccine

8 tablespoons unsalted
butter
2 garlic cloves, minced
4 teaspoons parsley,
minced
½ onion, diced
4 fresh mushrooms, sliced
4 tablespoons tomato,
peeled, seeded and
chopped

½ cup green onion,
chopped
2 teaspoons Creole
Seafood Seasoning *
¼ cup shrimp stock *
2 cups cooked fettuccine
noodles (12 ounces dry)
24 medium shrimp, peeled
and deveined
½ cup dry wine

Melt half the butter in a large saucepan and sauté garlic, parsley, onions, mushrooms, tomato, green onions, and seafood seasoning for 30 seconds, stirring gently. Add stock and simmer until onions are transparent. Add the cooked fettuccine, shrimp and wine; simmer until liquid is almost evaporated. Remove from heat, add remaining butter. Stir gently until butter is melted and sauce is creamy. Serve with French bread. * *Creole Seafood Seasoning on page 136. Shrimp Stock on page 139. Wine Suggestion: Sauvignon Blanc*
Yield: 4 servings   *Janice Gamel Tucker*

Shrimp Stock

To each quart of water add 1 medium onion, peeled and quartered; 3 stalks celery, coarsely cut; 1 whole garlic clove, peeled; fresh shrimp heads and or shells.

Bring the ingredients to a rapid boil, reduce heat to a slow simmer. Cook at least 2 hours, no more than 8. When making stock, the best flavors are achieved by making the stock as clear as possible. After stock is cooked, strain, and reduce it for additional flavor. Simmer, uncovered, until evaporation reduces it to half its original quantity.

Janice Gamel Tucker

Shrimp And Wild Rice

1 (6¼-ounce) package
long grain wild rice mix
1 pound medium shrimp,
cleaned and cooked
1 small onion, chopped
1 small green pepper,
sliced into thin strips
½ pound fresh
mushrooms

¼ cup butter
2 tablespoons flour
1 cup whipping cream
1 cup milk
1 tablespoon
Worcestershire sauce
4 drops hot sauce
¼ teaspoon pepper

Cook rice according to package directions. While rice is cooking, sauté onion, green pepper and mushrooms in a large skillet, over medium heat until tender. Stir in flour, cream and milk, bring to a boil. Reduce heat and cook stirring constantly until mixture begins to thicken. Remove from heat. Combine cream sauce, Worcestershire sauce, hot sauce, pepper, rice and shrimp. Stir well. Pour into lightly greased 12 x 8 x 2-inch dish. Bake at 350° for 10 to 15 minutes or until hot.
Yield: 8 servings   *Bonnie Mullen Murphy*

Shrimp Cabildo

1 pound shrimp, peeled
and deveined
½ pound thin spaghetti
noodles
¼ cup cooking oil
1½ cups sliced fresh
mushrooms
¼ cup sliced green
onions, including tops
3 tablespoons plain flour

1½ teaspoons salt
¼ teaspoon paprika
8 ounces Swiss cheese,
grated
1 cup milk
1 cup half and half
½ cup dry sherry
2 tablespoons pimento
2 tablespoons Parmesan
cheese

Cook spaghetti noodles, drain and keep warm. Heat cooking oil, add mushrooms and onions, cooking until tender. Add shrimp and cook until they turn pink. Stir in flour, salt and paprika. Add milk and half and half. Cook, stirring constantly until thick. Stir in Swiss cheese, sherry and pimentos. Spoon over spaghetti and sprinkle with Parmesan cheese. Place under broiler for three to four minutes until cheese is brown.
Yield: 6 servings   *Fran Adams Hammonds*

Shrimp Creole
"Very Spicy"

4 tablespoons butter
½ cup onion, chopped
2 cloves garlic, minced
12 green olives, chopped
3 cups canned tomatoes
1 green pepper, chopped
1 bay leaf
Pinch of thyme
2 teaspoons parsley,
  chopped

2 teaspoons sugar
⅔ teaspoon salt
1 teaspoon cayenne
  pepper or less if desired
2 pounds fresh raw
  shrimp, cleaned
Cooked rice

Melt butter over low heat. Add onions, garlic and green olives and simmer, covered for about two minutes. Add canned tomatoes, green peppers, bay leaf, thyme, parsley, sugar, salt and cayenne. Cook until the sauce is thick, about fifty minutes. When sauce is thick add shrimp and cook ten minutes. Serve over rice.
Yield: 6 servings   *Julie Beazel Flournoy*

Shrimp In Cognac And Cream
Rich!

2¼ pound raw shrimp,
  shelled and deveined
5 tablespoons butter
¾ cup cognac

4 egg yolks
¾ cup heavy cream
Salt and pepper
Nutmeg

Lay cleaned shrimp on a board and split them down the backs without cutting all the way through. Melt butter in a large skillet, add shrimp and sauté over medium heat for about five minutes or until they are pink. Season shrimp with the salt, pepper and nutmeg to taste. Heat cognac in a small pan, ignite and pour over shrimp. Tilt the pan back and forth until the flames die down. Simmer the shrimp over low heat for about five minutes and remove pan from heat. Beat together the egg yolks and heavy cream and very gradually stir the mixture into the pan juices. Reheat the pan if necessary - but do not let the sauce boil. Serve at once over wild rice. *Wine Suggestion: Schloss Vollrads*
Yield: 6 servings   *Martha Lyons Wagner*

Shrimp Mull

Use 2 large skillets for this recipe.

¾ to 1 pound streak o'lean - do not substitute
3 or 4 large white onions
2 pounds fresh Georgia shrimp, shelled and deveined

Approximately 1 cup flour
Approximately 1½ cups hot water
Salt and pepper to taste
Rice - enough cooked for at least 8 people

Cut streak o'lean into very thin strips. Brown and drain. Break into very small pieces and return to grease in the skillets. Cover meat with thin slices of onions broken into rings. Place shrimp on top of onion. Salt and pepper to taste. (Easy on the salt - streak o'lean is very salty!) Sift approximately 1 cup flour over all and stir gently to coat. Pour approximately 1½ cups of water over all and stir well again. Cover and cook for 20 minutes or until done. Check frequently and add more water if neccesary. Gravy should be of medium thick consistency. Serve over rice.
Yield: 8 servings   *Ann Konigsmark Johnson*

This is the recipe of Captain Ed Royal of Brunswick, Georgia. "Captain Ed" was, for many years, a shrimper and fisherman on the Georgia coast.

Southern Scallops

1 cup dry white wine
1½ teaspoons salt
2 pounds scallops
½ cup melted butter
¼ cup olive oil

2 tablespoons chopped parsley
1 teaspoon garlic salt
Grated Parmesan cheese

Combine wine and salt in a saucepan, bring to a boil. Add scallops, simmer for two to three minutes. Drain liquid and place scallops in a casserole. Combine butter, oil, parsley and garlic salt and pour over scallops. Sprinkle with cheese. Bake at 400° for 10 to 15 minutes.
Yield: 4 servings   *Betty Carithers*

Veal Piccata
Sure to get rave reviews

4 tablespoons butter
2 tablespoons oil
1 pound veal, thinly sliced
Flour to coat veal
¼ cup dry white wine

2 tablespoons lemon juice
2 tablespoons parsley, chopped
Lemon slices, optional
Parsley sprigs, optional

Place veal between wax paper and pound until ⅛ inch thick. Heat 2 tablespoons of butter and oil in skillet over medium heat. Dredge both sides of veal in flour and shake off excess. Cook veal until lightly browned on each side. Place on platter and keep warm. Season with salt and pepper. Over low heat, add wine to skillet drippings, scraping up brown bits with wooden spoon. Cook until wine begins to evaporate. Add lemon juice, remaining butter, and parsley. Return veal to skillet and turn to warm and coat with sauce. Remove to platter and garnish with lemon slices and parsley.*Wine Suggestion: California Gamay Beaujolais*
Yield: 4 to 6 servings   *Cindy Crockett Webster*

Veal Vermouth

2 pounds veal cutlets
Flour
2 teaspoons olive oil
2 teaspoons bacon grease
½ cup butter
¼ cup onions, diced
½ cup Vermouth

½ pound mushrooms, chopped
2 green peppers, chopped
2 large ripe tomatoes, chopped
1 clove garlic, diced
½ cup ham, finely diced

Pound the cutlets thin and sprinkle with flour on both sides. Place olive oil, bacon grease and butter in skillet. Add onion and sauté. Add veal and brown slowly about five minutes on each side. Add Vermouth, cover and simmer for five minutes. Add chopped mushrooms, green peppers and tomatoes. Cover and simmer 5 more minutes. Add diced garlic and ham and simmer, uncovered for 10 minutes until done. (If it gets dry too fast add more Vermouth.)
Yield: 4 to 6 servings   *Leckie Kern Stack*

Veal Forestier

1½ pounds veal cutlets, ¼ inch thick
1 garlic clove, halved
⅓ cup flour
¼ cup Italian bread crumbs
2 tablespoons grated Parmesan cheese
¼ cup butter
½ pound mushrooms, thinly sliced
½ cup dry vermouth
Salt and pepper to taste
Cooked egg noodles

Pound veal cutlets lightly, on each side, with meat mallet. Rub veal with cut garlic; discard garlic; set veal aside. Combine flour, bread, crumbs and cheese; coat veal lightly with flour mixture. In 10-inch skillet, melt butter over medium-high heat. Cook veal, few pieces at a time in butter until lightly browned. Add more butter if necessary. Return all meat to skillet and add mushrooms, vermouth, salt and pepper. Cover, reduce heat to low and cook for 15 minutes or until meat is fork tender. If more liquid is needed add 1 to 2 tablespoons of water. Serve with egg noodles. *Wine Suggestion: Fleurie*
Yield: 6 servings   *Susan Thomas Burney*

Pork tenderloins may be used instead of veal. Rub tenderloins with garlic before slicing into the ¾ inch thick medallions (do not pound the pork).

Frogmore Stew
Great for large casual dinner party!

3 pounds Polish sausage, cut in 1½ inch pieces
2 large onions, chopped
2 lemons, sliced
2 tablespoons seafood seasoning
Salt and pepper to taste
15 ears of corn, shucked
½ cup butter
4 pounds raw, unpeeled shrimp
2 gallons water

Into two gallons of water, add sausage, onion, lemons, seafood seasoning, salt and pepper. Bring to a boil and simmer 45 minutes. Add butter and let melt. Add corn and cook for 10 minutes. Add shrimp and cook about five minutes, or until shrimp are nice and pink. Drain water and serve on a large platter.
Yield: 12 servings   *Linda Allen Milligan*

VEGETABLES AND FRUITS

Accompaniments

Vegetables And Fruits

Artichoke-Spinach Casserole

4 (10-ounce) packages
frozen chopped spinach
2 (8-ounce) packages
cream cheese
¾ cup butter or margarine

2 (15-ounce) cans
artichoke hearts, drained
Crushed Ritz crackers
Grated Parmesan cheese

Preheat oven to 350°. Cook spinach according to package directions. Drain. Place in buttered 3-quart casserole. In top of double boiler, melt butter or margarine and cream cheese. Spread mixture over spinach. Arrange artichoke hearts over cheese mixture. Top generously with cracker crumbs and Parmesan cheese. Bake at 350° until bubbly, approximately 25 minutes. *May be assembled in advance. Reserve crumbs and cheese until ready to bake.*
Yield: 12 servings   *Paulette Riley Gebhardt*

Fresh Asparagus
With Sour Cream Sauce

1 pound fresh asparagus *
2 cups chicken broth
Hard boiled egg, grated

4 slices bacon, cooked
and crumbled

Sour Cream Sauce:
2 egg yolks, beaten
1 (16-ounce) carton sour
cream

Salt and pepper, to taste
5 teaspoons sweet
Vermouth

Cook asparagus in chicken broth until tender. Drain well. Using a wire whisk, prepare sauce in a double boiler. Do not bring to a boil. Pour sauce over asparagus and top with grated egg and crumbled bacon. * *May substitute 1 pound fresh broccoli.*
Yield: 6 servings   *Ginger Colquitt Autry*

Green Beans And Corn For A Crowd

2 (16-ounce) cans French style green beans
1 (17-ounce) can white corn
1 (5-ounce) can sliced water chestnuts
1 (8-ounce) carton sour cream
1 can cream of celery soup
3 tablespoons mayonnaise
⅓ cup onion
1½ cups Cheddar cheese
½ cup plus 2 tablespoons butter
1½ stacks Ritz crackers

Drain first 3 ingredients and layer them in a buttered casserole dish. Dot with butter. Mix next 5 ingredients and pour over vegetables. Melt butter and mix with cracker crumbs to cover the entire casserole. Bake at 325° for 40 minutes.
Yield: 10 to 12 servings   *Meredith Webb Dykes*

Green Bean-Sour Cream Casserole

2 tablespoons margarine
2 tablespoons flour
¼ teaspoon salt
⅛ teaspoon pepper
¾ cup milk
½ cup sour cream
2 tablespoons onions, chopped
1 (16-ounce) can French style green beans, drained
½ cup Swiss cheese, shredded
Toasted bread crumbs

Preheat oven to 325°. Melt margarine in saucepan over low heat. Blend in flour, salt, and pepper. Cook over low heat, stirring until mixture is smooth and bubbly. Remove from heat and stir in milk. Return to heat and stir until thick and smooth. Remove from heat and stir in sour cream and onion. Place green beans in 1½ quart casserole dish. Pour sauce over beans, stirring to mix well. Top with Swiss cheese and bread crumbs. Bake at 325° for 20 to 25 minutes.
Yield: 4 to 6 servings   *Rebecca Edenfield Lingerfelt*

Mom's Great Baked Beans
Can't beat these on the 4th of July, or anytime!

2 (1-pound) cans pork and
  beans
½ cup brown sugar
2 tablespoons prepared
  mustard
½ cup ketchup
1 large onion, chopped
3 to 4 slices bacon

Preheat oven to 350°. Combine first five ingredients, and pour into 2-quart casserole dish. Top with bacon slices. Cook at 350° for approximately 1 hour, or until bacon is cooked and bean mixture is thick.
Yield: 8 servings

Susan Knight Bentley

Pennsylvania Dutch Green Beans

3 slices bacon, diced
1 small onion, diced
2 teaspoons cornstarch
¼ teaspoon dry mustard
1 (16-ounce) can French
  style green beans
1 tablespoon brown sugar
1 tablespoon vinegar
Salt, to taste

Cook bacon until crisp and remove from skillet. Add onion to 1 tablespoon of the bacon drippings. Cook until tender. Blend in cornstarch and mustard. Drain beans, reserving ½ cup liquid. Stir in reserved liquid. Cook, stirring constantly, until thickended and translucent. Blend in sugar, vinegar, and salt. Add beans and heat. Top with bacon.
Yield: 6 servings

Carol Armbrust Fey

Pork And Beef Beans
Very Hearty

1 (21-ounce) can pork and
beans
1 (21-ounce) can kidney
beans
1 pound ground beef
1 envelope dry onion soup
mix

3 tablespoons ketchup
1 tablespoon yellow
mustard
1 tablespoon brown sugar

Preheat oven to 400°. Brown ground beef in a skillet, pouring off excess grease. Combine meat with remaining ingredients. Place in crock pot for one hour, or in a glass dish for 30 to 40 minutes at 400°, or until mixture thickens.
Yield: 8 to 10 servings   *Rebecca Edenfield Lingerfelt*

Southern Style Green Beans
(An old family recipe that has been handed down from generation to generation in its original version)

Green beans
Fat back

Salt, to taste
Sugar, a pinch

Pick beans early enough in the day to get on the stove by 8 o'clock for dinner at noon. Select very young tender beans and a few mature ones for shelling. Break up and wash well. Cover with water. Add a slab of fat back, cut to the rind in several places. When the beans have cooked about two hours, add salt and a pinch of sugar. Do not stir. Let the water boil down so that beans get sticky but do not scorch. *As told to Sherry McAdams by her grandmother, Mrs. Charles F. McLeese, who learned it from her mother, Mrs. Fred Bolt, who of course cooked on a woodstove.*

Sherry McAdams

Three Bean Bake

1 (32-ounce) can pork and
beans
1 (16-ounce) can lima
beans
1 (16-ounce) can kidney
beans
½ cup onions, chopped
2 tablespoons green
pepper, chopped
½ cup brown sugar
1 cup ketchup
1 tablespoon
Worcestershire sauce
1 tablespoon mustard
½ cup cream cheese

Brown onions, and combine with all remaining ingredients except for the cream cheese. Bake at 350° for 30 minutes, adding the cream cheese the last 10 minutes.
Yield: 10 servings   *Judy Gorrell Harper*

Broccoli Deluxe
Microwave

1 (10-ounce) package
frozen chopped broccoli
1 can cream of chicken
soup
1 (8-ounce) carton sour
cream
1 tablespoon minced
onion
¼ teaspoon salt
⅛ teaspoon pepper
¾ cup herb flavored
stuffing mix
2 tablespoons butter

Pierce broccoli package with fork. Place broccoli in microwave and cook 7 to 8 minutes. Cool slightly; drain and pour into a 2-quart casserole dish. Blend together soup, sour cream, onion, salt, pepper, and combine with broccoli. In a small glass bowl, melt butter 30 seconds and mix with stuffing mix. Sprinkle over broccoli mixture. Cook 7 minutes. Cover casserole with cover or plastic wrap.
Yield: 6 servings   *Carol Ann Evans Garrett*

Favorite Broccoli Casserole

2 (10-ounce) boxes frozen
chopped broccoli
1 can cream of mushroom
soup
1 cup mayonnaise
2 eggs, beaten
1 medium onion, chopped

Salt and pepper, to taste
1 cup Cheddar cheese,
shredded
¼ cup butter, melted
½ package of Pepperidge
Farm Herb Stuffing mix

Cook broccoli according to package directions. Drain well. Combine soup, mayonnaise, eggs, onion, salt and pepper. Add to broccoli and pour mixture into 1½ quart casserole dish. Sprinkle cheese on top and pour melted butter over cheese. Spread stuffing over entire casserole and bake, uncovered, 45 minutes at 350°.

Yield: 6 to 8 servings   *Karen Coleman Hirons*

Broccoli Milan

2 (10-ounce) packages
chopped, frozen broccoli
1 (16-ounce) can stewed
tomatoes
2 eggs, beaten
1 can cheese soup

Salt, pepper, and oregano
to taste
2 tablespoons butter
8 ounces mozzarella
cheese, shredded

Preheat oven to 350°. Cook broccoli according to package directions, drain well, and place in a 9 x 13-inch casserole dish. Mix in tomatoes with half of the liquid. Pour eggs over the mixture and then spread soup on top. Sprinkle with salt, pepper, and oregano. Dot with butter and cover with cheese. Bake at 350° for 45 minutes, or until bubbly and lightly browned on top.

Yield: 8 servings   *Chris Rinne Moyer*

Broccoli Pie

2 (10-ounce) boxes frozen
chopped broccoli
3 eggs, beaten
1 small onion, diced
Butter or margarine
1 (6-ounce) can sliced
mushrooms

2 tablespoons flour
½ cup American cheese,
grated
1 cup bread crumbs

Thaw broccoli. Do not cook. Sauté onions in butter. Combine beaten eggs and onions. Mix with broccoli, mushrooms, flour and cheese. Place in a greased 10-inch pie pan. Sprinkle with bread crumbs. Bake at 350° for 35 to 40 minutes.
Yield: 6 to 8 servings
Ann Hite Benson

Broccoli And Wild Rice

2 (10-ounce) packages
frozen chopped broccoli
1 (6-ounce) box long grain
and wild rice
1 can cream of chicken
soup

1 (8-ounce) jar Cheese
Whiz
1 (8-ounce) can sliced
water chestnuts

Preheat oven to 350°. Cook broccoli and rice according to package directions. Combine ingredients and pour into a greased casserole dish. Bake for 30 minutes or until bubbly.
Yield: 8 servings
Jennifer Johnson Cobb

Peppered Cabbage
"Quick and Easy"

1 medium head white
cabbage, grated
¼ cup butter
2 tablespoons sour cream

Dash salt
1 teaspoon freshly ground
pepper

Sauté cabbage in butter until tender crisp (about 2 to 3 minutes), stirring constantly. Stir in sour cream; season with salt and pepper. Serve hot.
Yield: 6 servings
Jeanne Powell Orman

Brussel Sprouts Casserole
Try it, you'll like it

Non-stick cooking spray
2 pounds brussel sprouts
4 medium onions, sliced
Cayenne pepper, to taste
Salt, to taste
1 cup Swiss cheese,
  grated
1 cup Romano cheese
1 cup Cheddar cheese,
  grated
1 cup Sauterne wine

Spray an oblong pan with non-stick cooking spray. Cook the brussel sprouts until tender and drain. Put a layer in pan, topped with a layer of onions, seasonings, and cheeses. Repeat layers and pour wine over assembled casserole. Bake at 375° for 1 hour.
Yield: 6 to 8 serivngs   *Ann Hite Benson*

Tex-Mex Cabbage

1 medium cabbage
2 tablespoons butter
1 medium onion, thinly
  sliced
1 green pepper, thinly
  sliced
1 tablespoon sugar
1 (28-ounce) can whole
  tomatoes, drained and
  quartered
½ teaspoon salt
¼ teaspoon pepper
¾ cup sharp Cheddar
  cheese, grated

Core cabbage and cut into six wedges. Put wedges into a pot with enough salted water to almost cover them. Place lid on pot and cook over medium heat for 10 minutes. Drain well and place in buttered 2 quart shallow baking dish. Sauté onion and green pepper in butter with sugar. Add tomatoes, salt and pepper. Pour over cabbage in baking dish. Sprinkle grated cheese on top and bake for 20 to 30 minutes at 350°.
Yield: 6 to 8 servings   *Linda Hiller LeSueur*

Carrots Clements

1 pound carrots, diced
½ cup onion, chopped
1 cup cheese, grated
¼ teaspoon salt

⅔ cup mayonnaise
1 teaspoon sugar
Pepperidge Farm Corn
Bread Stuffing

Preheat oven to 350°. Cook carrots in salted water until tender, approximately 18 minutes. Drain and cool. Combine next 5 ingredients and mix with carrots. Pour into a buttered casserole dish and sprinkle top with stuffing. Bake 30 minutes at 350°.
Yield: 6 servings   *Annette Clements*

Carrots Israeli
Unsurpassed

1¼ pounds young carrots
2 tablespoons butter or
   margarine
⅓ cup dry white wine
½ teaspoon ground
   nutmeg
½ teaspoon ground
   cinnamon

⅔ cup white raisins,
   optional
3 tablespoons light brown
   sugar
½ cup orange juice
4 slices unpeeled orange

Scrape carrots and cut into ¼-inch slices. Combine with butter, wine, nutmeg and cinnamon and cook over low heat until carrots are tender. Stir in raisins and sugar and continue cooking a few minutes longer, until raisins are plump and carrots are glazed. Stir in orange juice, and garnish with orange slices when ready to serve.
Yield: 6 servings   *Paulette Riley Gebhardt*

Cheese Scalloped Carrots

12 carrots, pared and
sliced
1 small onion, minced
1/4 cup butter
1/4 cup flour
1 teaspoon salt
1/4 teaspoon dry mustard

2 cups milk
1/8 teaspoon pepper
1/4 teaspoon celery salt
1/2 pound American
cheese, sliced
3 cups buttered soft bread
crumbs

Cook carrots, covered in 1-inch boiling, salted water until barely tender. Drain. Meanwhile in saucepan, gently cook onion in butter 2 to 3 minutes. Stir in flour, salt and mustard, then milk. Cook, stirring until smooth. Add pepper and celery salt. In 2 quart casserole dish, arrange layer of carrots, then layer of cheese. Repeat until all are used, ending with carrots. Pour on sauce. Top with crumbs. Bake 350° for 35 to 40 minutes.
Yield: 8 to 10 servings   *Judy Gorrell Harper*

Creamed Carrots

1 1/2 pounds carrots, cut
into fourths
1 1/2 cups water
1 tablespoon sugar
1 1/2 tablespoons butter
1/2 teaspoon salt
Pinch of pepper

1 1/2 cups whipping cream
Salt and pepper, to taste
2 tablespoons butter,
softened
1 tablespoon parsley
1 tablespoon chives

Bring carrots to a boil with sugar, water, butter, salt and pepper. Cover and boil slowly for 30 to 40 minutes or until carrots are tender and the liquid has evaporated. Correct seasonings. Meanwhile bring the cream to a boil in a saucepan and pour in enough to cover the carrots. Boil slowly uncovered for 15 to 20 minutes or until cream has been almost entirely absorbed by the carrots. Correct seasonings. Just before serving, gently toss carrots with butter, parsley and chives.
Yield: 4 serivngs   *Betty Neel Cobb Lawton*

Glazed Carrots
Microwave

1 pound carrots
2 tablespoons butter or margarine
¼ cup brown sugar

2 tablespoons cold water
1½ teaspoons cornstarch
¼ cup pecans, coarsely chopped

Wash and cut carrots into diagonal slices. Place in 1 quart casserole dish with butter and sugar. Cover and cook 9 to 11 minutes, stirring after 5 minutes. Mix the water and cornstarch until smooth. Stir into carrot mix and add pecans. Cover and cook in microwave 2 to 4 minutes until thickened. Stir before serving. *Can be doubled: Use 2 quart casserole dish. Cook 15 minutes, stirring after 7 minutes . . . . add thickeners and cook 4 to 6 minutes.*
Yield: 4 servings

Sharon McPherson Gordon

Velda's Carrot Custard
A favorite at Ella's Hemlock Inn, Bryson City

2 cups carrots, sliced
2 eggs
1½ cups milk
½ teaspoon salt
4 tablespoons butter or margarine, melted

1 teaspoon sugar
1 cup sharp cheese
1 cup bread crumbs
Paprika, optional

Cook and mash carrots. Beat eggs and mix together with milk, salt, butter and sugar. Grate cheese and add to the other ingredients, including the bread crumbs. Place mixture in a greased 1½-quart casserole and bake for about 30 minutes in a 350° oven.
Yield: 8 to 10 servings

Ella Jo Stevens Shell

Sunshine Carrots

When in a rush, substitute frozen carrots for fresh!

3 cups carrots, sliced
¼ cup sugar
½ cup orange juice

2 tablespoons flour
2 tablespoons butter, melted

Cook carrots in boiling salted water until tender. Drain. Combine sugar, orange juice, flour, and melted butter. Place carrots in buttered casserole dish and pour juice mixture over. Bake at 350° for 20 minutes.
Yield: 6 to 8 servings   *Pamela Cornett Platt*

Saucy Cauliflower

1 medium head cauliflower
8 cups water
1 teaspoon salt
1 tablespoon lemon juice
¾ cup mayonnaise

1 tablespoon prepared mustard
1 teaspoon dried mustard
4 ounces sharp Cheddar cheese, grated

Preheat oven to 350°. Add whole cauliflower, flower side down, to boiling water with salt and lemon juice added. Cook 8 to 10 minutes uncovered. Turn over and cook on the other side 8 to 10 minutes. Remove from water and drain on paper towel. Combine mayonnaise and mustards and spread over top of cauliflower. Sprinkle cheese on top and bake at 350° for 15 minutes or until golden brown.
Yield: 4 to 6 servings   *Dona Owenby Harbin*

Em's Cauliflower In Sauce
Microwave

1 head cauliflower	½ to 1 teaspoon mustard
½ cup mayonnaise	¼ teaspoon salt
1 tablespoon minced	6 slices processed
onion	American cheese

Loosely cover cauliflower with saran wrap, and steam in a small amount of water for 9 minutes (or until tender) on HIGH in the microwave oven. Drain. Combine the mayonnaise, onion, mustard and salt, and spoon on top of cauliflower. Place slices of cheese over the cauliflower. Be sure to cover the cauliflower, entirely. Microwave until melted.

Yield: 4 to 6 servings   *Marsha Brown Thomas*

Corn Soufflé

1 (16-ounce) can whole corn	½ cup corn oil
1 (16-ounce) can cream style corn	2 beaten eggs
1 (8½-ounce) box Jiffy corn muffin mix	1 (8-ounce) carton sour cream
	3 ounces Cheddar cheese, grated

Combine the first six ingredients together, mixing well. Pour mixture into a soufflé dish and bake at 350° for 45 minutes. Top with the grated cheese and bake another 10 minutes or until cheese is melted.

Yield: 8 servings   *Patricia Moore Caltabiano*

Escalloped Corn

2 (12-ounce) cans white corn, drained	½ cup Cheddar cheese, grated
3 eggs, beaten	½ cup cracker crumbs
1 cup milk	Paprika

Preheat oven to 350°. Combine corn, eggs, milk, and cheese. Place in a greased 7-inch round, or 9-inch loaf pan. Top with cracker crumbs and sprinkle with paprika. Bake uncovered for 30 minutes or until firm.

Yield: 8 servings   *Jennifer Johnson Cobb*

Far East Celery

4 cups celery, sliced
1 (15-ounce) can sliced
  water chestnuts, drained
1 can cream of chicken
  soup
1 (2-ounce) jar diced
  pimento

¼ cup margarine
1 cup bread crumbs
¼ cup slivered almonds,
  toasted

Cook celery in small amount of boiling water for 5 minutes. Drain and mix celery with water chestnuts. Add soup and pimento, and place entire mixture in a greased 1-quart casserole dish. Meanwhile melt margarine. Add bread crumbs and almonds. Top celery mixture with this and bake for 35 minutes at 350°.

Yield: 6 servings

Anne Mabie Crew

Eggplant Supreme

1 large eggplant, peeled
2 ribs celery, chopped
1 large onion, chopped
1 small bell pepper,
  chopped
¼ cup butter
1 teaspoon Worcestershire
  sauce

1 dash hot sauce
1 cup Cheddar cheese,
  grated
1 (6-ounce) can ripe
  olives, chopped
Salt, to taste
Ritz cracker crumbs

Cut up eggplant and steam in a small amount of water on low heat until tender. Sauté celery, onion, and bell pepper in butter. Add cooked eggplant. Stir in Worcestershire sauce and hot sauce. Add cheese and olives. Taste before adding salt. Put mixture in baking dish and cover with cracker crumbs. Bake 30 minutes in a 375° oven.

Yield: 4 servings

Carole Feledik Templeman

Ritzy Eggplant

2 large eggplants
2 eggs, beaten
¼ cup milk
Salt and pepper, to taste

Onion, to taste
¾ cup sharp cheese, divided
Ritz crackers, crushed

Wash eggplant, peel, and cut in pieces. Boil in salted water 30 minutes, until soft. Drain. Add eggs, milk, salt, pepper, and onion. Beat until fluffy. Add ¼ cup of the grated cheese. Top with crackers and remaining cheese. Bake at 350° for 30 minutes, or until bubbly.

Yield: 4 to 6 servings

Ann Hite Benson

Hot Hominy

South meets Southwest when this traditional Southern member of the corn family is prepared tex-mex!

4 slices bacon, fried and crumbled (reserve drippings)
1 large onion, chopped
1 (16-ounce) can tomatoes

2 jalapeño peppers, diced
3 (15½-ounce) cans hominy, drained
½ pound sharp Cheddar cheese, grated

Cook onion in bacon fat until limp. Add tomatoes and jalapeños and stir. Add hominy, stirring well to combine all ingredients. Place in a casserole and top with cheese and bacon. Bake at 350° for about 40 minutes, or until bubbly.

Yield: 6 to 8 servings

Leckie Kern Stack

Ken's Mushroom Casserole

1 pound fresh
  mushrooms, sliced
3 tablespoons butter
3 tablespoon flour
½ cup sour cream

1 cup milk
Salt and pepper to taste
1 box seasoned croutons
1 cup Cheddar cheese,
  diced

Sauté mushrooms in butter 3 minutes. Remove from heat, cover and let stand 2 to 3 minutes. Stir in flour. Slowly add sour cream and milk. Season to taste. Cover bottom of 13 x 9-inch casserole dish with croutons, and pour mushroom mixture over this. Top with cheese, but DO NOT STIR. Bake at 425° for 15 minutes.
Yield: 8 to 10 servings   *Ginger Byrd McPherson*

Mushroom Casserole
A great "do ahead" dish.

1 (16-ounce) carton
  mushrooms, washed and
  sliced
1 large green pepper,
  chopped
1 large onion, chopped
4 stalks celery, chopped
3 tablespoons butter or
  margarine

1 cup milk
4 eggs
Salt and pepper, to taste
8 slices white bread,
  buttered
1 can cream of mushroom
  soup
1 cup sharp Cheddar
  cheese, grated

Preheat oven to 350°. Sauté mushrooms, green pepper, onion and celery in butter or margarine. Mix milk and eggs; season with salt and pepper. Remove crusts from bread slices and layer ½ of the bread in a greased baking dish, top with the mushroom mixture and then with the remaining bread. Pour egg mixture over and bake at 350° for 30 minutes. Pour mushroom soup over the top and bake 20 minutes. Add grated cheese and bake an additional 5 minutes.
Yield: 8 servings   *Lisa Sterchi Faucette*

Scalloped Okra And Corn
Fresh, frozen or canned okra–whatever you have available

1 (14½-ounce) can cut
okra, drained
4 tablespoons butter,
divided
1 (15-ounce) can corn,
drained

2 tablespoons flour
1 cup milk
½ pound sharp Cheddar
cheese
1 cup dry bread crumbs

Stir fry okra in 2 tablespoons butter for 10 minutes. Place in baking dish alternating layers with drained corn. Make a white sauce by melting butter in a saucepan over low heat and blending in flour. Milk should be added all at once, cooking quickly and stirring constantly . Cheese is stirred in until blended. Pour this mixture over vegetables, and cover with crumbs topped with dots of butter. Bake at 350° for approximately 45 minutes until the casserole is heated through and the crumbs are brown.
Yield: 6 to 8 servings

Leckie Kern Stack

Baked Vidalia Onions
"This is one of the easiest ways to enjoy the Georgia Vidalia."
Microwave.

4 medium large Vidalia
onions *, peeled
4 beef bouillon cubes
4 tablespoons butter or
margarine, divided

Salt and pepper, to taste
Grated cheese, cracker
crumbs, parsley, or fresh
herbs, optional

Hollow out a small area in the top of each onion. Place onions in a glass baking dish. Put one bouillon cube and 1 tablespoon margarine into hollow of each onion. Season with salt and pepper. Cover with plastic wrap and microwave on HIGH for 10 to 12 minutes. Any one or more of the optional ingredients should be added during the last minute of cooking. * Any sweet onion may be substituted if Vidalias are not available.
Yield: 4 servings

Mary Ellen Miller Trippe

French Fried Onion Rings
A Georgia Favorite

1 cup flour
2 tablespoons corn meal
1 cup beer

½ teaspoon salt
2 jumbo Vidalia onions *
4 cups oil

4½ to 5 hours prior to serving: Combine flour, corn meal, beer and salt in a bowl using a whisk. Let sit for 4 hours at room temperature. Thirty minutes before batter is ready, preheat oven to 200°. Peel and slice onions. Separate into rings. Heat oil and batter onion rings. Fry in oil until brown, and then place in a casserole dish in oven until golden brown and crispy. Do not stack.
* If Vidalias are unavailable, any sweet onion may be substituted.
Yield: 4 servings   *Jennie Inglesby Adams*

Onion Pie
Great served with steaks!

1 cup Ritz crackers, finely
   crushed
¼ cup butter plus 2
   tablespoons, melted
2 cups Vidalia onions, *
   thinly sliced
2 eggs

¾ cup milk
¾ teaspoon salt
Dash pepper
¼ cup sharp Cheddar
   cheese, grated
Paprika
Parsley, optional

Mix cracker crumbs with ¼ cup butter. Press into 8-inch pie plate. Sauté onions in 2 tablespoons butter until translucent, but not brown. Spoon into crust. Beat eggs with milk, salt and pepper. Pour this mixture over onions, sprinkle with cheese and paprika, and bake at 350° for 30 minutes. Garnish with parsley if desired.
* Any sweet onion may be substitued if Vidalias are not available.
Yield: 6 to 8 servings   *Karin Maltenieks Werbell*

Cheese - Potato Casserole
This is very easy and can be made ahead!
Men and children love it!

8 potatoes, peeled, cooked
   and diced
1 pound American cheese,
   cut into strips
½ cup onion, chopped
1 cup mayonnaise
½ teaspoon salt
¼ teaspoon pepper
½ pound bacon, chopped
   and partially fried
¼ cup green olives, sliced

Combine potatoes, cheese, onion and mayonnaise. Add salt and pepper. Place in a 9 x 13-inch baking dish. Sprinkle bacon and olives on top. Bake for 1 hour at 325°.
Yield: 10 to 12 servings   *Pam Duncan Balsley*

Instant Potato Pancakes
A different way to serve potatoes!

1 cup instant mashed
   potato flakes
½ cup plus 1 tablespoon
   self rising flour
1¼ cups milk
3 tablespoons margarine,
   softened
3 teaspoons dried minced
   onions
½ teaspoon salt
1/16 teaspoon pepper
1/16 teaspoon nutmeg, or
   onion powder, or garlic
   powder

Preheat oven to 400°. Combine mashed potato flakes and self rising flour in medium mixing bowl. Add the remaining ingredients, and using a fork, blend together. Drop batter by "heaping" tablespoons, onto a non-stick baking sheet, forming 7 or 8 pancakes. Bake until golden brown, approximately ten minutes. Turn pancake over and bake until crisp, approximately 8 more minutes.
Yield: 4 servings   *Cheryle Johnson Kirk*

Creole Stuffed Potatoes

6 baking potatoes
1 green pepper, diced
1 onion, diced
⅓ cup butter

1 tomato, diced
* 1 to 2 tablespoons half
   and half
Salt and pepper, to taste

Bake potatoes. Meanwhile, sauté pepper and onion in butter. Add tomato and cook for 1 minute. Scoop out potato centers, and mash with milk and seasonings. Stir in onion, peppers, and tomatoes. Stuff shells with mixture. Bake at 400° until brown on top. (Approximately 20 minutes). * Milk may be substituted.
Yield: 6 servings   *Leckie Kern Stack*

Gourmet Potatoes

6 medium potatoes
¼ cup butter, melted
3 cups Cheddar cheese,
   shredded
⅓ cup green onions,
   chopped

1 teaspoon salt
¼ teaspoon pepper
1½ cups sour cream
2 tablespoons butter

Cook potatoes in skin. Cool. Peel and shred coarsely. Set aside. Melt butter in pan over low heat. Blend with cheese, onions, salt, pepper, and sour cream. Fold mixture into potatoes. Pour into greased 2-quart casserole dish and dot with butter. Bake 25 to 30 minutes at 350° until lightly browned.
Yield: 8 servings   *Mariam Thomas Richardson*

Delmonico Potatoes

9 medium-sized red
   potatoes
½ pound sharp Cheddar
   cheese, grated
1 teaspoon dry mustard

1½ teaspoons salt
Dash pepper
Pinch of nutmeg
1 cup heavy cream
1 cup milk

Preheat oven to 325°. Boil potatoes in large pot until nearly done. Remove potatoes and let cool. Peel and grate potatoes and place in a buttered 1½ quart casserole, being careful not to press the potatoes down firmly into dish. In a 1-quart saucepan combine cheese, mustard, salt, pepper, nutmeg, cream and milk, stirring over low heat until cheese melts. Pour over potatoes, Do not stir. Bake uncovered 45 to 60 minutes.
Yield: 8 servings   *Susan Struzzieri Burns*

Oyster Stuffed Potatoes
The oysters are a real surprise!

6 large baking potatoes
¼ cup butter
1 (8-ounce) carton sour
  cream
1 large onion, chopped
Salt, pepper, and garlic
  powder, to taste

½ to 1 pint of fresh
  oysters *
1 cup Cheddar cheese,
  grated

Bake potatoes for 1½ hours at 350° to 400°, until done. Cut off top of potatoes and scoop out pulp, reserving. Retain shells. Mash potatoes with butter, sour cream and onions. Add spices. Put half of the mixture into the shells. Place two or more * (to taste) oysters in each shell and fill to the top with potato mixture. Sprinkle cheese on top of each potato and bake at 400° for 30 minutes.

Yield: 6 servings   *Pat Holden Mozley*

Roasted Potatoes

2 to 3 pounds of new
  white, or red potatoes
6 tablespoons margarine
  or butter
3 tablespoons olive oil
3 cloves garlic, finely
  chopped
½ cup parsley, chopped

1 tablespoon fresh thyme
  or ½ teaspoon dried
  thyme
1½ teaspoons rosemary
1½ teaspoons paprika
Cayenne pepper to taste
Salt to taste
Pepper to taste

Preheat oven to 375°. Clean potatoes and pat dry. Potatoes may be sliced or cooked whole. In a roasting pan, melt margarine in oil. Add all spices except salt and pepper. Add the potatoes, mixing them well so that they are coated with mixture. Bake for about 40 minutes or until potatoes are tender, basting occasionally. Season with salt and pepper if needed.

Yield: 10 servings   *Stephanie Threlkeld Gill*

Poppy Seed Potatoes

3 cups potatoes, cooked
  and diced
1 cup Cheddar cheese,
  grated
1 tablespoon poppy seeds

2 tablespoons flour
1 teaspoon salt
Dash pepper
1 cup sour cream

Preheat oven to 375°. Combine all ingredients and put in greased 1½-quart casserole dish. Bake uncovered at 375° for 30 to 35 minutes.

Yield: 6 servings   *Dell Cochran James*

Potato Cheese Chips

4 medium baking potatoes
1 cup margarine, melted
1 cup Parmesan cheese,
  grated

Salt, pepper and paprika
  to taste

Preheat oven to 375°. Peel potatoes and slice into ⅛ inch rounds. Dip slices into melted butter then into the cheese. Place slices on a large baking sheet lined with greased foil. Sprinkle with salt and pepper and a dash of paprika. Bake at 375° for 20 minutes.

Yield: 4 to 6 servings   *Debbie Lewis Mitchell*

Potatoes And Cheese

8 medium-large potatoes,
  peeled and cooked
1 (8-ounce) package cream
  cheese, softened
1 (8-ounce) carton sour
  cream

1 stick butter or
  margarine, melted
1 teaspoon salt
Non-stick cooking spray
Paprika

Mash potatoes and combine with next 4 ingredients. Put mixture into a 9 x 13-inch glass dish which has been sprayed with non-stick cooking spray. Sprinkle top with paprika. Bake at 350° until potatoes are hot and fluffy, approximately 30 minutes.

Yield: 4 to 6 servings   *Marty James Hagood*

Scalloped Potatoes And Mushrooms

5 medium-to-large potatoes, thinly sliced	1 cup shredded Swiss cheese
Salt and pepper	½ cup snipped parsley
1 pound fresh mushrooms, sliced	3 green onions, sliced
	2 cups whipping cream

Preheat oven to 350°. Arrange ⅓ of the potatoes in a buttered 3-quart casserole dish. Sprinkle with salt and pepper. Top with half the mushrooms, cheese, parsley, and onions. Repeat layers, ending with potatoes, salt and pepper. Pour whipping cream over casserole. Cook in 350° oven for 45 minutes to 1 hour, or until potatoes are done when tested with a fork.
Yield: 8 servings   *Kaye Armitage DeJarnett*

Apples And Sweet Potatoes

1 (2 pound) can sweet potatoes or 2 pounds fresh ones that have been boiled and peeled	¾ cup maple syrup
	¼ cup melted butter
	1 teaspoon salt
2 cups apples, sliced and peeled	

Slice potatoes lengthwise and place them into a well greased 12 x 8 x 2-inch casserole. Arrange the apple slices on top of the potatoes. Combine the syrup, butter and salt pour over the potatoes and apples. Cover and bake at 350° for 45 minutes. Remove the cover and continue to bake for another 30 minutes or until apples are tender, basting frequently.
Yield: 8 servings   *Carol Reck Teem*

Cranberry Yams

2 (17-ounce) cans yams,
    drained
2 cups fresh cranberries
½ cup flour
½ cup brown sugar,
    packed

½ cup old fashioned or
    quick oats (uncooked)
1 teaspoon cinnamon
⅓ cup margarine
1½ cups miniature
    marshmallows

Preheat oven to 350°. Mix yams and cranberries. In a separate bowl, make a coarse crumb mixture by combining the flour, brown sugar, oats, cinnamon, and margarine (cut in). Toss 1 cup crumb mixture with yams and cranberries. Place in a 1½-quart casserole dish. Top with remaining crumbs and bake at 350° for 35 minutes. Add marshmallows, and broil until browned, approximately 2 minutes.
Yield: 4 to 6 servings   *Jeanne Powell Orman*

Supreme Sweet Potato Soufflé
A variation of a Southern favorite

2½ cups sweet potatoes,
    mashed
½ cup butter
1 cup sugar
½ cup brown sugar
¾ cup evaporated milk

4 egg yolks (save whites)
½ cup coconut
½ cup raisins
1 teaspoon vanilla
½ cup pecans, chopped
Pinch of salt

Topping:
⅓ cup butter
⅓ cup flour

1 cup pecans, chopped
1 cup brown sugar

Combine all ingredients, except for topping mixture. Beat egg whites stiffly and fold into potatoes. Pour into a 9 x 13-inch baking dish. Mix topping ingredients together and sprinkle over the top. Bake at 325° to 350° for 45 minutes.
Yield: 10 servings   *Cathy Colquitt*

Hawaiian Sweet Potatoes

2 cups mashed sweet
potatoes or (1 pound 13
ounce) can
½ teaspoon salt
1 cup sugar

2 eggs
1 cup milk
1 cup coconut
1 teaspoon vanilla

Topping:
1 (8-ounce) can crushed
pineapple with juice
1 large jar maraschino
cherries with juice

¾ cup sugar
2 tablespoons cornstarch
¼ teaspoon red food
coloring

Cook potatoes and salt until tender. Drain, mash and add remaining ingredients. Bake at 350° for 1 hour.
Topping: Mix all ingredients and bring to a boil. Cook and stir constantly until mixture is thick. Cool and spread over cooked potatoes.
Yield: 8 servings   *Anne Mabie Crew*

Special Spuds
Great for barbeques!

1 medium onion, chopped
1 can cream of chicken
soup
1 (8-ounce) carton sour
cream

1 (32-ounce) package
frozen hashbrown
potatoes
½ cup Parmesan cheese

Stir together onions, soup and sour cream. Put hashbrowns in the bottom of a large casserole dish. Pour mixture over and top with Parmesan cheese. Bake at 350° for 1 hour.
Yield: 10 servings   *Betty Brewer Munford*

Brazilian Rice

A good accompaniment for any meat or fish.

¼ cup butter or margarine
1 tablespoon onion, chopped
1 cup milk
4 eggs, beaten
1 tablespoon Worcestershire sauce
2 teaspoons salt
½ teaspoon marjoram
½ teaspoon thyme
½ teaspoon rosemary
2 (10-ounce) packages chopped spinach, thawed and drained
3 cups cooked rice
1 pound sharp cheese, grated

Preheat oven to 350°. Melt the butter or margarine and sauté the chopped onion. Add the milk, eggs, Worcestershire sauce, salt, marjoram, thyme, and rosemary. Stir in the spinach, rice and cheese. Bake in a greased 2-quart covered casserole at 350° for 35 to 40 minutes.
Yield: 8 to 10 servings   *Linda Marett Disosway*

Herb Rice

This spicy dish adds zest to plain meats!

3 tablespoons margarine
½ cup onion, finely chopped
1 cup white rice, uncooked
½ teaspoon marjoram
½ teaspoon summer savory
1 teaspoon rosemary
½ teaspoon salt
3 bouillon cubes (chicken OR beef) *
2 cups water

Melt margarine in a two-quart saucepan. Add the onion and rice. Cook until the rice begins to brown. Add spices and bouillon cubes. Add water and bring to a boil, stirring to dissolve cubes. Cover with lid, turn low and heat for 14 minutes. Remove from heat, but leave lid on for 10 additional minutes, or until ready to serve. * Use chicken bouillon with shrimp or chicken, beef bouillon with steak or roast.
Yield: 6 servings   *Patricia Wilson George*

Cumin Rice
A distinctive flavor

1 can cream of mushroom
soup
1 can cream of celery
soup
1 can cream of chicken
soup

1½ cups uncooked regular
rice
1½ cups water
½ to 1 teaspoon cumin

Combine all ingredients and place in a greased 1½-quart baking dish. Bake, uncovered, at 350° for 2 hours.
Yield: 6 servings   *Dorothy Elletson*

Gourmet Rice

¼ pound butter (not
margarine)
1 cup long grain and wild
rice, mixed *
½ cup almonds, slivered

1 small onion, chopped
1 (5-ounce) can
mushrooms
4 chicken bouillon cubes
2 cups water

Melt butter and cook everything, except bouillon and water, in heavy skillet for 5 minutes over low heat. Place rice mixture in casserole dish. Dissolve bouillon cubes in water and pour over rice. Cover and cook 1 hour at 325°. * Prepackaged mix may be used, but omit herb packet.
Yield: 6 to 8 servings   *Martha Williams Moore*

Parmesan Rice

7 tablespooons butter,
divided
2 onions, chopped
1½ cups rice

1 teaspoon salt
2¾ cups beef consommé
½ cup Parmesan cheese
¼ cup chopped parsley

Sauté onions in 3 tablespoons butter for 1 to 2 minutes. Add rice and salt. Stir fry 1 to 2 minutes or until rice starts to brown. Add beef consommé, bring to a boil, cover and simmer 30 minutes. At serving time, blend Parmesan cheese, parsley, and remaining butter into rice.
Yield: 8 servings   *Judy Thomas Ballard*

Spicy Spinach Madeline

A favorite with the "boys." They are pleasantly surprised that spinach can taste so good!

2 (10-ounce) packages
 chopped spinach
4 tablespoons butter,
 divided
2 tablespoons flour
2 tablespoons green
 pepper, chopped
½ cup evaporated milk
½ teaspoon black pepper

¾ teaspoon celery salt
1 teaspoon Worcestershire
 sauce
¾ teaspoon garlic salt
6 ounces; jalapeño
 cheese, cubed
Seasoned bread crumbs

Preheat oven to 350°. Cook spinach according to package directions. Drain well, reserving ½ cup of the liquid. Melt the butter in a skillet, and blend in flour until smooth. Add peppers and cook until slightly tender. Add ½ cup of the spinach juice and ½ cup of the canned milk. Stir until thick. Add pepper, celery salt, Worcestershire, garlic salt and cheese. Heat until smooth and pour over spinach. Mix well and pour into a buttered casserole dish. Top with bread crumbs and dot with butter. Bake at 350° until bubbly.
Yield: 8 servings

Stephanie Threlkeld Gill

Spinach-Artichoke Casserole

2 (10-ounce) packages
 frozen chopped spinach
½ cup green onions,
 chopped
½ cup butter
2 (8-ounce) cartons sour
 cream

½ teaspoon salt
¼ teaspoon pepper
2 (8-ounce) cans
 artichokes in water
½ cup grated Parmesan
 cheese

Cook spinach, drain, and set aside. Sauté onions in butter over low-to-medium heat. Mix onions and butter with spinach. Add sour cream, salt and pepper. Drain liquid from artichokes. Fold into spinach mixture, and pour into a 2-quart casserole dish. Sprinkle with Parmesan cheese. Bake at 350° for 20 to 30 minutes, or until bubbly.
Yield: 6 to 8 servings

Helen Clayton Shingler

Spinach And Carrot Medley

5 medium carrots, thinly
sliced
1 medium onion, sliced in
thin rings
1 (10-ounce) package
frozen leaf spinach
3 tablespoons butter
3 tablespoons flour

1½ cups milk
¼ teaspoon salt
1 cup American cheese,
shredded
Dash pepper
½ cup soft buttered bread
crumbs

Preheat oven to 350°. Cook the carrots and onions in a small amount of salted water until nearly tender (about 8 minutes). Drain and cool. Cook spinach according to package directions and drain thoroughly. While the vegetables cool, begin the sauce by melting butter in a pan. Blend in the flour to make a paste, and gradually stir in milk. Cook and stir until the sauce thickens. Add cheese, salt and pepper, and continue stirring until cheese melts. Place half of the spinach in a 1½ to 2 quart casserole dish, then cover with half of the carrots and onions. Top with half of the cheese sauce. Repeat. Sprinkle the bread crumbs on top. Bake in 350° oven for 15 to 20 minutes or until crumbs begin to brown.
Yield: 4 to 6 servings *Jeanne Powell Orman*

Spinach Savannah

3 (10-ounce) packages
frozen chopped spinach
2 (3-ounce) packages
cream cheese, softened
4 tablespoons butter,
melted

Salt and pepper to taste
Dash nutmeg
Grated rind of 1 lemon
1 (6-ounce) package herb
stuffing

Cook spinach and drain well. Return to low heat and immediately add cream cheese and 2 tablespoons of butter. Add salt, pepper, nutmeg and lemon rind. Pour into a buttered casserole. Spread the herb stuffing on top and then drizzle with the remaining butter. Bake at 350° for 25 minutes.
Yield: 8 to 10 servings *Beverly Webb McCollum*

Spinach-Zucchini Boats

1 (10-ounce) package
  frozen chopped spinach
3 zucchini
2 tablespoons flour
½ cup milk
⅓ cup Cheddar cheese,
  shredded

4 slices bacon, cooked
  and crumbled
Bread crumbs
Butter

Preheat oven to 350°. Cook spinach and drain. Cook zucchini in boiling water for 10 minutes. Drain well and half. Scoop out pulp, chop, and add to the spinach. Blend flour and milk and add spinach mixture, cooking until thick. Add cheese and bacon. Fill zucchini shells with mixture. Top with bread crumbs and dot with butter. Bake at 350° for 20 minutes.
Yield: 6 servings
Leckie Kern Stack

Cheesy Squash

4 to 5 medium squash, cut
  in pieces
2 large onions, sliced
1 can cream of mushroom
  soup
1 (8-ounce) carton sour
  cream

1 cup seasoned bread
  crumbs
2 eggs, beaten
¾ cup sharp cheese,
  grated

Preheat oven to 350°. Cook squash and onions until tender (approximately 15 to 20 minutes); drain well. Cool. Add the next 4 ingredients and mix well. Pour into a greased 1½ to 2 quart casserole dish, and bake at 350° for approximately 30 minutes, or until "set". Top with cheese and bake an additional 5 minutes.
Yield: 4 to 6 servings
Connie Meaders Kone

Clemson Squash

6 to 8 medium squash,
  chopped
2 small onions, chopped
  fine
Salt and pepper, to taste
1 (17-ounce) can cream
  style corn

2 eggs, beaten
3 tablespoons margarine
1 tablespoon sugar
Grated cheese or bread
  crumbs

Boil squash and onions for approximately 20 minutes. Drain and mash. Combine with next five ingredients in a greased casserole dish, and top with bread crumbs or cheese. Bake at 350° for 30 to 40 minutes.
Yield: 6 to 8 servings   *Mikell VonKolnitz Stribling*

Nel's Stuffed Squash Florentine

3 large yellow squash
2 (10-ounce) boxes
  chopped frozen spinach
1 (8-ounce) package cream
  cheese

1 envelope dry onion soup
  mix
Seasoned bread crumbs
Parmesan cheese

Preheat oven to 325°. Steam squash whole until tender, approximately 10 to 12 minutes or until the inside is tender but the outside is still firm. * Split squash lengthwise and remove the seed with a spoon. Cook spinach, adding no water. As the spinach begins to bubble, reduce heat and add cream cheese which has been cut into small pieces. Stir until it all melts. *Do not boil as this will crudle the cream cheese.* Add soup mix and blend well. Fill scooped out squash shells with spinach mixture. Top with seasoned bread crumbs and Parmesan cheese. Bake at 325° until heated through, approximately 15 minutes. * *To microwave the squash instead of steaming: Place squash in a glass dish with 3 tablespoons water. Cover with saran wrap, with one end open for steam to escape. Cook on high for 4 to 5 minutes and let sit for 4 minutes.*
Yield: 6 to 8 servings   *Betty Parrott Barnett*

Old Fashioned Squash Casserole

2 pounds yellow summer
squash, sliced
1 medium onion, sliced
½ cup butter or margarine
1 tablespoon sugar

1 teaspoon salt
2 eggs
1 cup bread crumbs,
divided

Boil squash and onions until tender, approximately 15 minutes. Drain and mash with a fork. Combine squash and onions with remaining ingredients, including ½ cup of the bread crumbs. Put in 1½-quart casserole dish, and sprinkle remaining bread crumbs on top. Bake 30 minutes at 300°.

Yield: 6 servings   *Cheryl Tilley Briscoe*

Settlement Squash

*This cherished recipe became part of
one couples divorce settlement!*

1½ pounds tender squash,
sliced
1 can condensed cream of
chicken soup, undiluted
1 (8-ounce) carton sour
cream
1 (4-ounce) jar pimentos,
drained and sliced
(optional)

1 (8½-ounce) can water
chestnuts, thinly sliced
2 medium onions, finely
chopped
½ cup butter or margarine,
divided
½ to 1 package herb
stuffing mix *

Cook squash in salted water until tender, approximately 12 to 15 minutes. Drain well, and add the next 5 ingredients. Meanwhile melt 6 tablespoons of the butter in a skillet, add stuffing and mix well. Press stuffing mixture into the bottom of a 2-quart baking dish, reserving some of the mixture for the top of casserole. Pour squash mixture over stuffing and sprinkle remaining stuffing over top. Dot with remaining butter. Bake at 350° for 30 minutes. * *½ package is usually sufficient, but more may be added to taste.*

Yield: 8 servings   *Rebecca Edenfield Lingerfelt*

Southern Style Squash Crêpés
Crepes freeze beautifully!

Squash Mixture:

3 cups yellow squash,
sliced

2 medium onions,
chopped

1 tablespoon bacon
grease

½ teaspoon salt

1 egg, beaten

1 (8-ounce) carton sour
cream

1 cup extra-sharp Cheddar
cheese, grated

Crêpés:

3 eggs

2 tablespoons all-purpose
flour

1 tablespoon water

1 tablespoon milk

Pinch of salt

1½ teaspoons butter

Squash: Add bacon grease to a small amount of water and simmer squash and onions covered until tender (approximately 6 to 8 minutes). Stir in salt. Drain well. Blend in egg and sour cream. Mash well. Place approximately 2 tablespoons of the squash mixture in each crêpé and fold twice (triangular in shape). Place filled crêpés on lightly greased cookie sheet. Sprinkle each crêpé with cheese. Bake in a 350° oven until cheese melts. (Approximately 15 minutes).

Crêpé: Mix first five ingredients well, to form the batter. Keep batter covered and refrigerated from three hours to overnight. Melt butter in skillet. When it bubbles, pour in enough batter to cover bottom of pan with a thin coating. Keep the pan moving. After about one minute of cooking, turn the crêpé. Turn crêpé over again and again until the crêpé is well browned. Crêpé may be stacked with foil or waxed paper in between.

Yield: Approximately 6 servings (ingredients may be tripled to fill more crêpés).

Patsy Spinks Dupree

Oberley's Ratatouille

½ cup vegetable oil
3 cloves garlic, sliced
2 medium zucchini
2 crook neck yellow
  squash
3 large onions, thinly
  sliced

4 green peppers, sliced
4 medium tomatoes,
  chopped
2 tablespoons parsley,
  chopped
1 teaspoon basil
Salt and pepper to taste

Heat oil in large Dutch oven. Add garlic and cook over low heat 2 minutes. Add vegetables, spices, salt and pepper. Cook, covered, over low heat 45 minutes. Uncover and simmer approximately 15 minutes.
Yield: 10 servings

Marsha Brown Thomas

Squash Casserole

This dish can be made a day or two ahead.
Great for company!

1½ pounds squash, sliced
1 teaspoon sugar
½ cup mayonnaise
½ cup onion, minced
¼ cup bell pepper, minced

1 egg, slightly beaten
½ cup cheese, grated
Salt and pepper, to taste
Cracker crumbs
¼ cup butter

Cook squash in boiling water, until tender, (approximately 15 minutes). Drain well, mash, and add next 7 ingredients. Pour entire mixture into a two-quart casserole dish. Top with crumbs and dot with butter. Bake at 350° for 40 minutes or until hot and bubbly.
Yield: 6 servings

Becky Worthington Dorsett

Stuffed Zucchini
Just as good reheated!

6 medium zucchini (2
large)
6 bacon slices
¾ cup onion, chopped
1 clove garlic, minced
1 (4-ounce) can
mushrooms, stems and
pieces, drained (reserve
liquid)

⅔ cup seasoned bread
stuffing mix
⅓ cup wheat germ
2 tablespoons Parmesan
cheese, grated
1 tablespoon ketchup
¾ teaspoon basil
½ teaspoon salt
⅓ teaspoon pepper

Cook zucchini in boiling water 5 to 10 minutes, or until tender. Drain. Let cool. Cook bacon until crisp and drain, reserving 3 tablespoons of the drippings. Sauté onion and garlic in drippings. Add mushrooms and cook 5 minutes, stirring occasionally. Set aside. Slice zucchini lengthwise. Scoop out centers and chop. Combine chopped zucchinni, mushroom mixture, and remaining ingredients, except bacon. Mix well. (Add 1 to 2 tablespoons of the mushroom juice if the mixture seems too dry.) Fill zucchini shells with mixture and crumble bacon over the tops. Place stuffed shells in a large shallow baking pan, and bake at 400° for about 20 minutes.
Yield: 6 to 8 servings *Linda Galt Best*

Zucchini And Walnuts

¼ cup olive oil
1 pound zucchini, cut into
½-inch slices
2 tablespoons onion,
minced

1½ tablespoons lemon
juice
1 cup walnuts, chopped
Salt and pepper, to taste

Heat the oil in a skillet and fry the zucchini and onions for 5 minutes, until tender. Add the lemon juice. Add nuts and salt and pepper, to taste.
Yield: 8 servings *Leckie Kern Stack*

Zucchini Strips Provencale

2 teaspoons olive oil
1 garlic clove, thinly sliced
½ cup onion, diced
4 medium zucchini, cut
  lengthwise into eighths
2 medium tomatoes, diced
½ teaspoon oregano
  leaves
¼ teaspoon salt
Dash pepper
2 tablespoons fresh
  parsley, chopped
1 tablespoon lemon juice,
  freshly squeezed
Parsley sprigs, optional

Heat oil in a 10-inch non stick skillet. Add garlic and sauté until golden. Remove and discard garlic. Add onion to same skillet and sauté until translucent. Add remaining vegetables, oregano, salt, and pepper. Cover and let simmer until zucchini is tender crisp, about 5 minutes. Sprinkle mixture with chopped parsley and lemon juice. Toss to combine. Garnish with parsley sprigs if desired.
Yield: 4 servings   *Mary Ellen Miller Trippe*

Fancy Tomato Casserole
A versatile side dish.

2 (14½-ounce) cans of
  tomato wedges
1 teaspoon salt
1 medium onion, finely
  chopped
10 tablespoons seasoned
  bread crumbs
1½ cups sharp cheese,
  grated
Parmesan cheese

Preheat oven to 350°. Empty tomatoes (do not drain) into a large mixing bowl and chop into smaller pieces. Mix in salt and onion. Place ½ of the mixture in a greased 1½-quart casserole dish. Cover with ½ crumbs and ½ the cheese. Add remaining tomatoes and cover with crumbs and cheese. Sprinkle generously with Parmesan cheese. Bake 30 minutes at 350°.
Yield: 4 to 6 servings   *Connie Meaders Kone*

Garden Fresh Tomato And Zucchini Casserole

This casserole adapts easily to serve 2 people or 200!

Butter
Zucchini, sliced
Salt and pepper
Saltine crackers, crumbled
Tomatoes, sliced

Sharp Cheddar cheese, shredded
Onions, sliced
Cheddar cheese soup

Begin by buttering an appropriately sized casserole dish. Add a layer of sliced zucchini. Salt and pepper to taste. Sprinkle with saltine cracker crumbs. Dot with butter. Add a layer of sliced fresh tomatoes. Sprinkle with saltine cracker crumbs. Dot with butter. Add a layer of shredded sharp Cheddar cheese. Layer sliced onions next. Salt and pepper to taste. Sprinkle with saltine cracker crumbs. Add another layer of shredded cheese. After layers are complete, cover with Cheddar cheese soup. (1 can soup with ½ can water for small casseroles, and 2 cans soup with about ¾ can water for larger casseroles.) Bake, uncovered, at 350° for 1 hour and 10 minutes.
Yield: Any amount you need! *Trish Rogers Elliott*

This recipe originated with a woman trying to use up the last of her tomatoes from her country garden. The one unbreakable rule is that the tomatoes must be fresh! She wouldn't use tomatoes unless they were straight from her garden.

Fresh Vegetable Casserole
Yummy

1½ pounds yellow squash, sliced
1 carrot, thinly sliced
1 onion, thinly sliced
1½ cups margarine or butter, melted
2 cups Pepperidge Farm stuffing mix divided
¾ cup sour cream
1 can cream of chicken soup
1 (2-ounce) jar chopped pimento

Combine squash, carrot and onion in salted water and cook until tender, approximately 8 to 10 minutes. Do not overcook. Drain. Meanwhile add butter to the stuffing mix. Mix sour cream, soup and pimento. Spread 1 cup of dressing mix in greased casserole dish. Put squash mixture on top, then sour cream mixture. Top with remaining dressing mix. Bake at 350° for approximately 45 minutes.

Yield: 8 servings   *Pamela Croy Newton*

Vegetable Vidalia Onion Combo

8 tablespoons butter, divided
1 tablespoon fresh lemon juice
1 pound fresh mushrooms, sliced
4 cups Vidalia onions, * sliced
3 cups tomatoes, diced
2 cups soft bread crumbs, divided
Salt and pepper, taste

Melt 3 tablespoons butter in a skillet. Add lemon juice and mushrooms and sauté for 3 minutes. Remove mushrooms. Melt an additional 2 tablespoons butter and sauté onion rings until tender. Place onions in a 10 x 6 x 2-inch baking dish. Arrange mushrooms over onion and sprinkle with salt and pepper. Combine tomatoes and 1 cup of the bread crumbs in the skillet. Season with salt and pepper. Simmer 15 minutes and pour over mushrooms. Top with mixture of 1 cup soft bread crumbs tossed with 3 tablespoons melted butter. Bake at 350° for 30 minutes. * *Sweet onions may be substituted if Vidalias are unavailable.*

Yield: 8 servings   *Dell Cochran James*

Veggie Kabobs

1 cup vegetable oil
½ cup lemon juice
1 teaspoon parsley flakes
2 broccoli spears, cut into
  1-inch pieces
2 yellow squash, cut into 8
  pieces each

3 small onions, quartered
8 cherry tomatoes
Cooked seasoned rice
  (optional)

Preheat broiler. Combine oil and lemon juice and parsley in medium bowl. Add washed and cut veggies. Let veggies marinate at least 5 minutes, but the longer the better. Alternate broccoli, squash, and onion on 4 skewers. Broil veggies 5 minutes. Remove. Add cherry tomatoes to skewers, and brush all veggies with marinade. Return to broiler for 3 minutes. Remove, brush again with marinade and serve with hot rice if desired. *Green peppers, mushrooms, corn on the cob chunks are other vegetables to try. This recipe is especially good because the hostess can fix the correct amount - one kabob per quest - without having any waste!*
Yield: 4 servings   *Debbie Lewis Mitchell*

Vegetable Surprise
A favorite of young and old

1 (10-ounce) package
  frozen broccoli spears,
  chopped
1 (10-ounce) package
  Fordhook lima beans
½ cup margarine
3 cups Rice Krispies
1 can cream of mushroom
  soup

1 package dried onion
  soup mix
1 (8-ounce) carton sour
  cream
1 (5-ounce) can sliced
  water chestnuts

Cook vegetables and drain. Meanwhile melt margarine and brown Rice Krispies. Mix the remaining ingredients with the cooked vegetables, topping with Rice Krispies. Bake at 350° for 30 minutes.
Yield: 6 to 8 servings   *Francine Adams Hammond*

Apples In Sauce
Microwave
A time saver

8 medium tart cooking
  apples (Granny Smith)
½ cup water
1 cup sugar
¼ teaspoon ground
  cinnamon

¼ teaspoon ground
  nutmeg
⅛ teaspoon salt

Peel, core and cut apples into small to medium size pieces. Place apples in 2-quart glass casserole dish with ½ cup water. Cover and microwave 15 to 20 minutes until tender. Stir once during cooking. Stir in sugar, spices and salt. Cover and let stand 15 minutes. Serve warm or cold.
Yield: 4 to 5 cups   *Angel Layne Daniel*

Cheesy Baked Apples

2 (16-ounce) cans apple
  pie filling
½ cup butter or margarine,
  softened

1 cup sugar
¾ cup flour
½ pound Velveeta cheese,
  grated

Preheat oven to 350°. In a mixing bowl cream butter, sugar and flour until fluffy. Set aside. Place both cans of apples into a greased 3-quart baking dish and top with butter mixture. Sprinkle the grated cheese over the entire dish. Bake at 350° for 30 to 40 minutes or until lightly browned.
Yield: 8 to 10 servings   *Inez Pou Bennett*

Holiday Apples

2 (29-ounce) cans
  Comstock apples,
  unsweetened with juice
4 cups bread cubes with
  crust
1 cup margarine

¾ cup sugar
¾ cup brown sugar
½ teaspoon nutmeg
¾ teaspoon cinnamon
½ cup apple juice
⅛ cup lemon juice

Preheat oven to 350°. Mix all ingredients and put in a 2-quart or 9 x 13-inch pan and bake for 45 minutes.
Yield: 12 servings   *Mary Mayes Suhr*

Brandied Fruit

12 macaroons, crumbled
4 cups drained fruit
(peaches, pears,
apricots, pineapples,
white cherries)

½ cup slivered almonds
¼ cup dark brown sugar
¼ cup melted butter
½ cup cream sherry

Preheat oven to 350°. Grease a 2½ quart dish. Cover bottom with a layer of macaroon crumbs. Alternate layers of fruit and crumbs, ending in crumbs. Sprinkle with brown sugar and almonds. Drizzle with butter and sherry. Bake uncovered at 350° until it bubbles on top, about 30 to 45 minutes.
Yield: 8 to 10 servings   *Carole Feledik Templeman*

Cranberry - Apple Casserole
*Great with Thanksgiving turkey in lieu
of traditional cranberry sauce.*

3 cups apples, chopped
and unpeeled
2 cups fresh, whole
cranberries
1 cup sugar

½ cup uncooked Quaker
Oats
½ cup pecans, chopped
½ cup brown sugar
½ cup butter, melted

Preheat oven to 325°. Grease a 2-quart casserole dish. In this dish combine apples and cranberries. Sprinkle with sugar. Combine the oats, nuts, brown sugar and butter, sprinkle over the fruit. Bake for 45 minutes. If more topping is preferred, use one cup each oats and pecans. Do not increase the brown sugar or butter.
Yield: 8 servings   *Kaye Armitage DeJarnett*

Cranberry Mousse

1 (12-ounce) can jellied
cranberry sauce
1 (5-ounce) can crushed
pineapple

1 (8-ounce) carton sour
cream
1 tablespoon mayonnaise

Mix together all ingredients and freeze in small molds, such as cup cake pan. Remove from molds and put in plastic bag and freeze until ready to use.
Yield: 10 to 12 small molds   *Dianne Davison Isakson*

Baked Apricots

2 (16-ounce) cans apricot
  halves, drained
⅔ cup brown sugar

1 cup Ritz crackers
½ cup butter, melted

Preheat oven to 300°. Grease a 1½-quart casserole. Layer apricots, sugar and cracker crumbs until all ingredients are used. Pour melted butter over all. Bake at 300° for 35 to 45 minutes.

Yield: 6 to 8 servings   *Betty Neel Cobb Lawton*

Cranapple Bake
Serve hot or cold.

6 apples, peeled and
  sliced
1 pound fresh cranberries
1 cup brown sugar
2 tablespoons cornstarch
1 cup chopped pecans or
  walnuts

1 tablespoon vanilla
2 ounces melted
  margarine
1 (12-ounce) jar apricot
  preserves

Spray a 8 x 12-inch dish with no - stick cooking spray. Preheat oven to 375°. Place sliced apples in dish, put whole cranberries on top. Mix sugar, cornstarch, vanilla, margarine and preserves and pour over berries. Sprinkle with chopped nuts. Bake at 375° for 50 minutes.

Yield: 6 to 8 servings   *Francine Adams Hammond*

Baked Fruit

1 pound pitted prunes
1 (5½-ounce) package
  dried apricots
1 (13-ounce) can pineapple
  chunks, not drained
1 (16-ounce) can cherry
  pie filling

1½ cups water
¼ cup dry sherry
⅓ cup slivered almonds,
  toasted (walnuts or
  pecans may be
  substituted)

Preheat oven to 350°. Put prunes, apricots and pineapple in deep 9-inch round casserole. Combine cherry pie filling, water, and sherry; pour over fruit. Stir in nuts; cover and bake at 350° for 1½ hours. This may be frozen.

Yield: 8 servings   *Carroll Ann Putzel*

Baked Fruit Compote

1 (15-ounce) can pineapple chunks, drained
1 (15-ounce) jar apple rings, drained
1 (16-ounce) can pear halves, drained
1 (16-ounce) can apricot halves, drained
1 (16-ounce) can sliced peaches, drained
½ cup butter
½ cup sugar
2 tablespoons all-purpose flour
¼ teaspoon ground cinnamon
1 cup white sherry
12 red maraschino cherries

Preheat oven to 350°. Arrange first five ingredients in layers in a 3-quart baking dish, set aside. Melt butter in top of a double boiler. Add sugar, flour, cinnamon, and sherry; mix well. Cook for 15 minutes or until mixture is slightly thickened. Pour sauce over fruit and arrange cherries on top. Refrigerate overnight. Bake at 350° for 50 to 60 minutes. Serve immediately.
Yield: 8 to 10 servings   *Sherry McAdams*

Fresh Curried Peaches
A Georgia Speciality

8 fresh peaches, unpeeled, halved and pitted
¼ cup butter, melted
1 cup brown sugar, packed
1 teaspoon curry
1 (14-ounce) can crushed pineapple, undrained
Maraschino cherries

Preheat oven to 350°. Arrange peach halves in greased casserole. Pour butter over peaches. Mix sugar and curry. Sprinkle mixture over peaches. Spread pineapple over the top of each peach half. Place cherry in the center of each peach. Bake at 350° for 30 minutes. Serve warm.
Yield: 8 to 10 servings   *Susan Workman Yielding*

Fruit Celebration

1 (29-ounce) can sliced peaches
1 (29-ounce) can pear halves
1 (15-ounce) can pineapple chunks
1 (29-ounce) can pitted plums
2 bananas
1 (16-ounce) can apple sauce

½ cup maraschino cherries
⅓ cup butter or margarine
¾ cup brown sugar (reserve 3 tablespoons)
½ cup slivered almonds (pecans may be substituted)

Drain all fruit. Put all fruit except bananas and apple sauce in a large bowl. Boil sugar and butter until sugar melts. Add apple sauce to butter and sugar mixture and pour over fruit. Refrigerate over night. Preheat oven to 350°. Butter a 2-quart casserole. Chop bananas and add to other fruit; pour all fruit into prepared casserole. Bake at 350° for 45 minutes. Mix 3 tablespoons of brown sugar with almonds. Sprinkle over fruit and bake 15 minutes longer.

Yield: 10 to 12 servings   *Patricia Wilson George*

Spiced Pear Bear
(A creative way with pears)

1 (14-ounce) can pear halves with syrup
1 cinnamon stick
Nutmeg to taste

Peel of 1 lemon rind
12 whole cloves
¼ cup sugar

Combine syrup from pears, sugar, cinnamon, lemon peel and cloves in a saucepan. Simmer 10 minutes or until thickened. Add pears and simmer 15 minutes until flavored. Sprinkle nutmeg on top and serve warm or cold. (For children use cloves as eyes, the pears take on a light brown color that reminds you of bears).

Yield: 4 to 6 servings   *Debbie Day*

Pineapple Casserole
Delicious with chicken, pork, or ham

1 (20-ounce) can crushed
pineapple, drained,
reserve juice
¼ cup sugar
3 tablespoons flour

1 cup sharp Cheddar
cheese, grated
½ cup Ritz cracker crumbs
½ cup buttter, melted

Preheat oven to 350°. In a blender or with a wire whisk, combine pineapple juice, sugar and flour. Add pineapple and cheese, pour into a buttered 9-inch pie plate. Top with cracker crumbs and pour melted butter over the top. Bake at 350° for 25 minutes. This dish is great for a brunch.
Yield: 4 to 6 servings   *Ginger Colquitt Autry*

Scalloped Pineapple

2 (20-ounce) cans
pineapple chunks,
undrained
5 cups bread cubes
(preferably a coarse
texture white bread with
crusts)

1 cup butter, softened
1½ cups sugar
2 eggs
½ cup heavy cream, not
whipped

Preheat oven to 350°. Cream butter and sugar. Add eggs and beat. Add pineapple with juice and add cream. Cut up bread with crusts into bite size cubes. Add bread to mixture and stir together. Place in a greased 2-quart casserole or a soufflé dish and bake at 350° for 1 hour. Toward the end of baking time over with foil so as not to burn bread. *Variation:* Drizzle a little extra melted butter over bread cubes before mixing with other ingredients.
Yield: 8 to 10 servings   *Pamela Croy Newton*

Apple Chutney
A good winter relish with roast, ham or turkey.

2 ounces garlic, ground
8 pounds apples
6 pounds sugar
2 pounds onions
Vinegar to cover
3 pounds raisins

1 pound crystallized
  ginger
Salt to taste (⅛ pound)
2 ounces mustard seed
3 dozen jelly jars

Peel and cut apples and onions. Run garlic through grinder. Combine apples and onions in Dutch oven. Cover with vinegar and let boil until apples are tender, but not mushy. Add sugar and boil 10 minutes. Add raisins and mustard seed and boil 20 minutes. Lower heat and simmer until mixture thickens and has rich golden color. Add ginger. Put chutney in sterilized jars and seal while still hot. Serve with curried dishes or as an appetizer over cream cheese with crackers.
Yield: 3 dozen jars   *Stephanie Threlkeld Gill*

Cranberry Orange Chutney
A wonderful holiday gift

1 cup fresh orange
  sections
¼ cup orange juice
4 cups fresh cranberries
1 cup sugar
1 cup apple, chopped and
  unpeeled

½ cup raisins
¼ cup walnuts, chopped
1 tablespoon vinegar
½ teaspoon ground ginger
½ teaspoon ground
  cinnamon

Combine all ingredients in a large saucepan. Bring to a boil; reduce heat and simmer 5 to 10 minutes or until cranberries begin to burst. Remove from heat and pour into a serving container. Chill until serving time. This may be frozen until ready to use.
Yield: Approximately 2 pints   *Phyllis Wallace Holley*

Hot Pepper Jelly
*Serve with pork or lamb or spread
on cream cheese and serve with crackers.*

½ cup hot peppers (red and green)
1½ cups green bell peppers (may use a few red)
1½ cups vinegar
6½ cups sugar (do not skimp)
1 or 2 pouches Certo
⅛ teaspoon red or green food coloring
6 or 7 half pint jars

Remove seeds and veins from peppers. (Wear rubber gloves when working with hot peppers). Chop some and grind in food processor or blender. You may use some of the vinegar with the peppers when grinding. In large pot, mix all ingredients except Certo and food coloring; bring to rolling boil and boil for 5 minutes. Add Certo and boil 1 minute. Remove from heat and let stand 5 minutes. Skim if necessary and add food coloring. Put in jars and seal. Turn upside down for a while to keep bits of peppers from rising to top.
Yield: 6 to 7 half pints

Mary Neal Pilcher

Pepper Relish
Colorful and festive

12 red peppers, medium to large
12 green peppers, medium to large
12 medium onions (Vidalia are best)
12 hot peppers
3 cups sugar
3 cups vinegar
3 tablespoons salt
Canning jars

Remove seeds and veins from peppers. (Use rubber gloves when working with hot peppers). Chop peppers and onions and grind in food processor. Cover with boiling water and let stand at least 5 minutes. Drain well; add sugar, vinegar and salt. Boil gently 5 to 10 minutes. Put in sterilized jars and seal.
Yield: 6 to 8 half pints

Mary Neal Pilcher

Strawberry Jam

2 quarts ripe strawberries
7 cups sugar
1 (1¾-ounce) box
  powdered fruit pectin

9 half pint jars

Wash, stem and thoroughly crush strawberries. Put berries and fruit pectin into large pot. Cook on high, stirring until mixture comes to a rolling boil. Add sugar and stir. Return to rolling boil and boil for 1 minute, stirring constantly. Remove from heat and skim off foam. Pour into scalded jars and seal.
Yield: 9 half pints   *Mary Neal Pilcher*

Squash Pickles
Great gift ideal!

12 cups yellow squash,
  thinly sliced
3 cups medium onions,
  thinly sliced
3 cups bell pepper, finely
  chopped

2 cups vinegar
2 cups sugar
2 teaspoons whole celery
  seed
2 teaspoons mustard seed

Cover squash and onions in salt water for 1 hour. Cover with foil. Drain and set aside. Bring bell pepper, vinegar, sugar, celery seed and mustard seed to a boil. Add squash and onions and bring to a boil again. Fill in hot, sterilized 1-pint jars and seal.
Yield: 6 to 8 pints   *Dona Owenby Harbin*

BREAD, CHEESE AND EGGS

Harmony

Breads, Cheese, Eggs And Pasta

Duke Dining Hall Biscuits
Beautifully high biscuits

2 cups flour
½ teaspoon salt
4 teaspoons baking
 powder
½ teaspoon cream of
 tartar

2 teaspoons sugar
½ cup shortening or
 margarine
⅔ cup milk, scant

Preheat oven to 450°. Sift dry ingredients; cut in shortening or margarine until mixture resembles course crumbs. Add milk all at once and stir until dough follows fork around the bowl. Roll dough ½ inch thick. (This may be done between two sheets of waxed paper dusted with flour, for easy clean up). Cut biscuits with cutter. Be careful not to roll dough too thin. Bake on ungreased cookie sheet at 450° for 10 to 12 minutes.
Yield: 10 to 12 biscuits   *Susan Smith Phillips*

Sour Cream Biscuits
Don't need to butter them, just enjoy!

1 cup butter, room
 temperature
1 (8-ounce) carton sour
 cream

2 cups self-rising flour

Preheat oven to 350°. Mix butter and flour by hand. Add sour cream. Grease small muffin tins. Drop 2 teaspoonfuls into muffin tins. Bake at 350° for 25 minutes or until barely golden brown.
Yield: 48 tiny biscuits   *Nancy Dendy Ryle*

Crisp Waffles

2 cups self-rising flour
½ cup vegetable oil
1½ cups milk

¾ cups pecans, finely
 chopped (optional)

Combine flour, oil and milk in a bowl. Beat with electric mixer until well mixed. Preheat waffle iron. Pour approximately ¾ cup of batter into hot iron. Sprinkle batter with pecans, if desired. Lower waffle iron lid and bake until well browned and crispy.
Yield: 3 to 4 waffles   *Esther Barnes Mulling*

Cinnamon French Toast For Two

½ cup milk
2 eggs, beaten
2 tablespoons honey
1 teaspoon ground
  cinnamon

¾ teaspoon vanilla extract
4 slices of French bread

Combine first five ingredients and mix well. Set aside. Dip both sides of bread slices into egg mixture. In a lightly greased skillet, cook bread until lightly browned.
Yield: 2 servings   *Allyson Ray Murphy*

French Toast
A Special Saturday Morning Treat

3 eggs, beaten
¾ cup milk
1 tablespoon sugar
¾ teaspoon vanilla
¼ teaspoon salt
1 teaspoon ground
  cinnamon (optional)

8 to 12 slices French
  bread, cut diagonally
  ¾-inch thick
Butter for frying

Optional toppings:
Powdered sugar
Honey

Syrup
Preserves

In a medium mixing bowl, beat eggs together; add remaining ingredients, except bread, and mix well. In a 9-inch square glass baking dish, arrange the bread on one layer (they will be squeezed together). Pour the egg mixture over the bread, turning to coat each piece. Cover and refrigerate overnight. Fry each slice in melted butter. Serve with any of the optional toppings.
Yield: 8 to 12 pieces   *Dianne Davison Isakson*

Oatmeal Pancakes
Mix the night before serving

2 cups quick cooking
   oatmeal, uncooked
2 cups buttermilk
½ cup whole wheat flour
2 tablespoons sugar

1 teaspoon baking soda
1 teaspoon baking powder
2 eggs, slightly beaten
¼ cup butter or margarine,
   melted

Mix oatmeal and buttermilk well and let soak in refrigerator for a few hours or overnight. Add remaining ingredients and mix well. Heat griddle and drop one large tablespoon of batter for each pancake. These may be wrapped individually, frozen and later cooked in the toaster.
Yield: 4 to 6 servings   *Sis Schmell Eastland*

Pancakes

2 cups buttermilk
1 teaspoon baking soda
2 eggs, beaten

1⅔ cups sifted flour
1 teaspoon salt

Heat griddle or frying pan. In a large mixing bowl, combine 2 cups buttermilk and baking soda. Mix in eggs. Gently add flour and salt; lightly mix until batter is lumpy. Drop batter on heated griddle by large spoonfuls. Cook until brown and turn. *Variation:* You may add 1 cup of blueberries to batter for blueberry pancakes.
Yield: 6 servings   *Kathy Dunn*

Buttermilk Biscuits

1 cup self-rising flour
½ cup shortening

¾ cup buttermilk

Preheat oven to 400°. Sprinkle ¼ cup flour on a flour board. Mix in shortening and remaining flour; add buttermilk a little at a time. Pour out mixture on to board and knead until it is a consistency to roll out. Roll out the dough and cut with biscuit cutter. Place on an ungreased cookie sheet. Bake at 400° for 15 to 20 minutes.
Yield: 12 biscuits   *Lois Barton Huggins*

Cream-Style Cornbread

1 (8-ounce) can creamed corn
1 (8-ounce) carton sour cream
1 cup self-rising corn meal
½ cup vegetable oil
2 eggs

Preheat oven to 400°. Grease and heat a black skillet. Mix corn, sour cream, corn meal, oil and eggs together. Pour into hot skillet. Bake at 400° for 20 to 30 minutes.
Yield: 8 servings   *Sara Moss Bentley*

Cornbread Casserole
Family will delight with this new twist to an old favorite!

1½ cups white corn meal
3 tablespoons sugar
3 teaspoons baking powder
4 eggs, well beaten
1 cup sour cream
1 cup New York sharp cheese, grated
1 cup green pepper, finely chopped
1 cup onion, finely chopped
½ cup oil
¾ teaspoon salt
1 cup creamed corn

Preheat oven to 450°. Sift dry ingredients together. Beat eggs with sour cream, oil and corn. Add cheese, pepper and onions to the dry ingredients. Blend in oil mixture. Pour into a 3 quart casserole and bake at 450° for 20 to 30 minutes. Casserole may be topped with ⅔ cup melted butter if desired.
Yield: 6 to 8 servings   *Ann Hite Benson*

Mexican Cornbread

3 eggs, beaten
1 (8-ounce) carton sour cream
1 (8-ounce) can cream style corn
½ cup shortening, melted
1½ cups self-rising corn meal
½ cup Jalapeño peppers
1 cup cheese, grated

Preheat oven to 375°. Combine all ingredients. Pour into a greased 9 x 13-inch pan and bake at 375° for 40 minutes.
Yield: 12 servings   *Betty Davis Haverly*

Grandmother's Cornbread

1 cup plain cornmeal
½ cup flour
1 teaspoon salt
1 teaspoon baking powder
1 teaspoon baking soda
1 egg
1¼ cups buttermilk
2 tablespoons cooking oil

Preheat oven to 450°. Sift together first 5 ingredients. Add egg, buttermilk, and oil; beat until blended. Pour into a greased and heated 9 x 9-inch pan and bake at 450° for 25 minutes or until golden brown on top. Remove from oven and cool in the pan. Cut into squares.
Yield: 6 servings   *Susan Mozley Haynie*

Thanks-Mama Cornbread Dressing

2 cups cornbread,
   crumbled
1½ cups dry, homemade
   bread crumbs
3½ to 4 cups homemade
   chicken stock
½ cup butter, melted
⅓ cup onion, finely diced
4 eggs
⅛ teaspoon salt
1 teaspoon sage, more if
   desired
1 cup celery, chopped,
   more if desired

Preheat oven to 450°. Beat eggs slightly; combine all ingredients and mix well. Pour into a well-greased 9 x 13-inch baking dish. Bake 30 minutes at 450°. *Note:* This is called Thanks-Mama Cornbread dressing because mama prepares this every year regardless of who hosts the Thanksgiving Dinner. Since all the ingredients are fresh and it takes some time to prepare, we all owe her a big thanks. It is usually doubled so we can all take some home.
Yield: 8 to 10 servings   *Cheryl Tilley Briscoe*

Ercelene's Spoon Bread
Good with Ercelene's Ham

2 cups milk
4 eggs, separated
1 cup white corn meal
2 teaspoons baking
  powder

¼ cup butter
½ teaspoon salt

Preheat oven to 425°. Heat milk in double boiler; add corn meal slowly, stirring constantly to keep from lumping. (If it lumps, remove from heat and stir until smooth.) Add butter to hot meal and stir. Let cool. Beat egg yolks and add to corn meal. Add baking powder and salt. Beat egg whites until stiff; then add to corn meal. Place in greased casserole dish. Bake at 425° for 30 to 40 minutes or until done.
Yield: 8 servings   *Adrian Winship Pressley*

Savannah Hush Puppies
Great for a fish fry

1½ cups corn meal
1½ cups water
⅓ cup milk
1 tablespoon vegetable oil
2 teaspoons salt
Grated onion to taste

2 eggs, beaten
1 cup flour
3 teaspoons baking
  powder
1 teaspoon sugar
Deep fat for frying

Cook corn meal and water until stiff. Remove from heat; add remaining ingredients. Drop from teaspoon into hot fat. Cook until golden brown and floating, turning once.
Yield: 24 to 30 hush puppies   *Georgie Keller Valentino*

Cherry Crescent Ring
Perfect Christmas brunch bread!

1 (10-ounce) jar
maraschino cherries,
drained (reserve 5
cherries for decoration)
1 (8-ounce) package cream
cheese, softened
¾ cup almonds, pecans or
walnuts, chopped

½ cup sugar
½ teaspoon almond
extract
2 (8-ounce) cans
refrigerated crescent
dinner rolls

Glaze:
1 cup confectioners' sugar
4 teaspoons milk

¼ teaspoon almond
extract

Garnish:
2 tablespoons chopped
nuts

5 maraschino cherries,
halved

Preheat oven to 375°. Grease a cookie sheet. Chop 1 cup cherries and combine with cream cheese, nuts, sugar and almond extract. Mix well and set aside. Separate crescent dough into two large rectangles. Overlap long sides of rectangles and firmly press edges and perforations to seal. Roll or pat out dough with hands to form a 13 x 15-inch rectangle. Spread cherry cheese mixture over dough. Beginning at long side, roll up rectangle pressing edges to seal. Place on cookie sheet seam side down. Form into a ring, firmly pressing ends together. With scissors or sharp knife, cut almost through ring at 1-inch intervals. Turn each section slightly on its side. Bake at 375° for 30 to 35 minutes, until golden brown. While ring is baking, prepare glaze. In small mixing bowl, combine all ingredients and mix well. After ring is removed from the oven and still warm, drizzle with glaze. Garnish with almonds and cherry halves.
Yield: 8 to 10 servings   *Paulette Riley Gebhardt*

Cherry Streusel Cake

1 cup plus 2 tablespoons butter, softened	2 teaspoons baking powder
1⅓ cups sugar	½ teaspoon salt
2 eggs	1 (20-ounce) can cherry
2⅓ cups flour	pie filling *

Preheat oven to 375°. In a bowl, cream together 1 cup butter and 1 cup sugar. Add eggs and mix. Sift together 2 cups flour, baking powder and salt. Gradually add this to the butter mixture. Beat until well mixed and butter has a smooth consistency. Take ¾ of the batter and spread it in a greased 9 x 13-inch pan. Pour pie filling over batter. Take the remaining mixture and drop small spoonfuls over the cherries. This batter will spread when cooking, but the smaller the drops, the more even the top layer will be. Take remaining butter, flour and sugar and blend together. Sprinkle evenly on top of the streusel. Bake at 375° for 45 minutes. Cool in the pan but can be cut and served while still warm. * *Blueberry pie filling is also good!*
Yield: 10 to 12 servings   *Bruce Goode Boling*

Sour Cream Coffee Cake
Perfect with morning coffee

1 cup margarine	2 cups flour
1 cup sugar	1 teaspoon baking soda
3 eggs	1 teaspoon baking powder
1 (8-ounce) carton sour cream	1 teaspoon vanilla

Filling:

1 cup nuts, chopped	2 tablespoons butter, melted
1 cup brown sugar	
2 tablespoons flour	

Preheat oven to 350°. Cream margarine, sugar, eggs, and sour cream. Gradually add sifted dry ingredients. Add vanilla and beat 10 minutes. Blend filling ingredients together. Pour half of cake batter into well-greased tube pan. Sprinkle with half of filling. Repeat once and bake for 45 minutes at 350°.
Yield: 12 servings   *Patricia Wilson George*

Coffee Ring
You'll be glad you invested the time

2 packages dry yeast (not
   rapid rise)
½ cup warm water
1½ cups warm milk
½ cup sugar

2 teaspoons salt
2 eggs, beaten
½ cup vegetable oil
6½ to 7½ cups all-purpose
   flour

Filling:
1 cup butter, softened
1 to 1½ cups brown sugar

Cinnamon to taste

Icing:
Confectioners' sugar
Milk

½ teaspoon vanilla

Dissolve yeast in warm water; set aside. Combine milk, ½ cup sugar, and salt. Add yeast mixture, eggs, and oil. Add enough flour to make a soft but slightly sticky dough and mix well. Cover and let rise in a warm place until doubled in bulk. Turn dough out on a floured surface and knead until smooth and elastic. Return dough to bowl; cover and again let rise until doubled. Place dough on a floured surface and divide into three equal portions. Roll each piece into an approximate 21 x 12-inch rectangle. On one piece at a time, smooth on some softened butter and sprinkle with brown sugar and cinnamon almost to edges. Roll as for jelly roll. Moisten edges and press together to seal. Form into a ring on greased baking sheet. Cut 2-inch slices with scissors on outer edge almost through ring. Turn slices cut-side up, overlapping the edges. Spread a little softened butter on top of each completed ring. Let rise for a short time (not doubled in size this time). Bake at 400° approximately 15 to 20 minutes or until very lightly browned. Cool for 10 or 15 minutes. For the glaze, mix just enough milk and confectioners' sugar to make a thick frosting and add vanilla. Glaze with this icing. These cakes freeze beautifully. *Variation:* Could also fill with nuts, raisins or dates, depending on your taste.
Yield: 3 large rings   *Pamela Croy Newton*

Eat One, Freeze One, Give One Away Coffeecake

Cake:
2 cups butter, softened
4 cups sugar
4 eggs
1 (16-ounce) carton
  sour cream
1 teaspoon vanilla

4 cups sifted flour
2 teaspoons baking
  powder
½ teaspoon salt

Topping:
2 cups pecans, chopped
2 teaspoons cinnamon

8 teaspoons sugar

Preheat oven to 350° and grease three round cake pans. Cream butter and sugar. Add eggs, one at a time, and beat until fluffy. Add sour cream, vanilla, baking powder and salt. Mix well. Fold in flour and mix. Pour half of the batter into the three cake pans. Mix remaining sugar and cinnamon. Sprinkle half the pecans on the first layer, then sprinkle half of the sugar and cinnamon mixture on top of the pecans. Dollop and spread the remaining mixture over the first layer, then top with remaining pecans and sugar and cinnamon mixture. Bake at 350° for 40 minutes or until done. Remove and cool. A great cake to freeze and take to the beach, to pull out once in awhile or for Christmas mornings.

Yield: 24 servings
Adrian Winship Pressley

Popover Pancakes

1 cup milk
1 cup flour
3 to 4 eggs
½ teaspoon vanilla

1 stick butter or margarine
¾ cup maple syrup
  (warmed)
½ teaspoon cinnamon

Preheat oven to 375°. Melt 1 stick of butter or margarine in a 13 x 9-inch glass baking dish. In bowl, combine milk, flour and vanilla. Whisk until smooth. Add eggs one at a time. Mix until smooth. Pour into pan with melted butter and place in oven for 20 to 25 minutes. When done cover with warm syrup and sprinkle with cinnamon.

Yield: 4 servings
Paula McClure Prentiss

Monkey Bread
A wonderful first bread for Mom's little helper

1¾ cups sugar
3 teaspoons cinnamon
3 cans biscuits (8 to 10
  per can)

¾ cup butter, melted

Preheat oven to 350°. Place ¾ cup sugar and 1½ teaspoons cinnamon in a bowl; seal with top and shake to mix. Cut biscuits in fourths and add to sugar mixture. Seal bowl and shake. Grease a Bundt pan and put biscuits in pan. Add 1 cup sugar and 1½ teaspoons cinnamon to melted butter. Stir and drizzle over biscuit mixture. Bake at 350° for 45 minutes. When cool, pull apart with hands to eat.
Yield: 12 servings   *Dona Owenby Harbin*

Agnes Paton's Lemon Bread
Easy bread with a delicate flavor

¾ cup margarine
1½ cups sugar
4 eggs, beaten
Rind of 1 lemon, grated
1 cup milk

3 cups sifted flour
1 teaspoon salt
1 cup pecans, chopped
2 teaspoons baking
  powder

Sauce:
Juice of 1 lemon

½ cup sugar

Preheat oven to 350°. Cream margarine and sugar together. Add the remaining ingredients and put in a large, greased loaf pan. Bake at 350° for about 30 minutes, or until toothpick inserted comes out clean. Combine lemon juice and sugar for the sauce topping; set aside for 30 minutes. Leave bread in pan to cool, but immediately after removing from oven, pour the topping sauce over the top and sides of bread.
Yield: 1 loaf   *Marsha Brown Thomas*

Poppy Seed Bread

3 cups flour
2⅓ cups sugar
½ teaspoon salt
1½ teaspoons baking
  powder
3 eggs, beaten
1½ cups milk
1⅛ cups oil

1½ tablespoons poppy
  seeds
1½ teaspoons vanilla
  extract
1½ teaspoons almond
  extract
1½ teaspoons butter
  flavoring

Glaze:
½ teaspoon vanilla extract
½ teaspoon almond
  flavoring
½ teaspoon butter
  flavoring

¼ cup orange juice
¾ cup confectioners'
  sugar

Preheat oven to 325° and grease and flour two (9¼ x 5¼ x 3-inch pans). Combine all dry ingredients together in a large bowl. Mix in beaten eggs, milk and oil until well blended. Add poppy seeds, vanilla, almond extract and butter flavoring and mix well. Pour mixture into loaf pans and bake one hour at 325°. Combine all glaze ingredients. Punch small holes in top of bread and drizzle glaze over cooling loaves.
Yield: 2 loaves   *Patricia Moore Caltabiano*

Blueberry Sally Lunn
Good with whipped cream

½ cup shortening
½ cup sugar
2 eggs
1¾ cups flour
3 teaspoons baking
  powder

½ teaspoon salt
1 cup milk
⅔ cup blueberries
½ teaspoon cinnamon
¼ cup firmly packed
  brown sugar

Preheat oven to 350°. Cream together shortening and sugar. Beat eggs and add. Sift together flour, baking powder and salt. Add this alternately with milk to creamed mixture. Carefully fold in blueberries. Pour into greased 8 x 8 x 2-inch pan. Mix brown sugar and cinnamon, sprinkle on batter. Bake at 350° for 50 minutes. Serve hot. May be reheated.
Yield: 6 to 8 servings   *Georgie Keller Valentino*

Banana Chocolate Chip Bread

2 cups flour
1½ teaspoons baking
  powder
1½ teaspoons baking
  soda
2 cups sugar
½ teaspoon lemon peel
⅔ cup shortening
1 cup buttermilk
1 teaspoon vanilla
  butternut flavoring

2 teaspoons coconut
  flavoring
3 medium ripe bananas,
  sliced
2 eggs
1 cup chocolate chips
1 cup plus 2 tablespoons
  flaked coconut
1 cup raisins

Preheat oven to 350°. Grease two loaf pans. Line pans with waxed paper and grease again. Sift all dry ingredients. Add shortening, buttermilk, two flavorings, lemon peel, bananas and eggs. Beat with electric mixer on medium speed. Fold in chocolate chips, 1 cup coconut and raisins. Fill pans about half full and top with the two tablespoons coconut. Bake in a 350° oven for 1 hour and 15 minutes. Leave unrefrigerated for 12 hours prior to serving. Freezes well.
Yield: 2 (12-inch) loaves   *Karen Smith Lockhart*

Grandmother's Blueberry Bread

2 eggs
1 cup sugar
1 cup milk
3 tablespoons shortening,
  melted
3 cups flour

1 teaspoon salt
4 teaspoons baking
  powder
1 cup blueberries
1 cup walnuts (optional)

Preheat oven to 350°. In a large mixing bowl, beat eggs and gradually add sugar. Add milk and melted shortening. In another mixing bowl sift dry ingredients and stir only until blended. Add dry ingredients to other mixture and mix. Carefully fold in blueberries and walnuts. Pour mixture into a large greased loaf pan and bake at 350° for 50 to 60 minutes.
Yield: 1 large loaf   *Kristine Reed Maedel*

Lemon-Blueberry Bread

¼ cup, plus 2 tablespoons
butter or margarine,
softened
1 cup sugar
2 eggs
1½ cups all-purpose flour

1 teaspoon baking powder
Pinch of salt
½ cup milk
2 teaspoons lemon rind,
grated
1 cup fresh blueberries

Glaze:
⅓ cup sugar

3 tablespoons lemon juice

Preheat oven to 350°. Cream butter and gradually add one cup sugar until blended. Add eggs, one at a time, beating well after each. Combine flour, baking powder and salt. Add this to creamed mixture alternately with milk, beginning and ending with flour mixture. Stir in grated lemon rind, then fold in blueberries. Pour batter into a greased loaf pan or two small pans. Bake at 350° for 55 minutes or until wooden toothpick inserted comes out clean. To make the glaze, combine sugar and lemon juice and heat until sugar dissolves. Puncture top of bread with wooden toothpick and pour lemon mixture over warm bread. Cool bread in pan 30 minutes.
Yield: 1 large or 2 small loaves   *Marsha Brown Thomas*

Super Strawberry Loaves

2 (10-ounce) packages
frozen strawberries,
thawed
1¼ cups oil
4 eggs
3 cups flour
2 cups sugar

2 teaspoons cinnamon
1 teaspoon salt
1 teaspoon baking soda
1 cup nuts, chopped
(pecans or walnuts)

Preheat oven to 375°. Grease and flour 2 (9 x 5 x 3-inch) loaf pans. Combine strawberries, oil and eggs; set aside. In large bowl combine flour, sugar, cinnamon, salt, soda and nuts. Add strawberry mixture and stir until blended. Pour into pans. Bake at 375° for 1 hour.
Yield: 2 loaves
Marilyn Simon Massey

Zucchini Bread

3 cups flour
2 teaspoons baking soda
1 teaspoon salt
½ teaspoon baking
  powder
¾ cup pecans, finely
  chopped

3 eggs
2 cups sugar
1 cup vegetable oil
2 teaspoons vanilla extract
2 cups zucchini, shredded
1 (8-ounce) can crushed
  pineapple, well drained

Preheat oven to 350°. Grease and flour 2 (8 x 4 x 3-inch) loaf pans. Combine flour, baking soda, salt, baking powder and pecans; set aside. Beat eggs lightly in large bowl; add sugar, oil and vanilla and beat until creamy. Stir in zucchini and pineapple. Add dry ingredients, stirring only until moistened. Spoon batter into 2 pans. Bake at 350° for 1 hour or until done. Cool 10 minutes in pan. Turn out on rack to finish cooling.
Yield: 2 loaves   *Betty Bickerstaff McRae*

Date Nut Bran Muffins

*This batter may be stored for up to six weeks
in the refrigerator in a covered container.*

5 cups flour, sifted
2 cups sugar
5 teaspoons baking soda
2 teaspoons ground
  cinnamon
1 teaspoon salt
2 cups all-bran cereal
2 cups wheat germ

2 cups bran flakes
2 cups dates, chopped
2 cups walnuts or pecans,
  chopped
1 cup oil
4 eggs, beaten
2 cups water
1 quart buttermilk

Preheat oven to 400° and grease muffin tins. Sift together flour, sugar, baking soda, cinnamon and salt. Set aside. In a separate bowl, combine remaining ingredients. Add dry ingredients gradually and stir just enough to moisten. Fill greased muffin cups ⅔ full and bake at 400° for 20 minutes or until done.
Yield: 12 to 14 dozen   *Pamela Croy Newton*

Blueberry Muffins

1¾ cups flour
2½ teaspoons baking
  powder
¾ teaspoon salt
¾ cup sugar
⅓ cup vegetable oil

½ cup milk
1 egg
1 cup blueberries, fresh or
  frozen (do not thaw)
Paper liners

Preheat oven to 400°. In large mixing bowl place flour, baking powder, salt and sugar. Stir lightly to mix. In small bowl beat together oil, milk, and egg. Pour liquid into flour mixture; mix slightly. Add blueberries and pour into lined muffin tins. Bake at 400° for 20 to 30 minutes or until brown and crispy on top.
Yield: 12 muffins   *Esther Barnes Mulling*

Date Nut Muffins

These will keep a week in a tin.

2 eggs
¾ cup sugar
1 teaspoon vanilla
5 tablespoons flour
⅛ teaspoon salt
¼ teaspoon ground
  cinnamon

¼ teaspoon ground
  allspice
1 cup pecans, chopped
1 cup dates, chopped

Preheat oven to 325° and grease 36 miniature muffin tins. Stir, do not beat, eggs, sugar, and vanilla. In a separate bowl, mix flour, salt, cinnamon and allspice. Add pecans and dates to flour mixture; combine the two mixtures. Fill greased muffin tins half full. Bake at 325° for 15 minutes.
Yield: 36 muffins   *Patricia Wilson George*

Sorrenson's Apple Pecan Muffins

1½ cups brown sugar
⅔ cup vegetable oil
1 egg
1 cup sour milk
1 teaspoon baking soda
1 teaspoon salt
1 teaspoon vanilla

2½ cups flour
1½ cups apples, diced
½ cup pecans, chopped
⅓ cup sugar
1 tablespoon butter,
   melted
Paper liners

Preheat oven to 325°. In large mixing bowl combine brown sugar, oil and egg; mix until blended; set aside. In small bowl combine milk, soda, salt and vanilla. Add flour to first mixture alternately with the second mixture; beat well. Fold in apples and pecans. Fill paper lined muffin tins ⅔ full. Combine sugar and melted butter; sprinkle over muffins. Bake at 325° for 30 minutes.
Yield: 15 muffins   *Beth Lamm Griffin*

Sweet Potato Muffins

½ cup butter
1¼ cups sugar
2 eggs
1¼ cups sweet potatoes,
   mashed
¼ teaspoon nutmeg
¼ cup pecans, chopped

1½ cups flour
2 teaspoons baking
   powder
¼ teaspoon salt
1 teaspoon cinnamon
1 cup milk
½ cup raisins

Preheat oven to 400° and grease muffin tins. Cream sugar and butter; add remaining ingredients, making sure not to over mix. Pour into muffin tins and bake 25 minutes at 400°.
Yield: 12 to 18 muffins   *Ann Mable Crew*

Cheddar Cheese Bread
Warms up any main dish

½ cup lukewarm water
2 packages yeast
4 cups Bisquick
4 ounces sharp Cheddar
  cheese, grated

1 (10¾-ounce) can onion
  soup

Preheat oven to 375°. Grease and flour 3 loaf pans. Mix ½ cup water with the yeast. In another mixing bowl, combine Bisquick and cheese. Add the onion soup to the yeast mixture. Combine the two mixtures. Put 1½ inches of water in a pan and bring to a boil. Turn stove off and put pan lid upside down on pan. Sit bowl of bread mixture on top of pan for 30 minutes, covering it with a towel. Put bread into pans. Bake at 375° for 40 to 50 minutes.
Yield: 3 loaves
Patricia Wilson George

Patsy's French Bread
A Cookbook Committee Favorite

1 long loaf of French
  bread, split horizontally
½ cup margarine
½ cup mayonnaise

1 cup Parmesan cheese,
  grated
Garlic, oregano and
  parsley to taste

Preheat oven to 300°. Mix all ingredients except bread. Spread mixture on bread. Wrap in foil. Bake 20 minutes at 300°. Uncover and broil until lightly browned.
Yield: 1 loaf
Virginia Jones Eubanks

Super Supper Bread

½ cup onion, chopped
1 tablespoon vegetable oil
1 egg, slightly beaten
¾ cup reserved fruit syrup
2 cups biscuit mix

1 cup Cheddar cheese, grated
1 tablespoon poppy seeds
1 tablespoon butter, melted

Preheat oven to 400°. Sauté onion in oil until clear. Mix together egg and fruit syrup. Blend in biscuit mix. Stir in onions and ½ cup cheese. Spread batter into a 9-inch round pie plate. Sprinkle top with remaining cheese and poppy seeds. Spoon melted butter on top. Bake at 400° for 20 to 25 minutes.
Yield: 6 servings   *Cheryl Tilley Briscoe*

Yorkshire Pudding
Serve with Prime Rib

2 eggs
1 cup milk
½ cup flour
Salt and pepper to taste

⅛ teaspoon nutmeg
½ cup beef drippings or melted fat

Preheat oven to 425° for 10 minutes. Beat eggs for 1 minute at highest speed of electric mixer. Add milk and slowly beat in flour. Add seasonings and 2 tablespoons of the drippings; beat for 1 minute at highest speed. Refrigerate for at least 30 minutes. Pour remaining drippings into a 7½-inch black cast iron skillet (or 8 heavy iron cupcake or muffin molds). Heat drippings in pan in the oven until sizzling hot. Add the chilled mixture to pan; bake at 425° for 30 minutes. Reduce oven temperature to 350° and bake an additional 10 to 15 minutes. The center may fall-this is O.K. Serve immediately; plain or with gravy. This is a light, puffy, brown "bread" more than a pudding.
Yield: 8 servings   *Dianne Davison Isakson*

Quick Company Rolls
Quick, easy and delicious

6 bake and serve rolls
¼ cup butter, melted
½ cup Cheddar cheese, grated room temperature
¼ cup Parmesan cheese
⅛ teaspoon onion, chopped
⅛ teaspoon salt
2 egg whites, beaten

Preheat oven to 350°. Cut rolls in half, crossway. Beat egg whites and mix with butter, cheese, onion and salt. Spread mixture on rolls. Bake at 350° for about 15 minutes or until brown.
Yield: 12 rolls   *Leckie Kern Stack*

Beau's Yeast Rolls

3 packages dry yeast
½ cup warm water
5 cups self-rising flour, unsifted
¼ cup sugar
1 teaspoon soda
1 cup shortening
2 cups lukewarm buttermilk

Dissolve yeast in warm water and set aside. Mix flour, sugar, and soda. Cut in shortening; add warm buttermilk and yeast mixture. Mix well. Place desired amount of dough on a floured cloth and pat out to a thickness of about ½ inch. Cut rolls with a biscuit cutter. Place on cookie sheet about 2 inches apart. Let them warm to room temperature before baking. Bake at 350° for 10 to 15 minutes. This will keep in refrigerator for several weeks so that you can pull off just enough for each meal.
Variation: Grease muffin tins. Roll dough into small balls and place 3 balls side by side in muffin tins. Increase cooking time by 5 minutes or until browned.
Yield: 1½ to 2 dozen   *Stephanie Threlkeld Gill*

Ice Box Rolls

*"When these come out of the oven, modestly
smile and take bows!"*

2 packages dry active
  yeast
1 cup lukewarm water
1 cup Crisco
¾ cup sugar
1 cup boiling water

2 eggs, beaten
7 cups flour (approximate)
1 teaspoon soda
1 teaspoon baking powder
1 tablespoon salt

⅛ cup oil
1 cup flour (for rolling out rolls)

Soak yeast in 1 cup lukewarm water, stir to mix well. Put Crisco
in a large mixing bowl, add sugar and boiling water. Use a large
spoon to help dissolve the shortening. Allow this mixture to cool
before adding yeast mixture and the eggs. Sift the remaining
dry ingredients together and add to yeast mixture until dough is
very sticky. Cover tightly and refrigerate overnight. Using ½
cup of flour, take out ½ the dough and knead on a floured board
or counter top until smooth. Roll out to ¼ to ½ inch thickness.
Cut with a biscuit cutter and dip one edge in oil and fold in half.
Place on a greased pan. Allow to rise about 4 hours (should be
high and light). Bake at 400° for about 8 minutes or until
golden brown.

Yield: 5 to 6 dozen
Estelle Elliott Bogle

Pumpkin Bread

1 teaspoon cinnamon
1 teaspoon nutmeg
1½ teaspoons salt
3 cups flour
3 cups sugar
1 cup oil

1 cup pumpkin, canned
4 eggs
½ cup nuts, chopped
2 teaspoons baking soda
⅔ cup water

Preheat oven to 350°. Mix ingredients in order given; beat
well. Grease and flour 3 (1-pound) coffee cans. Pour batter into
cans. Bake at 350° for 1 hour. Allow bread to cool 5 minutes in
cans before turning out. These freeze well.

Yield: 3 loaves
Sherry McAdams

Katie's Rolls

½ cup shortening
⅓ cup sugar
½ cup water, boiling
¼ cup water, just warm
1 package yeast
1 egg

3 cups plain flour, sifted
twice
½ teaspoon salt
2 tablespoons butter,
melted

Cream shortening and sugar. Add boiling water. Dissolve yeast in warm water and add to mixture. Add the egg. Add flour and salt gradually. When mixed, cover and refrigerate for two hours or until the next day. Make sure to keep it covered. When ready to bake, roll out dough and cut with a biscuit cutter. Fold each one over and brush tops with melted butter. Cover the rolls with a light cloth and let rise for 30 to 45 minutes in a warm spot or on top of oven. Cook about 15 minutes at 400°.
Yield: About 2 dozen

Lynn Stiles Foster

My Grandmother's Rolls
The best survive generations

1 cup Irish potatoes,
boiled and mashed
⅔ cup sugar
2 eggs, beaten
1 teaspoon salt
1 package yeast, dissolved
in ½ cup water used in
cooking potatoes

1 cup scalded milk
⅔ cup shortening
6 to 8 cups sifted flour
¼ cup butter, melted

Combine potatoes, sugar, salt and shortening. Add milk and eggs. When cool, add yeast mixture. Mix in flour to make a stiff dough. Put in a covered bowl and place in refrigerator. Use as needed to make rolls. Remove desired amount of dough and roll out and cut with a biscuit cutter. Place in baking pan and brush tops with melted butter. Fold over tops. Cover and let rise 1 hour. Bake at 400° about 15 minutes or until light brown.
Yield: About 4 dozen

Paula Fry Elmore

Onion Rolls

Great for sandwiches and well worth the effort.

6 cups flour
2 packages active dry yeast
2¼ cups milk
2 tablespoons sugar
4 tablespoon instant minced onions, divided
2 tablespoons cooking oil

1 tablespoon prepared mustard
1½ teaspoons salt
¼ teaspoon pepper
1 egg
¼ cup plus 2 tablespoons water
1 egg, beaten

In a large mixer bowl or food processor, combine 2½ cups flour and the yeast. In a saucepan, heat together the milk, sugar, 2 tablespoons dried onions, oil, mustard, salt and pepper just until warm, stirring occasionally. Add to dry mixture in the bowl. Add 1 egg; beat, with a mixer, on low speed for ½ minute, then on high for 3 minutes. Stir in, by hand, enough remaining flour to make a moderately stiff dough. On a lightly floured board, knead dough until smooth (about 5 minutes). Grease a large bowl and place dough in it, turning once to grease surface. Cover and let rise until doubled, about 1 to 1½ hours. Punch down and divide dough in half. Divide each half into 8 portions. Cover and let rise for 10 minutes. Shape each portion into rolls and flatten to 3½ inch circles. Place rolls on greased baking sheet. Cover and let rise 30 to 45 minutes. Preheat oven to 375°. Combine ¼ cup water and 2 tablespoons instant onion and let stand about 5 minutes. Combine beaten egg and 2 tablespoons water and brush onto rolls. Sprinkle with onion and water mixture. Bake at 375° for 20 to 25 minutes.
Yield: 16 large rolls   *Mikell Von Kolnitz Stribbling*

Whole Wheat Potato Rolls
Nourishing and flavorful

2 packages active dry
yeast
1½ cups water (water
used for cooking
potatoes)
⅔ cup sugar
1½ teaspoons salt

⅔ cup shortening
2 eggs
1 cup warm, smooth
mashed potatoes
4 cups white flour
3 cups whole wheat flour

Dissolve yeast in potato water which has been cooled to warm; add a dash of sugar. Stir in ⅔ cup sugar, salt, shortening, eggs and warm potatoes. Combine flours and mix with yeast mixture until dough is easy to handle. Turn onto lightly floured board and knead until smooth and elastic. Lightly grease a bowl and pour mixture into it turning to grease top. Cover with a damp cloth and refrigerate. About 2 hours before baking, shape into rolls and place on a greased baking sheet. Brush with melted butter and let rise until doubled. Bake 12 to 15 minutes in pre-heated 400° oven. *Note:* To shape into rolls, roll out dough on floured board to ¼ inch thick and cut with large cutter, fold and brush with melted butter.
Yield: 4 dozen
Pamela Croy Newton

Sally Lunn

1 cup milk
½ cup butter
¼ cup water
3½ cups unbleached white
flour
2 teaspoons salt (optional)
3 eggs, beaten

½ cup honey
2 packages dry yeast
1 teaspoon pure vanilla
extract
½ teaspoon pure almond
extract

Heat the milk in a saucepan and add the butter and water. Cool to lukewarm. Pour the mixture into a bowl and add the flour, salt, beaten eggs, honey, dry yeast and the flavorings. Beat with a mixer for three minutes or mix with floured hands or a wooden spoon until all ingredients are well blended. Cover and place in a warm place to rise for about one hour. Mix down and put in a greased 9 or 10-inch tube pan. Bake at 350° for about 50 minutes.
Yield: 1 round loaf
Sharon Wilson Carson

Grandmother's Loaf Bread

2 cups milk, scalded
4 tablespoons sugar
5 tablespoons solid
  shortening (heaping)
4 teaspoons salt
2 packages dry yeast (not
  rapid mix)

2 cups lukewarm water
10 to 12 cups flour
  (reserve some to flour
  board and to knead on)
2 tablespoons butter,
  melted

Scald milk; remove from stove and add sugar, shortening and salt. Let cool completely. Dissolve yeast with a pinch of sugar in the 2 cups of lukewarm water. Combine yeast mixture with cooled milk mixture and mix lightly. Add flour and mix until dough is sticky and elastic. Knead. Place dough in a large greased bowl; cover. Let rise to top of bowl 3 times and work down in bowl each time. This step may take a good part of the day. Turn dough out on a floured board and knead. Divide dough into 3 equal parts. Grease 3 (9 x 5 x 2¾-inch) loaf pans; place dough in each. Brush tops of loaves with the melted butter. Let bread rise about one hour, but not doubled. Preheat oven to 425°. Bake bread at 425° until it rises, then reduce heat to 375° for 50 minutes. Remove from pans and brush with butter.

Yield: 3 loaves
Pamela Croy Newton

Whole Wheat Walnut Bread
"Moist"

2 cups whole wheat flour
1 cup all-purpose flour
1 tablespoon baking
  powder
1 teaspoon salt

½ teaspoon baking soda
1½ cups milk
1 cup packed brown sugar
1 tablespoon vanilla
1 cup walnuts, chopped

Preheat oven to 300°. Mix together the flours, baking powder, salt, and baking soda. In a separate bowl, mix the milk, brown sugar and vanilla, stirring until the sugar dissolves. Pour over dry ingredients. Mix well. Add one cup chopped walnuts. Bake at 300° for 1 hour to 1 hour 10 minutes in a greased 8 x 4-inch loaf pan.

Yield: 1 loaf
Becky Boyd Walker

Onion Lover's Twist

1 package dry yeast	½ cup hot water
¼ cup warm water	½ cup milk
4 cups flour	¼ cup margarine, softened
¼ cup sugar	1 egg
1½ teaspoons salt	

Filling:

¼ cup margarine, softened	1 tablespoon poppy seeds
¼ cup dried minced onions	1 teaspoon garlic salt
1 tablespoon Parmesan cheese	1 teaspoon paprika

Blend filling ingredients and set aside. In a large bowl, dissolve yeast in warm water. Add 2 cups flour, sugar, salt, hot water, milk, margarine and egg. Blend with an electric mixer at low speed; beat 2 minutes at medium speed. By hand, stir in remaining flour to form a soft dough. Cover; let rise 1 hour. Stir down. Toss on a floured surface until no longer sticky. Roll dough into an 18 x 12-inch rectangle. Spread filling on top. Cut lengthwise into 3 (18 x 4-inch) strips. Fold over each strip and seal edges and ends. Place strips on greased cookie sheet and braid together. Cover and let rise 1 hour. Preheat oven to 350°. Bake 30 to 35 minutes. Two small loves may be made by cutting the strips in half and continue as directed.

Yield: 1 large or 2 small loaves   *Susan Bolen Sappington*

Cheese Grits

1 cup grits, cooked	½ garlic clove, minced
½ cup butter or margarine	Tabasco to taste
1½ tablespoons Worcestershire sauce	2 egg whites, stiffly beaten
¾ pound Cheddar cheese, grated	

Preheat oven to 400°. To hot grits, add butter, Worcestershire, cheese, garlic and Tabasco. When cool add stiffly beaten egg whites. Bake at 400° for 20 minutes.

Yield: 6 servings   *Cynthia Meredith Davenport*

Cheese Soufflé

3 tablespoons butter
¼ cup flour
1⅞ cup milk
1 teaspoon salt
Dash of cayenne pepper
1 teaspoon prepared
  mustard

2 drops Worcestershire
  sauce
1 cup grated Cheddar
  cheese
6 eggs, separated

Make a cream sauce by melting the butter and blending in flour. Add milk, salt, cayenne, mustard and Worcestershire sauce. Add cheese. Beat egg yolks until thick, add to cheese mixture, stirring constantly. Beat egg whites until stiff. Fold into cheese mixture carefully. Fill a well-buttered soufflé baking dish three-quarters full. Bake at 300°, in a pan of hot water, for 2 hours until a knife comes out clean.
Yield: 8 servings

Sybil Kendall Little

Strata Bake

16 slices white sandwich
  bread, trimmed and cut
  in 1½ inch cubes
½ pound cheese,
  shredded
2 to 3 cups ham, cubed or
  1 pound cooked bacon

6 extra large eggs
1 teaspoon salt
2 cups milk
½ cup butter, melted

Put one half of the bread cubes on bottom of greased 7 x 11-inch baking dish. Cover with one half of the cheese then one half of the meat. Repeat layers. Combine milk, salt, and eggs. Beat thoroughly. Pour egg mixture over meat. Drizzle melted butter over top. Cover and refrigerate 12 to 24 hours. Bake at 325° for 45 to 50 minutes covered, then 10 to 15 minutes uncovered.
Yield: 8 to 10 servings

Susan Thomas Burney

Mushroom Cheese Casserole

2 tablespoons butter or
margarine, softened
5 slices white bread,
crusts trimmed
2 cups sharp Cheddar
cheese, grated

5 eggs, beaten
2 cups milk
1 (4-ounce) can sliced
mushrooms, drained
1 teaspoon salt

Spread butter on one side of bread slices. Place bread slices, buttered side down, in a greased 10 x 6 x 2-inch baking dish. Sprinkle cheese over bread. Combine other ingredients; pour over bread. Cover and chill. Bake, uncovered, 45 to 50 minutes or until set.

Yield: 6 servings   *Donna Cates Robinson*

Eggs Florentine With Mornay Sauce

2 (10-ounce) packages
frozen chopped spinach
4 poached eggs

2 cups Mornay Sauce
Parmesan cheese

Mornay Sauce:
4 tablespoons butter
½ onion, minced
4 tablespoons flour
2 cups hot milk

3 egg yolks
¼ cup cream
½ cup Parmesan cheese
2 tablespoons butter

Cook and drain spinach. Season with salt and pepper. Spread in a shallow baking dish. Prepare Mornay Sauce. Place poached eggs on top of spinach. Cover with Mornay Sauce. Sprinkle with Parmesan cheese. Brown well under the broiler. Serve very hot.

Mornay Sauce: Melt 4 tablespoons butter in a saucepan. Sauté onion until transparent, not browned. Stir in flour until blended. Gradually add hot milk. Cook, stirring constantly until sauce is smooth and thick. Simmer for ten minutes, stirring occasionally, and strain through a fine sieve. Keep hot. Add egg yolks, beaten with cream and Parmesan cheese. Cook, stirring until sauce almost boils, but does not. Add 2 tablespoons butter and stir well.

Yield: 4 servings   *Ginger Colquitt Autry*

Country Morning
Make tonight, enjoy tomorrow!

Cheese Sauce:

2 tablespoons butter
2½ tablespoons
  all-purpose flour
2 cups milk

½ teaspoon salt
⅛ teaspoon pepper
1 cup shredded processed
  American cheese

1 cup ham, cubed
¼ cup green onion,
  chopped
3 tablespoons butter,
  melted
1 dozen eggs, beaten

1 (4-ounce) can sliced
  mushrooms, drained
¼ cup butter, melted
2¼ cups soft bread
  crumbs
⅛ teaspoon paprika

Cheese Sauce: Melt butter in a heavy sauce pan over low heat. Blend in flour and cook one minute. Gradually add milk. Cook over medium heat until thickened, stirring constantly. Add salt, pepper and cheese, stirring until cheese melts and mixture is smooth.

Sauté ham and green onion in 3 tablespoons butter in a large skillet until onion is tender. Add eggs and cook over medium high heat, stirring to form large soft curds. When eggs are set, stir in mushrooms and cheese sauce. Spoon eggs into a greased 13 x 9 x 2-inch baking pan. Combine ¼ cup melted butter and crumbs, mixing well. Spread evenly over egg mixture. Sprinkle with paprika. Cover and chill overnight. Uncover and bake at 350° for 30 minutes or until heated thoroughly.

Yield: 10 servings   *Laura Phillips Lewis*

Girl's Club Breakfast Pizza

*This "pizza" was served at the 10th
birthday party for the Cobb-Marietta Girl's club.*

1 pound pork sausage
1 (8-count) package
refrigerated crescent
rolls
1 cup frozen loose pack
hash brown potatoes,
thawed
1 cup sharp Cheddar
cheese, shredded (Swiss
or Monterey Jack may be
substituted)

5 eggs
¼ cup milk
½ teaspoon salt
⅛ teaspoon pepper
2 tablespoons grated
Parmesan cheese

Preheat oven to 375°. Cook sausage until browned, drain
well. Separate crescent rolls into 8 triangles. Place in ungreased 12-inch pizza pan with points toward the center. Press
to seal over the bottom and up sides to form a crust. Spoon
sausage over crust. Sprinkle with potatoes; top with cheese. In
a bowl beat together egg, milk, salt and pepper. Pour over
sausage. Sprinkle Parmesan cheese over the top. Bake at
375° for 25 to 30 minutes.
Yield: 6 to 8 servings   *Susan Smith Phillips*

Sausage Squares

4 eggs
½ teaspoon salt
½ teaspoon onion powder
Dash pepper
2 cups milk
½ teaspoon dry mustard

2 cups seasoned croutons
1½ cups mozzarella
cheese, grated
1 pound sausage, cooked
and drained

Preheat oven to 350°. Combine all ingredients except
croutons, cheese and meat. Put croutons on the bottom of an
oven proof square baking dish. Top with cheese. Pour the mixture of eggs and milk over the cheese. Top with sausage. Bake
at 350° for 55 minutes. Cover with foil for the last 15 minutes.
Cut into squares and serve warm.
Yield: 4 servings   *Judy Singletary Davis*

Apple Betty Quiche
A winner in the Apple Betty Cook-Off

½ pound bulk sausage
½ cup onion, chopped
¼ teaspoon thyme
2 Red Delicious apples, pared and cut into ½ inch cubes
1 tablespoon lemon juice
1 tablespoon sugar
½ cup Cheddar cheese, grated and firmly packed
4 eggs, beaten
1½ cups milk
Pastry for 1 single crust deep dish pie

In a large skillet, brown sausage, onion and thyme until onion is tender, about 10 minutes. Remove from heat. Drain off excess fat. In a bowl, toss apples with lemon juice and sugar. Add prepared sausage mixture, cheese, eggs and milk; mix well. Pour into pie shell. Bake at 350° for 40 to 45 minutes until set. Let stand 10 minutes. Can also be frozen before cooking.
Yield: 6 servings   *Beth Waterhouse Sams*

Elegant Vegetable Quiche

1 (16-ounce) package frozen mixed vegetables
1 cup onion, coarsely chopped
½ cup margarine
½ cup fresh parsley, chopped or 2 tablespoons parsley flakes
½ teaspoon salt
½ teaspoon pepper
¼ teaspoon garlic powder
¼ teaspoon sweet basil
¼ teaspoon oregano
2 eggs, well beaten
2 cups (8-ounces) mozzarella cheese, grated
1 (8-count) can refrigerator crescent rolls
2 teaspoons Dijon mustard

Preheat oven to 375°. In a large skillet cook vegetables and onion in margarine until tender. Stir in parsley and other seasonings. Set aside. In a large bowl blend eggs and cheese. Stir vegetables into cheese and egg mixture. Separate rolls into 8 triangles. Place dough into quiche pan and press to make a crust. Spread crust with mustard. Pour vegetable and cheese mixture into prepared pan. Bake at 375° for 18 to 20 minutes or until a knife comes out clean.
Yield: 6 servings   *Shari Bolen*

Sausage Quiche
"Do ahead and relax before your quests arrive"

1½ pounds mild sausage
1 cup onions, chopped
½ teaspoon marjoram
1 teaspoon Italian herbs, divided
2 cups Cheddar cheese, grated
1 (6-ounce) box Pepperidge Farm Garlic-Onion Croutons
2½ cups milk
5 large eggs
1 teaspoon mustard powder
1 can cream of celery soup
12 ounces mushrooms, sliced
Parmesan cheese
Butter
Bread crumbs

Sauté the sausage and onions. Season with marjoram, ½ teaspoon Italian herbs, and add cheese. Mix well. Spray a 14 x 8-inch baking dish with cooking spray. Layer the croutons in the dish and cover with the sausage mixture. In a separate bowl, mix the milk, eggs and mustard powder. Pour over the sausage mixture. When this has all come to room temperature, cover and refrigerate for 10 to 24 hours. When ready to serve, mix soup, mushrooms, and ½ teaspoon Italian herbs. Spread over casserole. Sprinkle heavily with Parmesan cheese and bread crumbs. Dot with butter. Bake at 325° for 1½ hours.
Yield: 12 servings
Gladys Wilbur Kennedy

Asparagus Quiche

2 (16-ounce) packages frozen asparagus, cooked
⅝ cup whipping cream
1¼ cups half and half
Salt and pepper to taste
8 eggs, beaten
6 tablespoons Parmesan cheese
1 (9-inch) pie shell, browned

Cut asparagus into bite size pieces leaving 6 to 8 stalks whole. Arrange the cut-up asparagus on the bottom of the browned pie shell. Lay the whole stalks on the top like spokes with the ends toward the center. Mix all other ingredients together and pour over the asparagus. Bake at 400° for 40 minutes.
Yield: 6 to 8 servings
Donya Smith Rickman

Crab Quiche

1 (6-ounce) can crab meat, drained
1 tablespoon green pepper, chopped finely
3 tablespoons onion, chopped finely
½ cup mayonnaise
2 tablespoons flour
2 eggs, well beaten
½ cup milk
6 ounces Swiss cheese, grated
2 ounces sliced mushrooms, drained
¼ teaspoon salt
¼ teaspoon pepper
Dash of paprika
1 9-inch deep dish pie shell

Mix first eleven ingredients. Pour into an unbaked deep dish pie shell, and sprinkle with paprika. Bake at 350° for 45 to 60 minutes.
Yield: 6 servings   *Lucy Rush McBee*

Baked Eggs For Brunch

3 tablespoons butter
1 small onion, chopped finely
1 (6-ounce) jar sliced mushrooms
12 hard boiled eggs
1 can cream of mushroom soup
1 cup sour cream
¼ cup dry sherry or white wine
1 teaspoon Worcestershrie sauce
Salt and pepper to taste
Tabasco sauce to taste
1 cup sharp Cheddar cheese, grated
Parsley
Paprika
Bread crumbs

Preheat oven to 350°. Melt butter in casserole dish with onions and mushrooms. Slice eggs over top. Combine soup, sour cream, sherry and seasonings. Pour over eggs. Spread cheese over top. Sprinkle casserole with parsley, paprika, and bread crumbs. Bake for 15 to 20 minutes or until bubbly.
Yield: 10 to 12 servings   *Pamela Croy Newton*

Easy Pasta Primavera

1 (12-ounce) package
fettucini noodles
1 (16-ounce) package
frozen vegetable medley
(carrots, zucchini, limas,
cauliflower, etc.)
2 tablespoons butter or
margarine

1 (4-ounce) package
instant ranch style
dressing
1½ cups milk
¾ cup mayonnaise
Parmesan cheese

Cook fettucini noodles according to package directions. Sauté
vegetables in butter. Meanwhile mix dressing, milk and mayonnaise together. Pour dressing over vegetables and heat
gently. Drain noodles, arrange in a bowl, and pour vegetables
and sauce over noodles, tossing gently. Generously sprinkle
with Parmesan.

Yield: 4 to 6 servings

Jeanne Powell Orman

Karter's Linguine

¼ cup olive oil
½ teaspoon garlic salt
½ teaspoon oregano
¼ cup white wine
2 (6½-ounce) cans minced
clams (juice too)

Salt and pepper to taste
Dash of cayenne pepper
8 ounces linguine

Combine first seven ingredients in a large skillet, bring to a boil
cooking over medium heat. While sauce is cooking, cook the
noodles according to package directions. When noodles are
done, drain and add to the sauce. Toss well and serve in
shallow bowls. This dish is excellent with a salad and fresh
bread.

Yield: 4 servings

Marsha Brown Thomas

Cheesy Manicotti
Vegetarian entreé

1 (8-ounce) package
manicotti shells
1 (32-ounce) jar extra thick
spaghetti sauce, divided
2 cups shredded
mozzarella cheese,
divided
1 (16-ounce) carton ricotta
cheese
12 (2-inch) saltine crackers,
crushed

2 eggs, beaten
¼ cup chopped chives
½ teaspoon dried whole
basil
½ teaspoon dried whole
marjoram
¼ teaspoon garlic salt

Cook shells, omitting salt; drain. Pour half of spaghetti sauce into a lightly greased 13 x 9 x 2-inch baking dish. Combine 1½ cups mozzarella and next 7 ingredients. Mix well. Stuff shells and arrange in sauce. Pour remaining sauce over manicotti, and bake at 350° for 25 minutes. Sprinkle with remaining ½ cup mozzarella. Bake an additional 5 minutes.
Yield: 8 servings   *Donna Cates Robinson*

Macaroni And Cheese
"Not just another macaroni and cheese recipe!"

1 (8-ounce) box small
macaroni, cooked and
drained
1 pound sharp cheese,
grated
1 cup mayonnaise
1 (10-ounce) can cream of
mushroom soup

2 (2.5-ounce) cans sliced
mushrooms, drained
1 (2-ounce) jar chopped
pimento, drained
1 teaspoon sugar
Pinch of curry
Ritz crackers (optional)

Combine first 8 ingredients, mixing well. Top with crackers if desired. Bake at 350° 20 to 30 minutes.
Yield: Serves 10   *Mary Mayes Suhr*

Pasta With Steamed Veggies

2 medium zucchini, sliced
2 medium yellow squash, sliced
1 cup fresh broccoli flowerettes
¾ cup onion, sliced
1 cup mushrooms, sliced
1 (12-ounce) package spaghetti, or other pasta
½ cup butter or margarine, melted
½ cup whipping cream
¾ cup grated Parmesan cheese
Fresh ground pepper, to taste
Salt, to taste

Place first 4 ingredients in a steamer over boiling water. Cover and stem 5 to 7 minutes or until almost tender. Add mushrooms; cover and steam 1 minute. Set aside. Cook pasta according to package directions and drain. Add butter, whipping cream, cheese, salt and pepper. Toss well. Add vegetables to pasta mix and toss gently. Serve warm.
Yield: 8 servings   *Allyson Ray Murphy*

Shrimp Pasta

1 pound medium-sized fresh shrimp
3 ounces spinach noodles
1 pound Cheddar cheese
1 (10-ounce) can cream of mushroom soup
1 (3-ounce) can sliced mushrooms
½ pint sour cream
1 cup mayonnaise
⅓ cup chopped chives

Cook shrimp in boiling salted water, just until pink. Cool, peel and devein, set aside. Cook noodles according to package directions. Drain. Mix soup, sour cream, mayonniase and chives. Slice cheese very thin and line the bottom and sides of a 2 quart casserole (leave enough cheese for top). To assemble layer noodles, mushrooms and soup mix. Add shrimp and top with cheese. Bake at 350° until cheese is bubbly.
Yield: 6 servings   *Nancy Dendy Ryle*

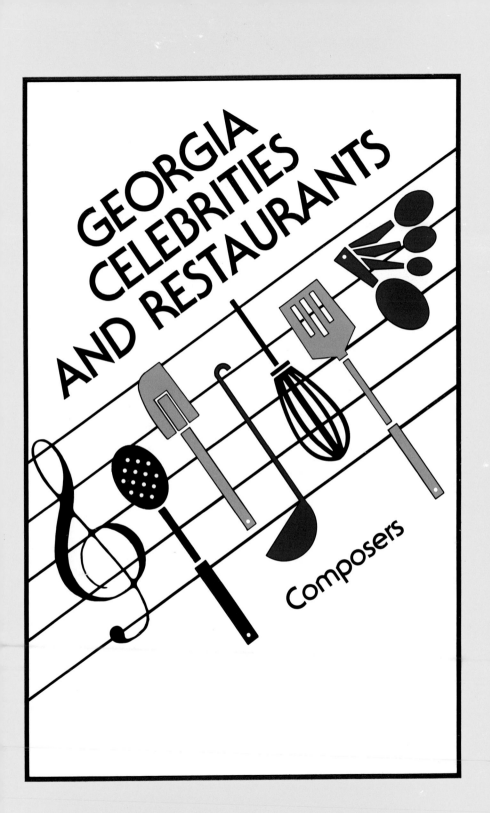

GEORGIA
CELEBRITIES
AND RESTAURANTS

Composers

Celebrities And Restaurants

Shrimp Scampi

2 cups butter
1 cup margarine
6 cloves of garlic, minced
3 shallots, chopped
6 tablespoons white wine
6 tablespoons lemon juice

2 tablespoons Tabasco
1 tablespoon dry mustard
½ cup chopped chives
2½ pounds jumbo shrimp,
   peeled, deveined and
   butterflied

Melt butter and margarine together in a saucepan. Add remaining ingredients except shrimp. Simmer over low heat for 4 to 5 minutes. Makes about 5 cups of sauce. Place shrimp in a broiler pan. Pour sauce over shrimp and broil for 6 to 8 minutes.
Yield: 6 servings

Glenn Burns
Meteorlogist, WSB-TV, Atlanta

Hershey Bar Cake

2 sticks margarine
2 cups sugar
2½ cups all-purpose flour
2 teaspoons vanilla
½ teaspoon soda (mix
   with flour)

1 cup buttermilk
4 eggs
1 (1-pound) can chocolate
   syrup
6 small plain Hershey bars

Melt chocolate bars in syrup over low heat. Cool. Cream sugar and margarine. Add eggs one at a time beating well after each one. Add cooled chocolate, then flour and milk alternately. Add vanilla. Bake 1½ hours at 300° in a lightly greased and floured Bundt pan.

The Honorable Vicki Chastain
Mayor of the City of Marietta, Georgia

Peanut Brittle

3 cups granulated sugar
1½ cups water
1 cup white corn syrup
3 cups raw peanuts

2 tablespoons soda
½ stick butter
1 teaspoon vanilla

Boil sugar, water and syrup until spins thread; add peanuts. After adding peanuts, stir continually until syrup turns golden brown. Remove from heat; add remaining ingredients stir until butter melts. Pour quickly on 2 cookie sheets with sides. As mixture begins to harden around edges, pull until thin.

First Lady Rosalyn Carter
Plains, Georgia

"Yellow Jacket" Oatmeal Cake

A must at the Bobby Cremins House.

½ cup butter
1 cup brown sugar
1 cup sugar
2 eggs, beaten
1 cup oatmeal
1½ cups boiling water
1½ cups flour

1 teaspoon baking soda
1 teaspoon cinnamon
1 teaspoon nutmeg
1 teaspoon salt
½ cup coconut (optional)
½ cup pecans, chopped

Pour water over oatmeal, cover and let cool. Cream butter and sugars. Add eggs, the dry ingredients and oatmeal. Stir in coconut and nuts. Bake in a 9x13-inch pan at 375° for 40 to 45 minutes. Does not need frosting. I sprinkle it with powdered sugar. Great for picnics or pot lucks.

Bobby Cremins
Georgia Tech Basketball Coach

Mac Davis' Favorite Spaghetti Sauce

2 tablespoons salad oil
1 minced clove of garlic
1 large onion, sliced
1 can beef consommée
1 can tomato soup
1 (6-ounce) can tomato paste
1 (8-ounce) can tomato sauce

1¼ pounds ground beef
¼ teaspoon seasoned salt
½ teaspoon accent
¾ teaspoon salt
1 (4-ounce) can mushrooms
1 teaspoon dried basil

Heat oil in a large skillet, sauté garlic and onion. Stir in next 4 ingredients. Simmer uncovered 1 hour, stirring occasionally. In another skillet sauté, just until pink disappears, the ground beef. Add rest of seasonings, except mushrooms and basil. Simmer 15 minutes then add mushrooms and basil. Simmer 15 more minutes.

Mrs. Edith Kimbrough
(Mac's Mom)
Atlanta, Georgia

An Atlantan, whose hit songs include "Baby Don't get Hooked on Me" and "I Believe in Music" Mac Davis was voted Country Music Association Entertainer of the Year.

Chili-O-Wyche

1 pound shredded/chopped beef (not ground)
1 large can tomatoes
2 large onions, chopped
2 bell peppers, chopped
1 large can of mushrooms, sliced

1 large can of tomato sauce
¼ cup chili powder
Salt and pepper to taste
1 cup sharp cheese, diced

Brown the shredded beef, add onions, bell peppers, chili powder, salt and pepper. Sauté for approximately 15 minutes. Add remaining ingredients and simmer for 1 hour.

Wyche Fowler, Jr.
United States Senator

Lillian's Sweet Georgia Brownies

Brownie:

½ cup butter or margarine
1 (1-ounce) square
  unsweetened chocolate
1 cup sugar
1 cup flour

½ to 1 cup nuts, chopped
1 teaspoon baking powder
1 teaspoon vanilla extract
2 eggs

Filling:

1 (8-ounce) package cream
  cheese, softened
  (reserve 2 ounces for
  frosting)
½ cup sugar
2 tablespoons flour
¼ cup butter or margarine,
  softened

1 egg
½ teaspoon vanilla extract
¼ cup nuts, chopped
1 (6-ounce) package
  semi-sweet chocolate
  chips (optional)

Frosting:

3 cups miniature
  marshmallows
¼ cup butter or margarine
1 (1-ounce) square
  unsweetened chocolate
Remaining 2 ounces of
  cream cheese

¼ cup milk
1 pound confectioners'
  sugar
1 teaspoon vanilla extract

Preheat oven to 350°. Brownie: Grease and flour a 13 x 9-inch pan. In large saucepan, over low heat, melt butter and chocolate. Add remaining brownie ingredients and mix well. Spread into prepared pan.

Filling: In small bowl, combine 6 ounces cream cheese and next 5 filling ingredients. Blend until smooth and fluffy. Stir in nuts. Spread over chocolate mixture. (* If desired, sprinkle with chocolate pieces.) Bake at 350° for 25 to 35 minutes, until a toothpick inserted in center comes out clean.

Frosting: Sprinkle marshmallows over brownie and bake 2 minutes longer. In a large saucepan, over low heat, melt butter, chocolate, remaining cream cheese, and milk. Stir in confectioners' sugar and vanilla extract until smooth. Immediately pour over marshmallows and swirl together. Cool and cut into bars. Store in refrigerator.

Yield: 3 dozen   *7th District United States Representative*
Buddy Darden

Harris Salad Supreme
Can be used as a dessert

1 (3-ounce) package
raspberry jello
2 cups boiling water,
divided
1 (21-ounce) can cherry
pie filling
1 (3-ounce) package lemon
jello
½ cup whipping cream

1 (2-ounce) package cream
cheese, softened
½ cup mayonnaise
1 (8¾-ounce) can crushed
pineapple, undrained
1 cup miniature
marshmallows
2 tablespoons chopped
nuts

Dissolve raspberry jello in one cup boiling water; stir in pie filling. Turn into a 9 x 9 x 2-inch baking dish; chill until partially set. Dissolve lemon jello in one cup boiling water. Beat together the softened cream cheese and mayonnaise. Gradually add lemon jello, then stir in undrained pineapple. Whip whipping cream; fold into lemon mixture with minature marshmallows. Spread on top of cherry layer; sprinkle with chopped nuts. Chill until set.
Yield: 12 servings   *Elizabeth Harris*
First Lady of Georgia

Stir Fry Shrimp With Fried Rice

3 tablespoons peanut oil
(do not substitute)
1 egg
4 green onions with tops,
sliced
1 clove garlic, minced

¾ pound shrimp, peeled
and deveined
½ cup sliced water
chestnuts
4 cups cooked rice, chilled
¼ cup soy sauce

Add 1 tablespoon of oil to skillet. Place on medium heat. When oil is hot, add egg and scramble. Remove and set aside. Increase heat - add remaining oil, onion and garlic. Stir-fry about 1 minute. Stir in shrimp and water chestnuts, cook until shrimp turns pink, about 5 minutes. Stir in cold rice and soy sauce until well mixed . . . . stir till heated through.
Yield:: 4 to 6 servings   *Barbara M. Dooley*

A much requested entrée from Vince Dooley, Athletic Director and Head Football Coach, University of Georgia.

Elberta-Deep-Dish-Georgia-Peach-Pie

6 cups peaches, peeled
and sliced
1 cup sugar
3 tablespoons cornstarch

1 tablespoon lemon juice
(optional)
1 pastry for one crust pie

Preheat oven to 400°. Mix all ingredients (except pastry) together lightly. Place mixture into a 9 x 9 x 2-inch square pan. Roll out pastry in a square to fit pan. Make small slits to let steam escape during baking. Lay crust over filling. Bake 60 minutes or until crust is browned.
Yield: 8 servings

Brenda Lee

Brenda's in-laws, Helen and Earl Shacklett, have a family homestead on Elberta Street hence the name. Since Brenda is from Georgia, this recipe is a sentimental and delicious favorite at her home.

Chilies Rellenos

3 (4-ounce) cans whole
Ortega chilies
1 pound Cheddar cheese,
grated
1 pound Monteray Jack
cheese, grated
4 eggs

3 tablespoons flour
2 (8-ounce) cans tomato
sauce
1 (13-ounce) can
evaporated milk
Small can diced black
olives, drained (optional)

Wash chilies and remove seeds. Drain well. In a 9 x 13-inch baking dish place ½ of the chilies flat and top with the Cheddar cheese. Then the other half of the chilies topped with the Monteray Jack cheese. Separate eggs. Beat yolks, add milk and flour and blend well. Beat whites separately and fold into yolks. Pour over chilies and cheese. Bake at 325° for 1 hour. Pour tomato sauce over hot casserole. (May mix the black olives with the tomato sauce.) Return to oven and bake ½ hour more. Can be prepared and frozen (uncooked).

Larry Nelson
1987 P.G.A. Champion
Marietta, Georgia

Tim McCabe's Infamous Baked Beans

1 (18-ounce) can of B&M
baked beans (It must be
B&M since I do
commercials for them
and this is part of the
deal)
1 teaspoon A-1 Sauce
¼ cup Kraft Barbeque
Sauce
1 teaspoon Lea & Perrin
Worcestershire Sauce

1 tablespoon ketchup
¼ cup maple (pancake)
syrup
Dash garlic powder
Dash cinnamon
4 slices bacon, cut in two
inch strips

Place the beans in a casserole dish. Add the remaining ingredients, except the bacon and stir throughly. Sample freely (this is the privilege of the cook). When you are throughly satisfied that these beans are fabulous, add the bacon, covering the top of the beans. Bake covered for 40 minutes at 400° (stir occasionally). Uncover and bake for 10 more minutes. Be sure and have the table set and ready because these beans smell so good, you'll drive your family crazy if they have to wait any longer than is absolutely necessary. (Microwave: Use high power, cook for 15 minutes with lid vented; stir. Cook of 10 more minutes with lid vented and let set for 5 minutes.)
Serves 4   *Tim McCabe*
                                                       Tim McCabe Productions

Avocado - Grapefruit Salad

1 (8-ounce) can grapefruit
sections or 1 large
grapefruit, sectioned
2 (3-ounce) packages
pineapple flavored
gelatin

1 cup boiling water
1 cup grapefruit juice
1 cup ginger ale
2 avocados, halved,
peeled and sliced
crosswise

Drain grapefruit and dice sections. Dissolve gelatin in water. Add fruit juice and cool. Add ginger ale, gently. Chill until partially set. Fold in grapefruit and avocados. Pour in mold or individual molds and chill until set.
Yield: 8 to 10 servings   *Zell Miller*
                        Lieutenant Governor of the State of Georgia

Georgia Pecan Pie
A favorite recipe of Senator Sam Nunn

1¼ cups sugar
½ cup light corn syrup
¼ cup butter or margarine
3 eggs, slightly beaten

1 cup pecans, coarsely
   chopped
1 teaspoon vanilla
Pastry for 9-inch pie

Preheat oven to 350°. Combine sugar, syrup and butter in a 2 quart saucepan. Bring to boil on high, stirring constantly until butter is melted. Remove from stove and gradually add hot syrup to eggs; stir all the while. Add pecans to mixture and cool to lukewarm. Add vanilla. Pour into pie shell and bake for 40 to 45 minutes.
Yield: 6 to 8 servings   *Senator Sam Nunn*
United States Senate
Chairman, Committee on Armed Services

Peach Pound Cake

1 cup butter or margarine,
   softened
3 cups sugar
6 eggs
3 cups flour
¼ teaspoon baking soda

¼ teaspoon salt
½ cup sour cream
2 cups fresh peaches,
   peeled and chopped
1 teaspoon vanilla extract
1 teaspoon almond extract

Preheat oven to 350°. Grease and flour a 10-inch tube pan and set aside. Cream together butter and sugar until light and fluffy. Add eggs, one at a time, beating well after each addition. Combine flour, soda and salt in separate bowl. Mix together sour cream and peaches, add dry ingredients to creamed mixture alternately with sour cream and peaches, beginning and ending with dry ingredients. Beat well after each addition. Stir in vanilla and almond extract. Pour batter into prepared pan and bake for 75 to 80 minutes or until cake tests done.
Yield: 10 to 12 servings   *Celestine Sibley*
Sweet Apple

*Celestine Sibley is a well-known columnist and journalist. Her books **Peachtree Street, U.S.A.; Christmas in Georgia; and Dear Store,** identify her as a loyal Atlantan and spokesman for Georgia.*

"When You're Hot You're Hot" Meatloaf
*"No special reason that the recipe is special.
It's just a favorite!"*

1 egg	Hand full bell peppers
Hand full rice	1 pound ground beef
Hand full onion	Large can tomato sauce
Hand full cornflakes	

Mix all together, shape into a loaf and bake at 350° until done.

Jerry Reed

A talented song writer and actor, Jerry Reed has written over 400 songs, starred in numerous films and won two Grammys. His hits include "A Thing Called Love" and "When You're Hot You're Hot"

Mexican Casserole

1 pound ground beef	1 (16-ounce) can chili beans, drained
1 onion, chopped	½ teaspoon dried marjoram
1 teaspoon salt	1 bay leaf
½ teaspoon black pepper	½ pound sharp Cheddar cheese, shredded
1 bell pepper, diced	Corn chips
1 (16-ounce) can tomatoes with juice	
1 (1¼-ounce) package taco seasoning mix	
1 (8-ounce) can tomato sauce	

In a 10-inch skillet, sauté beef and onion. Add salt, pepper, bell pepper, seasoning mix, tomatoes, tomato sauce, beans, marjoram and bay leaf. Let simmer for 30 minutes. Remove bay leaf and pour into a 2-quart casserole. Preheat oven to 350°. Sprinkle cheese over top. Top with corn chips. Bake for 20 minutes.

Ray Stevens

Ray Stevens, singer and songwriter, was inducted into the Georgia Music Hall of Fame in 1981. His hits include "Ahab the Arab" and "Everything is Beautiful".

Baked Brie And Apple Sandwich

1 apple, cored
6 to 8 ounces Brie
French bread or baguettes
Homemade or prepared
 mayonnaise

Almonds and grapes
(optional)

Preheat oven to 550°. Slice bread lengthwise and lightly spread mayonnaise on cut surfaces. Slice cored apple thinly and place slices on each side of bread. Slice Brie and place over apples. Bake on sheet pan 3 to 5 minutes until cheese melts and bread becomes crusty. Do not broil. Garnish with almonds and grapes if desired.

Yvette Greune
Once Upon A Stove
Marietta, Georgia

Gnocchi - Italian Potato Dumpling

1 pound potatoes, freshly
 boiled
1½ cups flour
1 egg beaten

Salt
Freshly ground pepper
Freshly grated nutmeg

Drain the potatoes well and shake over the heat to dry throughly. Mash very finely (there must be no lumps) and add the flour, egg, salt, pepper and nutmeg to taste. Mix to a dough and turn onto a floured board. With floured hands, roll pieces of the dough into long sausages, about 1-inch in diameter. Cut into 1 inch lengths and, using your little finger, make a dent in the center of each one to make them curl slightly. Drop the gnocchi, a few at a time, into a large pan of gently boiling salted water. Cook until they rise to the surface, about 3 to 5 minutes. Lift out with a slotted spoon, drain, put into a buttered dish and keep hot until all are cooked. Reserve liquid for the Pesto Sauce. Dot with butter and sprinkle with cheese. Serve warm with Pesto Sauce.
Yield: 4 to 6 servings

Scalini's
Marietta, Georgia

Pesto Sauce

Fresh basil is essential for this famous Italian speciality.
A little parsley can be added to enchance the green color.

2 ounces fresh basil
leaves
¼ cup pine nuts or
walnuts
2 cloves garlic
Large pinch of salt
Freshly ground black
pepper

¼ cup olive oil
(approximately)
⅓ cup grated Parmesan or
Pecorino cheese
(Romano)
Reserved liquid from
Gnocchi

Chop the basil and nuts roughly and put in a mortar with the garlic, salt and pepper. Pound together until reduced to a thick paste. Add the oil, a tablespoon at a time, stirring constantly, until the sauce is the consistency of thick cream. Alternately, put the basil paste into a blender with 2 tablespoons of the oil and blend at low speed adding the remaining oil gradually until a sauce of thick cream consistency is formed. Stir in the cheese. Before mixing with Gnocchi thin the Pesto Sauce with a spoonful or two of the reserved liquid. Pour over the Gnocchi and serve at once.

Yield: 4 to 6 servings

Scalini's
Marietta, Georgia

Aunt Fanny's Baked Squash

3 pounds yellow summer
squash
½ cup chopped onions
½ cup cracker meal or
bread crumbs

½ teaspoon black pepper
2 eggs
1 stick butter
1 tablespoon sugar
1 teaspoon salt

Wash and cut up squash. Boil until tender, drain throughly then mash. Add all ingredients except ½ of butter to squash. Melt remaining butter. Pour over top and sprinkle with cracker meal or bread crumbs. Bake in 375° oven for approximately 1 hour or until brown on top.

George "Pongo" Poole
Aunt Fanny's Cabin
Smyrna, Georgia

Bone's Triple Layer Chocolate Cake

Chocolate Cake:

2¼ cups Swansdown Cake Flour
1¾ cups sugar
2 sticks butter, room temperature
¾ cup milk
4 ounces (4 squares) unsweetened baking chocolate, melted
1½ teaspoons baking soda
1 teaspoon salt
¾ cup milk
4 eggs
1¼ teaspoons baking powder
1 teaspoon vanilla
1½ cups toasted walnut halves

Preheat oven to 350°. Grease 3 9-inch layer cake pans. Sift flour into large bowl. Add sugar, butter, ¾ cup milk, chocolate, baking soda and salt, and beat with electric mixer two minutes at medium speed. Add remaining milk, egg, baking powder and vanilla and beat two minutes more. Pour into prepared pans and bake in middle of oven 30 minutes, or until cakes test down and have pulled away slightly from sides of pan. Allow to cool completely on rack(s). Place first layer on plate and frost. Sprinkle with half the chopped nuts, if desired. Repeat with second layer, using remaining chopped nuts. Top with third layer and frost top and sides of cake. Decorate top of cake with toasted walnut halves.

Chocolate Frosting:

1 cup plus 2 tablespoons Baker's cocoa
⅓ cup cooking oil
¾ cup (1½ sticks) butter
4 cups sifted powdered sugar
5 tablespoons strongly brewed coffee
2 eggs
1 tablespoon vanilla
Pinch of salt

Soften chocolate and butter in top of double boiler over hot, not boiling, water. Stir in remaining ingredients. Place top of double boiler in bowl of ice and beat frosting with electric mixer about 5 minutes, or until it reaches spreading consistency.

Bone's Steak and Seafood
Atlanta, Georgia

Chart House Mud Pie

½ package Nabisco
chocolate wafers
½ stick butter, melted

1 quart coffee ice cream,
softened
1½ cups fudge sauce

Crush wafers and add butter, mix well. Press into 9-inch pie plate. Cover with soft coffee ice cream. Put into freezer until ice cream is firm. Top with cold fudge sauce (it helps to place in freezer for a time to make spreading easier). Store in freezer approximately 10 hours. Slice Mud Pie into eight portions and serve on a chilled dessert plate with a chilled fork. Top with whipped cream and slivered almonds.

The Chart House
Savannah, Georgia

Baklava

1 pound Fillo (strudel
leaves)
4 cups English walnuts
1½ cups sweet butter,
melted

½ cup sugar
½ teaspoon cinnamon
½ teaspoon cloves,
ground

Syrup:
1 cup sugar
1 cup honey
2 cups water

1 cinnamon stick
Juice of one small lemon

Grind walnuts; add sugar, cinnamon and cloves. Mix well. How a tray of Baklava is made: Brush baking tray with melted butter. Place strudel leaves at bottom of pan and brush or sprinkle with butter. Spread chopped walnuts evenly. Place 2 or more strudel leaves on top. Brush or sprinkle with butter and proceed as above until baking tray is filled. Place the last 3 strudel leaves on top, baste with melted butter and with a pointed knife, score top sheets in a square or diamond shape. Bake in a moderate oven; then increase heat and continue baking until top becomes golden brown, approximately 1 hour. Let cool. While Baklava cools prepare the syrup by combining all ingredients and boil for 10 minutes. After Baklava has cooled, pour warm syrup over the top.

Mary and Jimmy Duvlaris
Jimmy's on the Square
Marietta, Georgia

Poached Bass "Sea Island"

4 (5-ounce) fresh red bass
fillets, skinned
2 large shallots, peeled
and chopped
4 ounces fresh
mushrooms, cleaned and
sliced

3 egg yolks
4 ounces butter
6 ounces dry Vermouth
Salt and white pepper to
taste

(You will need a casserole type pan, good quality, thick bottom, at least 1½-inches high and of the right size: Fish fillets should cover bottom, with not too much empty space or too crowded.) Melt butter in above pan. Add shallots and mushrooms and cook until shallots are transparent. Add bass fillets. Add Vermouth and bring to a quick boil. Season with small amount of salt and white pepper. Cover with lid or foil. Reduce heat and simmer for 6 to 8 minutes. Then check by making a small cut into thickest part of the fillet. If done remove fish with a skmimer and hold until serving time - on heated platter in preheated oven. The mushrooms may be removed and placed on top of fish. Increase heat to reduce cooking liquid to ⅓ of original volume, this may take 5 minutes. Do not allow to darken. Carefully and slowly add this reduction to the cold uncooked egg yolks, whipping as fast as you can to prevent curdling; adjust seasoning with lime juice and freshly chopped parsley. Pour over fish, brown lightly in broiler and serve.
Yield: 4 servings

The Cloister Hotel
Sea Island, Georgia

Dante's Down The Hatch Chocolate Fondue

6 to 8 (3-ounce) bars Toblerone (or comparable Dutch, Danish or Swiss milk chocolate with almonds and honey)

Dash of instant coffee	Dash of cinnamon
Up to 1 pint of half and half (12% cream)	⅓ ounce Cointreau (or another favorite Liqueur)

Using a double boiler, cover the bottom of the pan with cream. (Low heat.) Add chocolate, breaking in small chunks. Melt it, adding more cream as is necessary, until mix is consistent. Do not scorch. Add the dash of coffee and the dash of cinnamon. Suggest simmering 6 to 8 hours adding cream as needed, to keep it from getting too thick. Pour Cointreau into the bottom of a ceramic pot and then pour in chocolate mixture. Serve hot in ceramic pot with candle under it to keep it warm.

Suggested FRESH fruits to serve with Chocolate Fondue:

Sliced strawberries	Cantaloupe
Hawaiian pineapple	Honey dew melon
Banana chunks	Seedless grapes

Other items:

Rum-soaked cake	Pound cake
Small marshmallows	Mandarin orange
Angel food cake	sections

Excellent fresh fruit in season:

Cherries	Tangerines
Peaches	Blackberries
Blueberries	Raspberries
Pears	

Dante S. Stephenson
Dante's Down the Hatch
Atlanta

Stuffed Jumbo Shrimp With Tomatoes

2 ounces butter
1 medium onion, chopped fine
3 to 4 stalks celery, chopped fine
12 ounces mushrooms, chopped
1 teaspoon lemon pepper
¼ teaspoon salt
1 teaspoon chicken base
2 tablespoons dry sherry
1½ cups dry stuffing
1 egg
18 jumbo raw shrimp/3 per person
4 ounces butter, melted
3 medium tomatoes
Garlic pepper to taste
Celery salt to taste
1 (8-ounce) package frozen LeSeur peas, thawed
Dill weed

Spray pan with Pam. Melt 2 ounces butter. Sauté onions, celery and mushrooms until juice comes out. Add lemon pepper, salt, chicken base and sherry, bring to a boil and remove from heat and add stuffing and egg. Mix well. Refrigerate. Cut and flatten shrimp, flat side down and dip in melted butter. Put on a glass pyrex dish. When stuffing is very cold place 1 scoop of stuffing on top of shrimp. Cut tomatoes into quarters and put between shrimp and sprinkle with garlic pepper and celery salt. Add thawed peas to the center of the dish and sprinkle with dill weed and salt. Cover airtight and refrigerate. Preheat oven to 400°. Bake 10 to 12 minutes or until shrimp are white.
Yield: 6 servings

Harrom Baker
Lickskillet Farm Restaurant
Roswell, Georgia

A charming old farmhouse, filled with delightful antiques, Lickskillet Farm offers old fashioned service and Southern hospitality.

Maximillians Shrimp And Crab Imperial

½ pound blue crab claw meat or lump crab
½ pound bay shrimp, cooked
2 heaping serving spoons mayonnaise
1 serving spoon heavy cream
½ serving spoon Worcestershire sauce
½ teaspoon white pepper
½ teaspoon Old Bay Seasoning
½ teaspoon salt
2 serving spoons parsley flakes
½ serving spoons diced pimento
1½ serving spoons finely diced onion
1½ serving spoons finely diced green pepper
1 egg

Add all ingredients together except crab and shrimp. Mix throughly. Then add crab and shrimp and mix again. Shrimp and Crab Imperial can be served hot or cold. Makes an excellent stuffing for avocado, served cold, or as a stuffing for flounder or grouper. Can also be served as a casserole topped with Cheddar cheese and baked until bubbly.

Maximillians Continental - American Cuisine
Marietta, Georgia

Ernies' Spicey Honey

2 gallons mayonnaise
48 ounces Karo syrup
1 gallon Guldens mustard
7 pounds honey

Mix all together and use as a barbeque sauce on ribs or steaks. Stores for several weeks in the refrigerator.

Ernies' Steak House
Marietta, Georgia

Pano's And Paul's

Short Smoked Salmon Filet Grilled:

4 (8-ounce) thick salmon filets (boneless and skinned)	**1 cup teriyaki sauce** **¼ cup lemon juice** **¼ cup orange juice**

Marinate the salmon filets for 30 minutes in teriyaki sauce, lemon juice and orange juice. Smoke on a very low heat in smoker for aproximately 8 minutes under heavy smoke. Make sure the salmon filets are still raw but have a nice smoked flavor. Sprinkle lightly with salt and freshly ground pepper and chargrill the filet to a nice medium.

Sesame Spinach:

1 pound fresh spinach (stems removed and washed) **2 tablespoons sesame oil**	**1 teaspoon ground sesame seeds** **Salt and pepper to taste**

Sauté the cleaned spinach in the sesame oil till wilted. Season with salt and pepper and sprinkle with freshly toasted and ground sesame seeds.

Pommery Honey Cream:

8 ounces yogurt **2 ounces Pommery Mustard** **1 ounce honey** **½ teaspoon Coleman's Mustard**	**Juice of 1 lemon** **1 teaspoon prepared horseradish** **Salt and pepper to taste**

Dilute mustard with lemon juice. Add honey, Pommery and yogurt. Mix and add salt and pepper to taste. Place the Salmon steak on top of the Sesame Spinach and drizzle the Pommery Honey Cream over salmon.

Yield: 4 servings

Pano's and Paul's
Atlanta, Georgia

Roast Loin Of Pork

Loin of pork
½ cup softened butter
Crumbled thyme and bay leaf

2 crushed garlic bulbs
Dijon mustard
Salt and freshly ground pepper

Mix softened butter, crumbled thyme, bay leaf, garlic and Dijon mustard to a smooth paste and rub well into the pork about 2 hours before roasting. Sprinkle to taste with salt and pepper and let stand at room temperature to absorb flavors. Arrange the meat, fat side up, and brown in a hot oven (450°) for about 15 minutes. Reduce heat to 350° and roast until done, about 1½ hours. Remove excess fat from pan and thicken pan drippings with a little flour. Garnish with watercress or parsley and serve with roast potatoes. It's the best!!

Tommy Roe

A successful nightclub and concert singer, Tommy Roe began his music career in Atlanta. This country rocker's music includes hits "Sheila" and "Dizzy".

Scallops Top Of The Square

1½ cups butter, melted and divided
½ cup flour
Pinch of salt
2 cups half and half
¼ cup Parmesan cheese

2 cups sea scallops, drained well
½ cup white wine
1 garlic clove
Paprika

In saucepan, combine ½ cup butter, flour and salt. Cook 4 to 5 minutes on low heat, stirring continuously. Add half and half, continue cooking until mixture thickens. Add Parmesan cheese; cook on low heat for 5 minutes. Set aside. Preheat oven to 350°. Sauté the scallops in remaining butter, wine and juice from the garlic clove. Cook for 2 to 3 minutes. Drain and place in shallow dish; cover with white sauce. Sprinkle with paprika. Cook 10 to 15 minutes. Serve warm.

Yield: 6-8 servings

Dan and Dave Reardon
Shillings on the Square
Marietta, Georgia

Pirates' House Escargots

2 dozen snails (2 cans)
24 mushroom caps

1 recipe Snail Butter, see below

Melt half the snail butter in a skillet and sauté mushroom caps until tender. Remove from skillet and place in 4 individual casserole dishes. Prepare snails for cooking according to instructions on can. Place a snail in each mushroom cap. Cover each snail with about 1 teaspoon snail butter. Broil until butter melts and snails are hot. Serve with lots of crusty French bread.

Snail Butter:
1 cup butter, softened
2 tablespoons minced shallots

2 cloves garlic, crushed
1 tablespoon finely chopped fresh parsley

Combine in bowl or food processor until well-blended.
Serves 4

Herb Traub
The Pirates House
Savannah, Georgia

Pecan Soufflé With Frangelico Sauce

Frangelico Sauce:
2 cups light cream
5 egg yolks, from large eggs

2 tablespoons sugar
1 teaspoon vanilla
3 tablespoons Frangelico

Soufflé:
1 tablespoon unsalted butter
1½ cups plus 2 tablespoons sugar
2 cups pecans, chopped into ¼-inch pieces
4 tablespoons water
2 large eggs

1 egg yolk, from a large egg
½ cup flour
2 cups milk
2 to 4 tablespoons dark rum
12 egg whites, from large eggs

(Cont.)

Making The Sauce: In a bowl, combine ⅔ cup of the cream with the egg yolks and mix well. Mix the remaining 1⅓ cups of cream with the sugar and vanilla in a saucepan. Cook this mixture over medium heat for 5 minutes. Remove the pan from the heat and slowly add the yolk mixture to it. Return the pan to low heat and cook, stirring constantly, until the sauce thickens enough to coat the back of a spoon. Do not boil or the egg yolks will curdle! Cooking can take up to 30 minutes. The end result should be a lovely, silky sauce, about the consistency of heavy cream. Add the Frangelico to the sauce and keep it warm while you make the soufflé. Preheat oven to 425°. Coat a 3-quart soufflé dish with 1 tablespoon of butter and then dust it with 2 tablespoons of the sugar. Put the chopped pecans in a roasting pan and roast in the oven for 7 to 10 minutes. Be careful - they burn easily. Set aside. Combine ½ cup of the sugar with 2 tablespoons of the water in a heavy-bottomed saucepan. Place the pan over medium heat and cook, without stirring, until the sugar has melted and caramelized to a golden brown (about 7 minutes). Remove the pan from the heat and add the remaining 2 tablespoons of water. Taking care not to splatter molten caramel on yourself, stir until the sugar has completely dissolved. Stir in the roasted pecans. Keep the caramelized mixture warm so it doesn't harden while you make the soufflé. Mix the 2 eggs, the egg yolk, ½ cup of the sugar and the flour together in a cool saucepan to make a paste. Slowly add the milk to the paste, taking care to avoid lumps. Put the pan over medium heat and bring the mixture to a boil, stirring constantly (about 15 minutes). The mixture should be quite thick. Stir in the caramelized sugar and pecans and add rum to taste. Allow the mixture to cool. Whip the egg whites until they start to foam. Beat the remaining ½ cup of sugar into the egg whites in a slow, steady stream. Continue until the whites hold stiff (but not dry) peaks. Fold the whites into the cooked mixture. Gently pour the batter into the prepared dish. Bake in the center of the oven until the soufflé puffs above the 3 quart soufflé dish (about 25 minutes). To Serve: The soufflé will remain puffed up for only a few minutes, so serve it immediately. Ladle ¼ cup of the Frangelico sauce onto each dessert plate, then top with a generous serving of soufflé.

Josef Lageder
Executive Chef
The Ritz - Carlton, Atlanta

Sautéed Veal Scallops
With Morel Sauce

Morel Sauce:

2 ounces fresh morels or 1
ounce dried
4 tablespoons unsalted
butter
1 tablespoon shallots,
chopped fine

1 cup dry white wine
1 cup cognac
3 cups heavy cream
Salt and ground white
pepper to taste

Garnish:
¼ bunch chopped fresh
chives

Rinse dried morels under cold running water in a small strainer until they are free of all dirt and grit. Transfer morels to a bowl, cover with cold water, and allow to soak for approximately two hours. After soaking, drain morels, rinse, and set aside (cut very large morels in half). If morels are fresh, wipe with damp paper towel. Cut off stems and save for another use. Slice large mushroom caps in half, and set aside. Melt 1 tablespoon of butter in a large skillet, and sauté the shallots for approximately two minutes (do not brown). Add morels to skillet and heat thoroughly. Add wine and cognac, and heat on high flame until liquid has reduced to one cup. Add cream to skillet and reduce liquid to half again on high heat. Add remainder of unsalted butter to skillet and whip with a wire whisk until sauce has thickened. Lower heat, add salt and white pepper to taste, and reserve sauce.

Veal Scallops:

2 pounds boneless veal
loin, skinned and
trimmed of all fat
6 tablespoons butter,
preferably clarified

2 tablespoons vegetable
oil
Salt and ground white
pepper to taste

(Cont.)

Cut trimmed boneless veal loin into 1½ ounce medallions. Pound veal between two pieces of wax paper, into ¼ inch thick scallops. Heat oil in a heavy skillet until pan is very hot. Add butter to the skillet and allow to melt. Add the veal scallops a few at a time (do not crowd the pan), and season lightly with salt and pepper. Sauté the scallops quickly, about 30 seconds per side, until lightly browned. Place veal scallops on serving platter. Spoon heated sauce over scallops, top with fresh chopped chives, and serve.

Serves: 4

Trotters
Atlanta, Georgia

Creme de Brie
Creamy, rich, French Brie soup

1 cup dry white wine
2 ounces flour
2 ounces butter
10 ounces Brie, cut into 1 ounce slices
1¼ pints heavy whipping cream
3½ cups chicken stock or broth
1 pound onions, diced

½ pound mushrooms, sliced
¼ teaspoon garlic, diced
1 bay leaf
A pinch of freshly chopped thyme
1½ to 2 ounces sherry
Salt and pepper to taste
12 toasted croutons

Melt butter in a heavy, 2 quart saucepan. Sauté onions, garlic and mushrooms in melted butter. Add wine and reduce until almost dry. Add flour and work into paste over low heat. Add chicken stock and bay leaf, bring to moderate boil; cook until soup consistency is achieved. Add thyme and whipping cream strain and return to heat. Slowly, with whisk, blend in 4 ounces of Brie, whipping until smooth consistency is achieved. Add salt and pepper and sherry to taste. Pour into bowls, place croutons on top, lay remaining slices of Brie on croutons and brown lightly under broiler and serve. Enjoy!!

Yield: 6 servings

The Abbey
Atlanta, Georgia

Dishwasher Salmon Filets
Your guest must see you remove this
from the dishwasher to believe you!

6 (8 to 10-ounce) salmon
filets or 6 (10 to
12-ounce) salmon steaks

6 teaspoons butter
Lemon pepper

Spray a glass plate with Pam. Place salmon on plate. Put thin slices of butter (1 teaspoon) on each piece and sprinkle with lemon pepper. Place plate on foil and cover fish air tight. Put large piece of foil on top and tuck under so water cannot get into foil seams. Put in dishwasher on lowest rack or if your dishwasher shoots water only in the middle, you have to set it on the top rack. Set the dishwasher on its highest setting. Fish should go through wash-rinse, wash-rinse, hot dry (complete cycle should not be longer than 1 hour) and your fish is ready. Open foil, drain juice in a pot. Cover fish with foil and keep warm in oven while making Creamy Dill Sauce. Decorate fish with fresh dill sprigs and lemon wedges

Ursula Knaeusel
Ursula's Cooking School, Inc.
Atlanta, Georgia

Creamy Dill Sauce

¼ cup juice from fish
2 tablespoons white wine
½ package Knorr
  Hollandaise Sauce
1 egg yolk
⅓ to ½ cup whipping
  cream

1 tablespoon fresh dill or 1
  teaspoon dry dill
½ teaspoon lemon pepper
½ tablespoon horseradish
  (optional)

Mix juice, wine, hollandaise sauce mix and egg yolk together. Stir over medium heat. When it comes to a boil add so much whipping cream till you have a nice, creamy consistency. Add dill, lemon pepper and horseradish. Taste for salt. Serve with Dishwasher Salmon Filets and fresh asparagus.

Ursual Knaeusel
Ursula's Cooking School, Inc.
Atlanta, Georgia

Desserts

A Classic Cake
An elegant dessert for company!

4 egg whites, room
temperature
1 cup Super Fine sugar
½ teaspoon vanilla
1 quart raspberry sherbet,
softened
3 cups whipping cream
2 to 3 tablespoons Creme
de Cassis liqueur

2 to 3 tablespoons
strawberry preserves
1 quart fresh strawberries
(3 whole berries for
garnish, remaining
berries sliced)

Sauce:
1 (10-ounce) package
frozen raspberries in
syrup, thawed

2 to 3 tablespoons Cream
de Cassis

Trace 3 (9-inch) circles on waxed paper. Place and secure on cookie sheets. Beat egg whites until soft peaks form. Gradually add sugar, 2 tablespoons at a time. Add vanilla and continue beating until stiff and glossy peaks form. Preheat oven to 275°. Spread beaten whites evenly on each circle. Bake 55 minutes at 275°. Turn off oven and leave meringue layers in until cool. Line a 9-inch springform pan with foil and spread sherbet evenly in pan. Freeze until firm (about 3 hours). Beat cream in a large bowl until soft peaks form. Add Cream de Cassis and preserves (you can add some fresh sliced strawberries too); beat until stiff. Remove 1 meringue layer from paper to cake plate. Invert sherbet layer onto meringue; remove foil. Top with another meringue. Layer and cover with 1 cup of whipped cream mixture; top with remaining meringue. Frost entire cake with whipped cream mixture and pipe whipped cream mixture with rosette tip on sides and top. Garnish the top with 3 whole strawberries and around the base with cut berries. Freeze. Purée raspberries in blender; strain to remove seeds. Add remaining sliced strawberries and Cream de Cassis. Toss gently. Slice cake and serve with raspberry sauce.
Yield: 8 to 10 servings   *Nancy Finke Rambasek*

Almond Pound Cake

1 cup margarine
½ cup shortening
3 cups sugar, divided
5 eggs
2 teaspoons almond
  extract

1 teaspoon vanilla extract
1 teaspoon salt
1 teaspoon baking powder
3 cups flour, divided
1 cup milk

Preheat oven to 325°. Grease and flour a Bundt pan. Cream together margarine and shortening. Add ¼ cup of the sugar and stir; add one egg and stir again. Repeat until all the remaining sugar and eggs are stirred into creamed mixture. Mix in extracts, salt and baking powder; add ¾ cup of the flour. Continue to mix adding milk alternately with remaining flour. Pour batter into prepared pan and bake at 325° for one hour. Lower temperature to 300° for 15 minutes. Cool completely.
Yield: 12 to 15 servings   *Deborah Grosser Anthony*

Apricot Brandy Pound Cake

1 cup butter, softened
3 cups sugar
6 large eggs
3 cups flour
¼ teaspoon baking soda
½ teaspoon salt
1 (8-ounce) carton sour
  cream

½ cup apricot brandy
1 teaspoon orange extract
1½ teaspoons vanilla
  extract
1 teaspoon lemon extract
1 teaspoon rum extract
½ teaspoon almond
  extract

Preheat oven to 325°. Grease and flour a 10-inch tube pan. Cream butter and add sugar, beating until mixture is light and fluffy. Add eggs, one at a time, beating well after each addition. Combine flour, soda and salt; mix well and set aside. Combine sour cream, brandy and extracts. Add to creamed mixture alternately with flour mixture. Mix well. Pour batter into prepared pan. Bake for 1 hour and 20 minutes or until done. Cool in pan, then remove from pan and place on cake platter. *(Better after having been frozen. May substitute Peach Brandy for the Apricot Brandy.)*
Yield: 12 servings   *Pamela Croy Newton*

Apple Cake

5 small or 4 large cooking
   apples
5 tablespoons sugar
2 teaspoons cinnamon
3 cups flour
2½ cups sugar
½ teaspoon salt
4 eggs

1 cup oil
2 teaspoons vanilla
⅓ cup orange juice
1½ teaspoons baking
   soda
1½ teaspoons baking
   powder

Glaze:
1½ cups confectioners'
   sugar
2 tablespoons butter,
   softened

1½ teaspoons vanilla
1 to 2 tablespoons water

Preheat oven to 350°. Grease and flour a 10-inch tube or
Bundt pan. Peel apples, core and thinly slice. In bowl, toss
apples with 5 tablespoons sugar and 2 teaspoons cinnamon.
Set aside. In large bowl, mix together flour, sugar, salt, eggs, oil,
vanilla, orange juice, baking powder and soda. Blend 1 minute,
then 3 more. This mixture will be very thick. Layer in pan ⅓
dough mixture, ½ apple mixture, ⅓ dough, remaining apples,
ending with dough mixture. Bake 1½ to 1¾ hours or until tester
comes out clean. Cool on rack 10 minutes, then invert. Remove
cake from pan and continue to cool. Mix glaze ingredients and
drizzle over cake.
Yield: 10 to 12 servings   *Leigh Ellen Carlson*

Dr. Byrd's Cake
Requires few steps and no mixer

3 cups flour, sifted
2 cups sugar
1 teaspoon soda
1 teaspoon cinnamon
1 teaspoon salt
2 cups ripe bananas, diced
1 small can crushed
  pineapple with juice

3 eggs
1 cup oil
1½ teaspoons vanilla
  extract
1 cup confectioners' sugar
Lemon juice

Preheat oven to 350°. Grease and flour a 10-inch tube pan. Combine the first five ingredients in a large bowl and mix well by hand. Add remaining ingredients and mix well by hand. Do not beat with mixer. Pour into prepared tube pan and bake at 350° for 1 hour 15 minutes. (Time will vary slightly, depending on individual ovens.) Cool in pan, on rack, until cool enough to handle easily. In small bowl, add enough lemon juice to powdered sugar to spread easily. Drizzle over cake.
Yield: 12 to 16 servings   *Kaye Armitage DeJarnett*

Apple Meringue Cake

Crust:
1¾ cups flour, sifted
¼ cup sugar
¼ teaspoon cinnamon
1 teaspoon salt

½ cup blanched almonds,
  finely ground
½ cup butter or margarine

Filling:
3 eggs, separated
½ cup brown sugar, firmly
  packed
3 tablespoons apple cider
  or apricot brandy
1 tablespoon lemon rind,
  grated

6 cups apples, thinly
  sliced and peeled
1 cup apricot preserves
3 tablespoons apple cider
  or apricot brandy
1 tablespoon fresh lemon
  juice

Meringue:
3 egg whites
Pinch of salt
3 tablespoons sugar

½ cup blanched almonds,
  slivered or ground

(Cont.)

Preheat oven to 350°. Sift flour, sugar, cinnamon and salt in bowl; mix in ground almonds; cut in butter until coarse crumbs form. Reserve 1 cup mixture. Pat remainder into a buttered 9-inch springform pan to line bottom and sides. Bake 20 minutes at 350° or until golden brown. Cool before filling. Leave oven on. Beat egg yolks (reserve whites for meringue). Add brown sugar, cider and lemon rind to egg yolks. Mix thoroughly. Add to sliced apples; toss and mix. Spoon apple mixture on to cooled crumb crust. Sprinkle with the reserved crumb mixture. Return to oven and bake 55 minutes or until apples are tender. Remove and leave oven on. Combine apricot preserves with apple cider or apricot brandy and lemon juice in small bowl. Gently spread preserve mixture over apple crumb layer. Beat 3 egg whites with salt until foamy. Beat in sugar slowly until soft peaks form. Spread meringue over hot cake, spreading to the edge of the pan. Sprinkle with almonds. Return to oven and bake 15 minutes until golden brown. Cool on wire rack 30 minutes. To remove from pan, gently slip a small spatula between meringue and side of pan to loosen. Release clamp, then lift off. Serve warm.

First place winner in the Cobb Marietta Junior League's 1986 Apple Betty Bakeoff
Yield: 10 to 12 servings   *Laura Powell Whitlock*

Chocolate Pound Cake

⅔ cup cocoa
3 cups sugar
1 cup margarine
½ cup shortening
5 eggs

3 cups flour
½ teaspoon baking powder
½ teaspoon salt
1 cup milk

Preheat oven to 325°. Grease and flour a tube pan. Blend cocoa with sugar and cream with the margarine and shortening. Add the eggs, one at a time, beating well after each addition. Sift together dry ingredients; add alternately with milk to creamed mixture. Bake for 1½ hours.
Yield: 12 to 14 servings   *Meredith Webb Dykes*

Carrot Cake
A classic

3 cups carrots, grated
1¾ cups sugar
1¼ cups vegetable oil
4 large eggs, room
  temperature
2 cups flour
2 teaspoons baking
  powder

2 teaspoons soda
1 teaspoon salt
2 teaspoons cinnamon
1 teaspoon lemon extract
1 teaspoon vanilla extract
½ cup pecans, chopped

Icing:
1 (16-ounce) box
confectioners' sugar
4 tablespoons butter,
  softened
8 ounces cream cheese,
  softened

1 teaspoon lemon extract
2 teaspoons vanilla extract
1 (8-ounce) can crushed
  pineapple, drained

Preheat oven to 350°. Grease, flour and line 3 (8-inch) layer pans with wax paper circles. Cream sugar and oil until light (2 minutes). Add eggs, and beat on high for 2 minutes. Sift dry ingredients and add to creamed mixture, 1 heaping tablespoon at a time. Add flavorings to batter; fold in carrots and nuts. Pour into prepared pans. Bake in 350° oven for 30 minutes. Cool on rack for 10 minutes. Cream confectioners' sugar, butter, and cream cheese. Add flavorings and pineapple. Icing spreads on cake easier if chilled. Chill the cake to set the icing.
Yield: 12 servings   *Adrian Winship Pressley*

Chablis Blanc Cake

A boxed mix never tasted so homemade.

½ cup pecans, chopped
1 small box vanilla instant
    pudding mix
½ cup Chablis Blanc wine
½ cup water

1 (18¼-ounce) box butter
    recipe golden cake mix
½ cup vegetable oil
4 eggs

Topping:
1 cup sugar
¼ cup Chablis Blanc wine

¼ cup water
½ cup margarine

Preheat oven to 325°. Grease and flour Bundt pan. Place nuts in bottom. Mix remaining cake ingredients together for 2 minutes. Pour batter over nuts. Bake for 55 to 60 minutes at 325°. Boil the topping ingredients for 2 minutes. Remove the hot cake from the Bundt pan. Place on a large cake plate or carrier. Spoon the hot topping over the cake. The cake will remain moist.
Yield: 10 to 12 servings   *Carol Head Wells*

Chilled Sherry Cake

4 eggs, separated
½ cup sugar
½ cup sherry
1 package unflavored
    gelatin

⅓ cup milk
1 angle food cake
2 pints whipping cream
Shaved chocolate
    (optional)

In top of double boiler, combine 4 well-beaten egg yolks, ½ cup sugar and sherry. Cook in double boiler until thick. Soften gelatin in milk and add to hot sauce; cool mixture in refrigerator. Shred angel food cake into small pieces and reserve. Whip 1 cup whipping cream and fold into 4 stiffly beaten egg whites. Add egg white mixture to cool sauce; mix together with angle food cake pieces in large bowl. Line a 9¼ x 5¼ x 2¾-inch loaf pan with wax paper on the bottom; pack sherry cake mixture into pan. Smooth the top surface and chill overnight or several hours. Whip 1 cup of whipping cream. Turn cake onto platter, ice with whipped cream, and decorate with shaved chocolate. Slice and enjoy!
Yield: 10 servings   *Adrian Winship Pressley*

Amaretto Cheesecake

1½ cups graham cracker
  crumbs
2 tablespoons sugar
1 teaspoon ground
  cinnamon
¼ cup plus 2 tablespoons
  butter or margarine,
  melted
3 (8-ounce) packages
  cream cheese, softened
1 cup sugar
4 eggs

⅓ cup Amaretto
1 (8-ounce) carton sour
  cream
1 tablespoon plus 1
  teaspoon sugar
1 tablespoon Amaretto
¼ cup toasted almonds,
  sliced (optional)
1 (1.2-ounce) chocolate
  candy bar, grated
  (optional)

Preheat oven to 375°. Combine graham cracker crumbs, 2 tablespoons sugar, cinnamon, and butter; mix well. Firmly press mixture into bottom and ½ inch up sides of a 9-inch springform pan. Beat cream cheese with electric mixer until light and fluffy. Gradually add 1 cup sugar, mixing well. Add eggs, one at a time, beating well after each addition. Stir in ⅓ cup Amaretto; pour into prepared pan. Bake at 375° for 45 to 50 minutes until set. Combine sour cream, 1 tablespoon plus 1 teaspoon sugar and 1 tablespoon Amaretto; stir well and spoon over the cheesecake. Bake at 500° for 5 minutes. Let cool to room temperature; then refrigerate 24 to 48 hours. (Cheesecake is best when thoroughly chilled and flavors have time to ripen). Garnish with almonds and the grated chocolate.
Yield: 10 to 12 servings   *Laura Phillips Lewis*

Milk Chocolate Cheesecake
With Custard Sauce

Crust:

1 package plain chocolate
  wafers (May substitute 1
  cup graham cracker
  crumbs)

1 tablespoon sugar
¼ teaspoon cinnamon
½ cup butter, melted

(Cont.)

Filling:

3 (8-ounce) package cream
  cheese, softened
4 eggs
1 cup sugar
1 (6-ounce) package milk
  chocolate morsels,
  melted

1½ teaspoons vanilla
  extract
2½ tablespoons cocoa
3 cups sour cream
¼ cup unsalted butter,
  melted

Custard Sauce:

7 egg yolks
¾ cup sugar
1 cup hot milk
2 cups heavy cream
1½ teaspoons vanilla
  extract

4 tablespoons orange
  liqueur
Toasted slivered almonds,
  chopped finely (optional)

Crust: Very lightly grease a 10-inch springform pan. Crush chocolate wafers and mix with sugar, cinnamon and butter. Press into the springform pan; refrigerate.

Filling: Preheat oven to 350°. Beat cream cheese until fluffy; add eggs and sugar mixing well. Add melted chocolate to egg mixture. Blend in vanilla, cocoa and sour cream. Beat well and add melted butter. Mix well and pour into springform pan. Bake at 350° for 45 to 60 minutes. Cool. Refrigerate overnight. Remove from pan before serving. Serve with Custard Sauce.

Custard Sauce: Beat yolks and sugar. Blend in milk and cream. Cook in a double boiler until thickened, stirring frequently. To keep from curdling, add some of the hot milk to egg mixture and mix well before adding other ingredients. Strain custard. When cool, add orange liqueur and vanilla extract. Refrigerate overnight.

To serve: Serve a small slice of cake on a dessert plate and spoon custard around the slice but not on top. Garnish the sauce with almonds.

Yield: 16 servings   *Pamela Croy Newton*

Praline Cheesecake
A Southern tradition

1 cup graham cracker
  crumbs
3 tablespoons sugar
3 tablespoons margarine,
  melted
3 (8-ounce) packages
  cream cheese, softened

1¼ cups dark brown sugar
2 tablespoons flour
3 eggs
1½ teaspoons vanilla
½ cup chopped pecans
Pure maple syrup
Pecan halves for garnish

Preheat oven to 350°. Combine graham cracker crumbs, sugar and margarine; press into the bottom of a 9-inch spring-form pan. Bake for 10 minutes. Remove from oven and increase oven temperature to 450°. Combine cream cheese, brown sugar and flour and beat in an electric mixer, at medium speed, until mixture is well blended. Add eggs, one at a time, beating well after each addition. Blend in vanilla; stir in nuts. Pour over crust and bake for 10 minutes at 450°. Reduce oven temperature to 250° and continue baking for 30 minutes. Cool before removing rim of pan. Chill, brush with pure maple syrup and garnish with pecan halves.
Yield: 8 to 10 servings   *Betty Davis Haverly*

Mocha Cake

Cocoa (unsweetened)
2 cups flour
1⅔ cups sugar
1⅓ cups water
⅔ cup butter or margarine,
  softened
3 eggs

2 teaspoons instant coffee
1½ teaspoons baking
  soda
1 teaspoon vanilla extract
½ teaspoon baking
  powder
½ teaspoon salt

Preheat oven to 350°. Grease two (9-inch) round cake pans. Coat bottoms and sides of pan lightly with cocoa. Into a large bowl, measure ⅔ cup cocoa and remaining ingredients. Beat with mixer at low speed to blend; increase speed to high and beat 4 minutes. Pour batter into pans. Bake 30 minutes or until inserted toothpick comes out clean. Cool in pans 10 minutes, remove to wire racks and cool completely. Frost with Mocha Butter Frosting.
Yield: 16 servings   *Patricia Rusinek Macchia*

Mocha Butter Frosting

1 (16-ounce) package
  confectioners' sugar
½ cup butter or margarine,
  softened
¼ cup cocoa

¼ cup water
1 teaspoon instant coffee
1 teaspoon vanilla extract
⅛ teaspoon salt

Combine all ingredients in a bowl; beat with mixer at low speed until blended. Increase speed to high and beat for 3 minutes or until light and fluffy.
Yield: Enough to frost one two layer cake

Patricia Rusinek Macchia

Rachel's Chocolate Cake

2 cups flour
2 cups sugar
½ cup butter
½ cup shortening
4 tablespoons cocoa

1 cup water
1 teaspoon baking soda
½ cup buttermilk
2 eggs
1 teaspoon vanilla extract

Icing:
6 tablespoons cocoa
⅓ cup butter
½ cup buttermilk
1 (16-ounce) box powdered
  sugar

½ teaspoon vanilla extract
Nuts (optional)

Preheat oven to 350°. Grease and flour a 13 x 9-inch pan. Mix together flour and sugar; set aside. Combine butter, shortening, cocoa and water and bring to a boil; pour over flour and sugar. Mix. Add the baking soda, buttermilk, eggs and vanilla extract; beat well and pour into prepared pan. Bake for 45 minutes. Five minutes before cake is done prepare icing. Combine cocoa, butter and buttermilk. Bring to a boil and pour over the box of powdered sugar. Beat; add the vanilla extract. Add nuts, if desired. Pour icing over hot cake.
Yield: 10 to 12 servings

Donya Smith Rickman

Kahlua Chocolate Cake

2 (6-ounce) packages
  semisweet chocolate
  chips
½ cup sugar
¼ teaspoon salt
½ cup Kahlua

4 eggs, separated
1½ teaspoons vanilla
2 cups whipping cream,
  whipped
3 dozen large ladyfingers

Melt chocolate in top of double boiler. Add 4 tablespoons of sugar, salt, and Kahlua. Cook, stirring constantly over boiling water until slightly thickened. Add beaten egg yolks; beat well. Cook for 2 minutes longer. Stir in vanilla. Remove from heat. Beat egg whites until foamy; add remaining sugar gradually and continue beating until stiff. Fold into chocolate mixture. Chill. When thoroughly chilled, fold in one cup whipping cream. Line a springform pan on bottom and sides with ladyfingers. Pour half of chocolate mixture into pan. Add another layer of ladyfingers; add remaining chocolate mixture. Chill for 24 hours. Serve topped with remaining whipped cream.
Yield: 12 servings   *Phillis Royster Rivers*

Chocolate Decadence
With Raspberry Sauce

Cake:

1 pound dark sweet
  (German) chocolate,
  broken into pieces
10 tablespoons butter,
  unsalted

4 eggs
1 tablespoon sugar
1 tablespoon flour

Whipped Cream Frosting:

2 cups heavy cream
2 tablespoons
  confectioners' sugar

1 teaspoon vanilla extract
Chocolate shavings
  (optional)

Raspberry Sauce:

1 (10-ounce) package
  frozen raspberries,
  thawed; or ½-cup fresh
  raspberries

1 tablespoon
  Kirschwasser
2 tablespoons sugar

(Cont.)

Cake: Preheat oven to 425°. Butter an 8-inch springform pan. (It is important that you use this size pan.) Place an 8-inch round of wax paper on the bottom. Butter the wax paper and flour the pan. Melt the chocolate and butter together in a heavy-bottomed sauce pan over low heat. Mix to blend. Cool. Place the eggs and sugar in the bowl of an electric mixer; and place the bowl over (but not touching) hot water, stirring with a whisk until the sugar is dissolved and the eggs are warm to the touch. Remove to the mixer and beat at high speed until the whipped eggs are cool and tripled in volume. Fold in the flour. Fold half of the whipped egg mixture into the melted chocolate and butter. Carefully fold in the remaining egg mixture. Pour the batter into the prepared springform pan. Bake 15 minutes. Remove from the oven and cool in the pan. Place the cake, still in the pan, in the refrigerator or freezer until very firm.

Frosting: Whip the cream with sugar and vanilla until stiff. Remove the cake from the refrigerator or freezer. Carefully remove it from the pan; invert onto a serving platter and peel off the wax paper. Working quickly, frost the top and sides of the cake with two-thirds of the whipped frosting. Place the rest of the cream in a pastry bag fitted with a star tube and make decoratives rosettes around the perimeter. Decorate the center of the cake with chocolate shavings and return to the refrigerator. Chill until firm.

Raspberry Sauce: Place thawed raspberries and juices in a food processor fitted with a steel blade. Process until puréed. Strain into a bowl. Add Kirschwasser and sugar and stir to blend. Serve a small slice of Decadence with several spoonfuls of raspberry sauce on the side.

Yield: 12 to 16 servings   *Mary Pressley Clayton*

Praline Cake

1 cup butter, softened
½ cup shortening
1 pound light brown sugar
5 eggs
3 cups unsifted flour
¼ teaspoon baking soda

½ teaspoon baking powder
¾ cup milk
2 teaspoons vanilla extract
2 cups pecans, chopped
Confectioners' sugar

Grease a 10-inch Bundt pan. Cream butter, shortening and brown sugar until light and fluffy. Add eggs, one at a time, beating well after each addition. Add sifted dry ingredients alternately with milk, beating until smooth after each addition. Stir in vanilla and nuts. Pour into prepared pan. Put in cold oven and turn heat control to 300°. Bake about one hour and 40 minutes. Let stand 5 minutes, then turn out on rack to cool. Before serving, sift confectioners' sugar lightly over top. Store in an airtight container.

Yield: 10 to 12 servings   *Mary Beth Brown Soignet*

Chocolate Chip Chocolate Cake

1 (18.5-ounce) package devil's food cake mix
1 small package instant chocolate pudding
4 eggs
½ cup cooking oil

1 cup sour cream
½ cup warm water
1 (6-ounce) package semi-sweet chocolate chips

Glaze:
2 cups confectioners' sugar
1 teaspoon vanilla
2 tablespoons butter

3 to 4 tablespoons water
2 ounces unsweetened chocolate

Preheat oven to 350°. Grease and flour Bundt pan. Combine first 6 ingredients in large bowl. Beat three minutes at medium speed. Add chips and beat 1 minute more. Pour into prepared pan. Bake 55 to 60 minutes at 350°. Cool on rack.

Glaze: Melt chocolate and butter together. Add sugar, vanilla then water. Blend well and pour over cake.

Yield: 10 to 12 servings   *Leigh Ellen Carlson*

Mama's Coconut Cake
Make this for people you really love

Cake:

1 cup butter
2 cups sugar
4 eggs, separated
3 teaspoons baking
  powder

3 cups cake flour
1 scant cup milk or water
½ teaspoon lemon extract
½ teaspoon vanilla extract

Coconut Filling:

3 eggs, beaten
1½ cups sugar
1 cup milk

2½ cups coconut, ground
  or grated (can use fresh
  frozen)
1 teaspoon vanilla

Icing:

2 egg whites
1½ cups sugar
⅓ cup water

1½ teaspoons white corn
  syrup
1 teaspoon vanilla

Preheat oven to 330°. (Not a misprint). Cream butter, sugar and egg yolks. Sift baking powder with flour; add to creamed mixture, alternating dry ingredients with the scant cup of milk or water. Add extracts and fold in stiffly beaten egg whites. Grease, flour and fill 3 (9-inch) cake pans. Bake at 330° about 25 minutes. Test for doneness.

Filling: Beat eggs; add sugar, milk and 2¼ cups of coconut. Stir and cook over medium heat to custard consistency. Add vanilla, cool and spread between layers and on top of cake. Sprinkle top with remaining coconut.

Icing: Combine unbeaten egg whites, sugar, water and corn syrup in top of double boiler. Beat just enough to blend ingredients. Place over rapidly boiling water and beat with mixer until light, fluffy peaks form (about 7 minutes by hand or 3 to 4 minutes by mixer). Remove from heat and add vanilla. Beat until stiff enough to stand in peaks. Spread over entire cake. Store in refrigerator.

Yield: 12 servings   *Cheryl Tilley Briscoe*

Special Occasion Ice Cream Cake

15 ladyfingers, split
1 (6-ounce) can frozen orange juice, undiluted
2 quarts vanilla ice cream, softened
2 (10-ounce) packages frozen raspberries
2 (9-ounce) cans crushed pineapple, drained
1 tablespoon frozen lemonade concentrate
1 teaspoon almond flavoring
1 teaspoon rum flavoring
6 Maraschino cherries, chopped
3 tablespoons nuts, chopped
1 cup whipping cream
4 tablespoons confectioners' sugar
1 teaspoon vanilla extract
Fresh strawberries
Mint leaves

This is prepared in 3 parts.

First: Line the bottom and sides of a springform pan with the split ladyfingers. Mix the undiluted can of orange juice with 1 quart of the softened ice cream. Spread this over the ladyfingers as the bottom layer. Freeze.

Second: Crunch the raspberries and strain to remove seeds. Add pineapple, and lemonade concentrate. Freeze this mixture until partially frozen and then beat. Spoon this mixture over the orange - ice cream mixture and refreeze.

Third: Add the almond and rum flavorings, cherries and nuts to remaining quart of softened ice cream. Pour over raspberry layer and freeze overnight. To serve, first whip together whipping cream, confectioners' sugar and vanilla extract. Take dessert out of freezer and remove from springform pan. Place on serving dish and cover with sweetened whipped cream. Decorate with strawberries and mint leaves. *This dessert freezes well and can be prepared a week ahead, except for garnishes.*

Yield: 12 to 16 servings   *Phyllis Royster Rivers*

Tennis Team Cake

3 cups sugar
1 cup butter, softened
½ cup shortening
5 large eggs
1 teaspoon vanilla extract
1 teaspoon coconut
   extract
1 teaspoon almond extract

1 teaspoon lemon extract
1 teaspoon rum extract
3 cups sifted flour
½ teaspoon baking
   powder
Pinch of salt
1 cup evaporated milk

Glaze:
1 cup sugar
½ cup water

½ teaspoon of each of the
   five extracts used in the
   cake

Preheat oven to 300°. Grease and flour a 10-inch tube pan, set aside. Cream sugar, butter, shortening at medium speed of electric mixer. Add eggs, one at a time, beating well after each addition. Add extracts, mix thoroughly. Combine flour, baking powder and salt. Add alternately with milk, blending well at low speed. Pour into prepared pan and bake at 300° for 1 hour and 45 minutes. Prepare glaze. When done, pierce top of cake with toothpick. Pour cooled glaze over warm cake before removing from pan. Let stand 15 to 20 minutes. Turn onto cake plate; cool completely before serving. Cake is very moist.
Glaze: Combine all glaze ingredients in saucepan; cook over low heat, stirring constantly, until sugar melts. Cool.
Yield: 10 to 12 servings   *Barbara Gully Allen*

Caramel Icing

2 cups brown sugar
½ cup evaporated milk
½ cup butter

¼ teaspoon salt, scant
1 teaspoon vanilla

In medium saucepan, mix the sugar, milk, butter and and salt. Bring to a rapid boil, stirring constantly. Boil one minute. Pour into a bowl and add vanilla; beat until lukewarm. If icing becomes hard, add one tablespoon of milk.
Yield: Icing for one (2-layer) cake or one tubecake.
                    Marvina Wallingford Northcutt

Yellow Layer Cake
"A good basic cake"

½ cup butter
1½ cups sugar
2 eggs
2½ cups cake flour
2½ teaspoons baking
  powder

¼ teaspoon salt
1 cup milk
2 teaspoons vanilla

Preheat oven to 350°. Grease and flour 2 (9-inch) cake pans. In a large mixing bowl, beat butter, sugar and eggs at high speed for 5 minutes. Sift together the flour, baking powder and salt. Reduce speed to low and alternately add flour mixture, then milk, to butter and sugar mixture. Add vanilla. Pour into prepared cake pans. Bake at 350° for 30 to 40 minutes. Perfect with Mother's Chocolate Icing.
Yield: 8 to 10 servings   *Vonnie Brand Heaton*

Mother's Chocolate Icing

¼ cup margarine
⅓ cup plus 1 tablespoon
  evaporated milk
1 (6-ounce) package
  semi-sweet chocolate
  chips

1 teaspoon vanilla
1 (16-ounce) box
  confectioners' sugar

Melt margarine in large saucepan over medium heat. Stir in milk and continue stirring until mixture is boiling rapidly. Remove pan from heat and add chocolate chips, stirring until melted. Add vanilla. Add sugar and stir until dissolved. If icing becomes too stiff, add few drops or hot water.
Yield: Icing for one (2-layer) 8-inch or 9-inch cake.
                                          Vonnie Brand Heaton

Very Moist Coconut Pound Cake

1 cup butter
½ cup Crisco
2¼ cups sugar
5 eggs
3 cups flour
1 teaspoon baking powder

¼ teaspoon salt
1 cup milk
2 teaspoons coconut
    flavoring
1 (6-ounce) package
    frozen coconut, thawed

Syrup:
¾ cup water
1½ cups sugar
2 tablespoons butter

1½ teaspoons coconut
    flavoring

Grease and flour a 10-inch tube pan. Cream butter and Crisco with 2¼ cups sugar. Add eggs, one at a time and beat on high speed, with an electric mixer, for 10 minutes (a must). Combine 3 cups flour, baking powder, and salt; add to creamed mixture alternately with milk, beginning and ending with flour. Add coconut flavoring and coconut. Bake in a cold oven at 325° for 1 hour and 25 minutes. Check with toothpicks for doneness. Must cool in pan for five minutes.
Syrup: Boil first 3 syrup ingredients for 5 minutes, then add coconut flavoring. Pour syrup over hot cake. Cool completely before inverting cake to a plate. This cake is even better after having been frozen.
Yield: 10 to 12 servings   *Pamela Croy Newton*

Chocolate Puffs

2 tablespoons cocoa
1 cup confectioners' sugar
¼ cup creme de cacao
2 tablespoons light corn
    syrup

2 cups cinnamon graham
    crackers, crushed
1 cup pecans, finely
    chopped
Confectioners' sugar

Mix together cocoa and sugar. In a small bowl mix together creme de cocoa and corn syrup; add to sugar mixture. Add graham crackers and nuts; stir until well mixed. Shape dough into walnut-sized balls; roll in confectioners' sugar. Place on a cookie sheet for several hours or until dry. Store at room temperature to serve. Also freezes well.
Yield: 3 dozen   *Bruce Goode Boling*

Chocolate - Peanut Clusters

2 tablespoons peanut
butter
1 (6-ounce) package
butterscotch morsels
1 (6-ounce) package
semisweet chocolate
morsels

2 cups salted Spanish
peanuts

Combine first 3 ingredients in a heavy saucepan; place over low heat and cook, stirring constantly, until melted. Stir in peanuts. Drop by rounded teaspoonfuls onto waxed paper. Chill until firm. Store in a covered container in refrigerator.
Yield: 4 dozen   *Cathy Colquitt*

Microwave Peanut Brittle
An easy recipe for children.

1 cup raw peanuts
1 cup sugar
½ cup light corn syrup
⅛ teaspoon salt

1 teaspoon butter or
margarine
1 teaspoon vanilla extract
1 teaspoon baking soda

In a 1½ quart glass bowl, stir together peanuts, sugar, syrup and salt. Cook for 8 minutes on HIGH, stir after 4 minutes. Stir in butter and vanilla extract. Cook on HIGH for 2 minutes. Add soda and stir until light and foamy. Pour onto lightly greased cookie sheet. Break into pieces when cool.
Yield: 1 pound   *Becky Webster Dykes*

White Chocolate Pretzels

2½ pounds white
chocolate
1 (10-ounce) bag stick
pretzels

30 ounces Spanish
peanuts

Spray turkey roaster with vegetable oil spray. Melt chocolate in roaster for 20 minutes in a 200° to 250° oven. Place peanuts and pretzels in chocolate. Stir until well mixed. Turn out by teaspoonfuls on a greased cookie sheet. When hardened, store in air tight container. Can be kept in the refrigerator, but not necessary. Freezes well.
Yield: 3 dozen   *Diana Palmer Huffstutler*

"Baby Heath" Bars

4 cups oatmeal, uncooked
1 cup brown sugar
¼ cup light corn syrup

¾ cup peanut butter
1 teaspoon vanilla extract
¾ cup butter, softened

Topping:
1 (6-ounce) package
chocolate chips
1 (6-ounce) package
butterscotch chips

1 cup peanut butter

Preheat oven to 400°; grease a 9 x 13-inch pan. Combine oatmeal, brown sugar, corn syrup, ¾ cup of peanut butter, vanilla extract and butter. Spread in prepared pan. Bake in preheated oven for 12 minutes.
Topping: Melt, in a double boiler or in a microwave oven, chocolate chips, butterscotch chips and the peanut butter. Spread the topping over the oatmeal mixture after removed from oven. Let cool, refrigerate and cut into squares.
Yield: 2 dozen   *Linda Allen Milligan*

Butterscotch Brownies

2 cups flour, unsifted
2 teaspoons baking
powder
1½ teaspoons salt
1 (12-ounce) package
butterscotch morsels

½ cup butter
2 cups light brown sugar,
firmly packed
4 eggs
1 teaspoon vanilla extract
1 cup pecans, chopped

Preheat oven to 350°. Combine flour, baking powder and salt. Set aside. Melt butter and butterscotch morsels in double boiler. Pour in large bowl and stir in brown sugar. Cool at room temperature for five minutes. Beat in eggs and vanilla extract. Stir in flour mixture and nuts. Spread into greased 15 x 10 x 1-inch baking pan. Bake at 350° for 30 minutes. Cool. Cut into 2-inch squares.
Yield: 3 dozen   *Jane Waters Stoddard*

Chess Bars

1 (18.5-ounce) box yellow
cake mix with pudding
½ cup butter, softened
1 cup pecans, chopped
1 (8-ounce) package cream
cheese, softened

1 (16-ounce) box
confectioners' sugar
2 eggs
½ teaspoon vanilla extract

Preheat oven to 350°. Mix cake mix and butter together by hand. (If the butter seems too hard, place in microwave for a few seconds and then mix with cake.) Press this mixture into a 9 x 13-inch pan. Sprinkle chopped pecans evenly over the cake mixture. Combine the remaining ingredients and blend together until smooth and well mixed. Pour over pecans and tip pan to distribute mixture evenly. Bake for 40 minutes at 350°. Let cool completely before cutting. This recipe freezes well.
Yield: 2 dozen   *Bruce Goode Boling*

Chocolate Pecan Pie Bars

1¼ cups flour
¼ cup sugar
½ teaspoon baking
powder
½ teaspoon ground
cinnamon
½ cup butter, softened
1 cup pecans, chopped
¼ cup butter

1 square semi-sweet
chocolate
3 eggs, beaten
1¼ cups brown sugar,
packed
2 tablespoons bourbon or
water
1 teaspoon vanilla

Preheat oven to 350°. In a mixing bowl combine flour, granulated sugar, baking powder and cinnamon; cut in ½ cup butter until mixture resembles coarse crumbs. Stir in pecans. Press into the bottom of ungreased 13 x 9-inch pan. Bake at 350° for 10 minutes. Combine ¼ cup butter and chocolate; heat and stir over low heat until chocolate is melted. Combine eggs, brown sugar, bourbon or water and vanilla in a small bowl, then mix with the melted chocolate. Pour over crust and bake 20 to 25 minutes more, or until set. Cool and cut into bars.
Yield: 3 dozen   *Meredith Webb Dykes*

Chocolate Peanut Butter Brownies

Cake:

1 cup margarine
¼ cup cocoa
1 cup water
½ cup buttermilk
2 eggs, well beaten

2 cups sugar
2 cups flour
1 teaspoon baking soda
1 teaspoon vanilla

Filling:

1 (12-ounce) jar crunchy
   peanut butter

1½ tablespoons oil

Icing:

½ cup margarine
¼ cup cocoa
6 tablespoons buttermilk
1 (16-ounce) box
   confectioners' sugar

1 teaspoon vanilla
Cream

Preheat oven to 350°. Grease and flour jelly roll pan.
Cake: Mix margarine, cocoa, water, buttermilk and eggs; heat and stir until boiling. Remove from heat; add sugar, flour, baking soda, and vanilla. Pour into prepared pan and bake at 350° for 25 minutes. Cool.
Filling: Mix peanut butter and oil. Spread on top of cake.
Icing: Heat margarine, cocoa and buttermilk on medium heat; bring to boil while stirring. Remove from heat; with hand mixer, blend in sugar and vanilla. Add enough cream to make icing smooth. Spread on top of filling. Refrigerate after frosting. These freeze well.
Yield: 2 to 3 dozen   *Pamela Croy Newton*

Candied Popcorn And Peanuts
Everthing but the prize!

5 quarts unsalted popped
popcorn
1 cup raw peanuts
1 cup butter or margarine
2 cups firmly packed light
brown sugar

½ cup dark corn syrup
½ teaspoon baking soda
½ teaspoon salt
½ teaspoon vanilla extract

Combine popcorn and peanuts in a lightly greased roasting pan; mix well and set aside. Melt butter in a large saucepan; stir in sugar and corn syrup. Bring mixture to a boil and boil for 5 minutes, stirring occasionally. Remove from heat; stir in soda, salt and vanilla. Pour sugar mixture over popcorn mixture, stirring until evenly coated. Bake in a 250° oven for 1 hour, stirring every 15 minutes. Cool and store in an airtight container.
Yield: 5 quarts   *Susan Henderson Chandler*

Coco - Grahams
Very rich!

1 cup margarine
1 egg, beaten
1 cup sugar
½ cup milk

Icing:
6 tablespoons margarine
1 teaspoon vanilla extract

1 cup pecans, chopped
1 (6-ounce) can coconut
1 box graham crackers,
divided

2 cups confectioners'
sugar
1 to 3 tablespoons milk

Place margarine, egg, sugar and milk in a saucepan; boil. Remove from heat. Add pecans, coconut and 1 cup graham cracker crumbs. Line the bottom of a 13 x 9-inch pan with whole graham crackers. Pour margarine mixture over graham crackers. Top with another layer of whole graham crackers.
Icing: Mix togther margarine, vanilla, confectioners' sugar and milk to spreading consistency. Spread icing on top layer of graham crackers. Refrigerate overnight. Cut into small bars.
Yield: 2 to 3 dozen bars   *Cheryl Tilly Briscoe*

Confection Squares a l'Almond

1¼ cups butter or
margarine, divided
½ cup unsweetened cocoa
powder
3½ cups confectioners'
sugar, sifted and divided
1 egg, beaten
1 teaspoon almond extract
2 cups graham cracker
crumbs

⅓ cup Amaretto
1½ cups semi-sweet
chocolate chips
Fresh strawberries
(optional)

Bottom Layer: In saucepan, melt ½ cup of butter; add cocoa and blend well. Remove from heat. Add ½ cup confectioners' sugar, egg and almond extract. Add graham cracker crumbs and mix well. Press into bottom only of ungreased 9 x 13-inch pan.

Middle Layer: Melt ½ cup butter; combine with Amaretto in a mixing bowl. Beat in remaining 3 cups of confectioners' sugar until smooth, using low speed of electric mixer. Spread over the crumb layer. Chill 1 to 2 hours.

Top Layer: Combine remaining ¼ cup butter and chocolate chips in small saucepan. Heat and stir over low heat until melted. Spread over the middle layer. Chill 1 to 2 hours. Cut in small squares. Garnish with fresh strawberries.

Yield: 7 to 8 dozen   *Cassie Kelly Cunningham*

Creole Porcupines
A traditional New Orleans cookie

3 tablespoons butter,
melted (no substitute)
1 cup brown sugar, firmly
packed
2 eggs, well beaten

1½ cups pecans, chopped
1 cup dates, chopped
3 cups coconut, shredded
and divided

Preheat oven to 300°. Melt butter and stir into sugar; beat in eggs. Add pecans, dates and 1 cup of the coconut. Form into small balls and roll in the remaining 2 cups of coconut. Place on a greased baking sheet and bake until cookies just begin to brown lightly, about 25 minutes.

Yield: 4 dozen   *Donna Owenby Harbin*

Creme De Menthe Brownies
As featured in Southern Living!

1 cup butter or margarine,
   softened and divided
1 cup sugar
4 eggs
1 cup flour
½ teaspoon salt
1 (16-ounce) can chocolate
   syrup

1 teaspoon vanilla extract
2 cups powdered sugar,
   sifted
2 tablespoons creme de
   menthe
1 (6-ounce) package
   semi-sweet chocolate
   morsels

Preheat oven to 350°. Grease and flour a 13 x 9 x 2-inch baking pan. Cream ½ cup butter; gradually add 1 cup sugar, beating until light and fluffy. Add eggs, one at a time, beating well after each addition. Combine flour and salt; add to the creamed mixture alternately with chocolate syrup, begining and ending with flour mixture. Stir in vanilla. Pour batter into prepared pan. Bake at 350° for 25 to 28 minutes. Cool completely. (Brownies will shrink from sides of pan while cooling.) Cream ¼ cup butter, gradually add 2 cups powdered sugar and creme de menthe, mixing well. Spread evenly over brownies; chill about 1 hour. Combine chocolate morsels and remaining ¼ cup butter in top of double boiler; bring water to a boil. Reduce heat to low; cook until chocolate melts. Spread over brownies; chill for at least 1 hour. Cut into squares. *Variation:* Grand Marnier can by substituted for creme de menthe.
Yield: 3½ dozen brownies   *Susan Gann Brasfield*

Forgotten Cookies
Bake while you sleep

2 egg whites
⅔ cup sugar
Pinch of salt
1 cup chocolate chips

½ cup nuts, finely
   chopped
1 teaspoon vanilla

Preheat oven to 350°. Beat the egg whites until stiff. Gradually add sugar, beating well. Add a pinch of salt. Fold in chocolate chips, nuts and vanilla. Drop by teaspoonfuls onto ungreased foil lined cookie sheet and place in preheated oven. Turn oven off, close the door and leave cookies inside for about 8 hours.
Yield: 3 dozen   *Leckie Kern Stack*

1898 Tea Cakes
Featured in the Marietta Daily Journal

Cake:

1 cup butter (no substitute), softened
2 cups sugar
1 teaspoon soda
1 egg

½ cup buttermilk
4 cups flour
2 teaspoons vanilla extract
1 teaspoon almond extract
½ teaspoon salt

Icing:

3 cups confectioners' sugar
6 tablespoons half and half
1½ teaspoons vanilla extract
1½ teaspoons almond extract

Food colorings of your choice
Decorations of your choice
Paintbrushes

Preheat oven to 350°. Cream butter and sugar; add egg, almond and vanilla extracts and mix well. Dissolve soda in buttermilk; add salt to flour. Alternate adding buttermilk and flour to creamed mixture. Refrigerate for at least one hour before rolling out. Roll out on floured board until ⅛ inch or less in thickness. Cut out with cookie cutters and place on a greased cookie sheet. Bake at 350° for 10 minutes.

For icing, mix sugar, half and half, and extracts. Divide between several bowls. Add different food colorings to each bowl; leave one bowl white. Cover kitchen table well with brown paper. Put out paint brushes, icings, a variety of decorations and cookies, and let the kids be creative!

Yield: 3 to 4 dozen

Lanier Scott Hoy

Emily's Almond Cookies

1 cup sugar	1 teaspoon almond extract
1 cup margarine, softened	2 cups flour, unsifted
1 egg	½ teaspoon salt
½ teaspoon vanilla extract	½ teaspoon baking soda

Preheat oven to 400°. Cream together sugar, margarine and egg, add vanilla and almond extracts. Blend together flour, salt and baking soda, add these ingredients to the creamed mixture. Stir. After dough is thoroughly mixed, pinch off enough to make a walnut-sized ball. Place balls on an ungreased cookie sheet about 2 inches apart. Dip the bottom of a juice glass in water, then in a bowl with sugar. Press each ball with glass just until dough forms a circle. Dip glass into sugar each time. Bake for 8 minutes. Cool on rack.

Yield: 4 dozen
Barbara Gully Allen

Fruitcake Cookies

2 pounds dates, chopped	2 teaspoons cinnamon
½ pound candied red cherries, chopped	1 teaspoon allspice
1 pound candied mixed fruit	1 teaspoon nutmeg, freshly grated
4 cups English walnuts, chopped	1 cup butter, softened
3½ cups flour	1½ cups sugar
1 teaspoon soda	2 eggs
1 teaspoon salt	

Preheat oven to 325°. Mix fruits and nuts in a large bowl. Combine flour, soda, salt, cinnamon, allspice and nutmeg, sift over fruit and nuts. Stir well. Cream butter and sugar until light and fluffy. Add eggs, beat well. Add to fruit mixture and mix well by hand. Drop by teaspoonfuls onto a lightly greased cookie sheet. Bake for 15 to 17 minutes. Do not overcook, these cookies should be chewy, not hard.

Yield: 12 dozen
Pamela Croy Newton

Jelly Tart Cookies

2½ cups flour
¼ teaspoon baking
  powder
½ teaspoon salt
1 cup shortening
2 teaspoons vanilla extract

½ cup confectioners'
  sugar, sifted
2 tablespoons milk
Strawberry jelly or
  preserves

Sift together flour, baking powder and salt. Mix shortening, vanilla and sugar until creamy. Blend into flour mixture; add milk. Chill until easy to handle. Preheat oven to 350°. On lightly floured board, roll dough to ¼ inch thickness. Cut 2½ inch rounds. Cut ¾ inch circle from the center of half of the rounds. Place on an ungreased cookie sheet 1 inch apart. Bake at 350° for 15 minutes. Cool. Place 1 teaspoon of jelly on whole rounds, top with rounds with hole in center. Sprinkle with sifted confectioners' sugar.
Yield: 1 dozen   *Carole Feledik Templeman*

Kids' Favorite Chocolate Cookies

1 (18.5-ounce) package
  chocolate cake mix with
  pudding
1 (8-ounce) container
  whipped topping, thawed

1 egg
Confectioners' sugar

Preheat oven to 350°. Grease cookie sheets lightly. Combine cake mix, whipped topping and egg in large bowl. Stir until well mixed. (This will be a very sticky mixture). Drop by teaspoonfuls on cookie sheet. Sift confectioners' sugar over cookies. Bake 10 to 12 minutes at 350°. Do not overbake....the best cookie is a soft cookie! *Variation:* Lemon cake mix may be substituted for the chocolate mix.
Yield: 4 dozen   *Debbie Lewis Mitchell*

Kookie Brittle

1 cup margarine, softened
1½ teaspoons vanilla
1 teaspoon salt
1 (6-ounce) package
  semi-sweet chocolate
  chips

1 cup sugar
2 cups flour, sifted
½ cups pecans, finely
  chopped

Preheat oven to 375°. Combine margarine, vanilla and salt in large bowl; blend well. Gradually beat in sugar. Add flour and chocolate chips; mix well. Press evenly into ungreased 15 x 10 x 1-inch pan. Sprinkle pecans over top. Bake at 375° for 25 minutes. Allow to cool and break into pieces, or cut into even squares while still hot.
Yield: 5 dozen

Nancy Marlow

Melt-A-Ways
These are guaranteed to melt in your mouth

¾ cup butter, no
  substitutes
½ cup confectioners'
  sugar, sifted

1 teaspoon vanilla extract
1 cup flour
½ cup cornstarch
Confectioners' sugar

Cream butter; gradually add confectioners' sugar and beat until light and fluffy. Stir in vanilla. Combine flour and cornstarch; add to creamed mixture and stir well. Chill for 1 hour. Divide dough in half. Shape each half into a 5 inch long roll. Wrap in wax paper, then in aluminum foil; freeze for 24 hours. Preheat oven to 375°. Cut dough into ¼ inch slices; place 1 inch apart on an ungreased cookie sheet. Bake for 8 to 10 minutes. Cool. Dust finished cookies with confectioners' sugar.
Yield: 3 dozen

Lynn Stiles Foster

Oatmeal Caramel Brownies

1 (14-ounce) package
  caramels
⅓ cup milk
2 cups flour
2 cups oats, uncooked
1 cup brown sugar, firmly
  packed
1 teaspoon baking soda

½ teaspoon salt
1 egg, slightly beaten
1 cup butter or margarine,
  softened
1 (12-ounce) package
  semi-sweet chocolate
  chips

Preheat oven to 350°. Combine caramels and milk in saucepan; cook over low heat, stirring constantly, until caramels melt. Set aside. Combine flour, oats, brown sugar, soda and salt. Add egg and butter, stirring until mixture is crumbly. Press half of mixture into greased 9 x 13-inch pan. Bake at 350° for 10 minutes. Sprinkle chips over crumbs and pour caramel mixture evenly on top. Sprinkle on remaining crumb mixture. Return to oven for 20 to 25 minutes. Cool and cut into bars. Chill 8 hours, then store at room temperature. These freeze well.

Yield: 3 dozen   *Ann Bramblett Fowler*

Never Fail Divinity

A microwave version of an old favorite

4 cups sugar
1 cup light corn syrup
¾ cup water
Dash of salt

3 egg whites
1 teaspoon vanilla
½ cup pecans, chopped

Combine sugar, corn syrup, water and salt in 2 quart casserole. Microwave on high for 19 minutes, stirring every 5 minutes or to 260° on candy thermometer. Beat egg whites until very stiff. Pour hot syrup gradually over egg whites, beating at high speed for about 12 minutes or until thick and candy begins to lose gloss. Fold in vanilla and pecans. Drop by small spoonfuls onto wax paper.

Yield: 6 dozen   *Carol Ann Evans Garrett*

Potato Chip Cookies

1 pound butter, softened
1 cup sugar
3¼ cups flour
1 teaspoon vanilla

1½ cups potato chips,
coarsley crushed
Confectioners' sugar

Preheat oven to 300°. Cream butter and sugar. Slowly blend in flour and vanilla. Gently fold into potato chips. Drop dough by well-rounded teaspoons onto ungreased cookie sheet. Wet a fork to prevent sticking and flatten cookies gently. Bake 15 to 20 minutes until just barely browned. Cool and sprinkle with confectioners' sugar.

Yield: 4 to 5 dozen   *Stephanie Threlkeld Gill*

Sand Tarts

5 tablespoons
confectioners' sugar
¾ cup margarine, softened

2 tablespoons vanilla
2 cups flour
1 cup nuts, finely chopped

Preheat oven to 275°. In food processor, chop nuts and add flour to mix well. Set aside. In mixing bowl, mix margarine, sugar and vanilla. Add the flour and nuts and mix well. Dough will be stiff. Roll a small amount of dough (about 2 teaspoons) in hands to form half moon shape. Bake on ungreased cookie sheet at 275° for 30 minutes. Roll crescents in confectioners' sugar while hot. *Great for Christmas goodies.*

Yield: 4 to 5 dozen   *Martha Jones Byrd*

Sour Cream Apple Squares

2 cups flour
2 cups firmly packed
  brown sugar
½ cup margarine, softened
1 cup English walnuts,
  chopped
1 to 2 teaspoons
  cinnamon
1 teaspoon baking soda

½ teaspoon salt
1 cup sour cream
1 teaspoon vanilla
1 egg
2 cups peeled apples,
  finely chopped
Whipped cream or ice
  cream (optional)

Preheat oven to 350°. Lightly spoon flour into measuring cup and level off. In large bowl, combine first three ingredients and blend until crumbly. Stir in nuts. Press 2¾ cups crumb mixture into ungreased 13 x 9-inch pan. To remaining mixture, add cinnamon, soda, salt, sour cream, vanilla and egg. Blend well, then stir in apples. Spoon evenly over base. Bake 25 to 35 minutes. Cut into squares. Serve warm or cold with whipped cream or ice cream.
Yield: 2 to 3 dozen   *Donya Smith Rickman*

Sabre Meringues
Very fancy and different

½ cup butter, softened
1 cup sugar
2 eggs, separated
1 teaspoon vanilla
2 cups flour

1 teaspoon baking powder
1 teaspoon salt
1 jar raspberry jelly
½ cup sugar
Chopped nuts

Preheat oven to 350°. Cream butter and sugar. Add egg yolks and vanilla. Sift flour, baking powder, and salt; add to creamed mixture. Pat into greased jelly roll pan. Bake 10 minutes. Remove from oven and spread jelly on top of first layer. Beat two egg whites until stiff adding ½ cup sugar. Spread over jelly. Sprinkle with chopped nuts. Bake for 20 to 25 minutes. Cut into bars and cool.
Yield: 2 dozen   *Ruth Ellen Philpot Compton*

Toffee Bars
These freeze well!

2 cups flour
1¾ cups light brown sugar
1½ cups butter (no
  substitute)

1 cup pecans, chopped
1 (6-ounce) package
  semi-sweet chocolate
  chips

Preheat oven to 350°. Mix flour and 1 cup brown sugar; cut in ½ cup butter. Press mixture into a 9 x 13-inch ungreased metal pan. Sprinkle pecans over this mixture. Bring to a boil butter and remaining sugar and boil exactly one minute, stirring constantly. Pour over pressed mixture and bake exactly 20 minutes. Let sit one minute; then sprinkle with chocolate chips. When completely softened, spread the chocolate with a spatula. Chill thoroughly; return to room temperature before cutting.

Yield: 3 dozen
Meredith Webb Dykes

Apple Sour Cream Pie

2 (9-inch) pie shells,
  unbaked
4 cups apples, diced
1½ cups sugar

4 tablespoons flour
2 cups sour cream
2 eggs, beaten
1 teaspoon vanilla

Topping:
1 cup sugar
2 teaspoons cinnamon

6 tablespoons flour
½ cup butter

Preheat oven to 400°. In large mixing bowl, mix sugar and flour; add apples, sour cream, eggs, and vanilla. Pour into pie shells and bake for 30 minutes at 400°. Mix all topping ingredients and set aside. Remove pies from oven and sprinkle with topping; replace in oven for 10 additional minutes.

Yield: 2 (9-inch) pies
Kristine Reed Maedel

Bama Chess Pie
Even Georgia fans will be delighted!

6 tablespoons butter or
  margarine, melted
1 cup sugar
3 eggs, beaten

1 tablespoon vanilla
1 tablespoon white vinegar
1 (9-inch) unbaked pie
  shell

Preheat oven to 325°. Mix sugar, beaten eggs and butter. Add vanilla and vinegar; mix well. Pour into unbaked pie shell and bake at 325° for 45 minutes to one hour.
Yield: 8 servings   *Patricia Wilson George*

Coconut Pie
So easy and so delicious!

2 eggs
1 cup sugar
¼ cup margarine, melted
½ cup buttermilk

1 teaspoon vanilla extract
½ cup coconut (or more if
  desired)
Unbaked pie shell

Preheat oven to 350°. Beat eggs and add remaining ingredients, mix well. Pour into unbaked pie shell; bake 45 minutes.
Yield: 6 servings   *Roddy Thomas Hiser*

Cranberry Nut Pie
Great for the holidays

2 cups fresh cranberries,
  chopped
½ cup walnuts, chopped
½ cup sugar
1 cup flour
1 cup sugar

¾ cup margarine, melted
2 eggs
2 teaspoons almond
  extract
Whipped cream or vanilla
  ice cream (optional)

Preheat oven to 325°. Mix cranberries, walnuts and ½ cup sugar; spread in bottom of greased 10-inch pie pan. Mix remaining ingredients and pour over cranberry nut mixture. Bake 55 to 60 minutes at 325°. Serve with whipped cream or vanilla ice cream.
Yield: 8 to 10 servings   *Suzy Burt Crenshaw*

Chocolate Mousse Pie
"Elegant"

⅔ (8½-ounce) package
  chocolate wafers
2 tablespoons butter,
  melted
8 eggs, separated, at room
  temperature
1½ cups plus 3
  tablespoons sugar
2 teaspoons vanilla
¼ teaspoon salt

½ cup brandy
10 ounces unsweetened
  chocolate
2 ounces semi-sweet
  chocolate
¾ cup butter, softened
¼ cup coffee
1½ cups whipping cream
Cherry cordials (optional)

Preheat oven to 325°. Grind chocolate wafers until very fine. Combine butter with crumbs and pat sides and bottom of buttered 9-inch springform pan. Bake at 325° for 10 minutes. Remove and cool. Combine egg yolks, 1½ cups sugar, vanilla, salt and brandy in top of double boiler. Place over simmering water and beat until pale yellow and thick, about 8 to 10 minutes. Remove from water and set aside. Melt both types of chocolate in top of double boiler over hot water. When melted, remove from water and beat in butter, a little at a time. Gradually beat chocolate into egg yolk mixture until smooth. Chocolate mixture will congeal and be stiff. Beat in coffee. Beat egg whites (egg whites should be room temperature) into soft peaks. Gradually beat in 3 tablespoons sugar until soft peaks form. Beat 1 cup of beaten egg whites into chocolate mixture to thin it; carefully fold in remaining beaten egg whites until well blended. Whip the cream until stiff and fold into chocolate mixture. Pour into prepared crust and chill overnight in refrigerator. Garnish with cordials (optional—directions follow).

Cherry Cordials:
10 to 15 maraschino
  cherries with steams
½ cup brandy

5 ounces semi-sweet
  chocolate

Soak cherries in brandy and put in freezer. Melt 5 ounces semi-sweet chocolate. When cherries are frozen, dip into chocolate until cherry is covered. Place on wax paper and refrigerate until needed.

Yield: 10 servings   *Nancy Finke Rambasek*

Captiva Key Lime Pie

1 (20-ounce) can
  sweetened condensed
  milk
2 eggs
¾ cup key lime juice (may
  substitute regular lime
  juice)

1 (9-inch) graham cracker
  pie shell
Whipped cream (optional)
Lime slices (optional)

Preheat oven to 350°. Mix first 3 ingredients well and pour into pie shell. Bake at 350° for 20 minutes. Chill for 4 to 5 hours. Garnish with fresh whipped cream and/or lime slices.
Yield: 6 to 8 servings   *Beth Rambo Drew*

Deep Dish Peach Cobbler

2 cups fresh peaches,
  peeled and sliced (fresh
  peaches are best but
  when they cannot be
  found use frozen)

1 to 1½ cups sugar
½ teaspoon cinnamon
½ teaspoon almond
  flavoring

Crust:
½ cup butter
¾ cup flour
2 teaspoons baking
  powder

Pinch salt
¾ cup milk

Preheat oven to 350°. Put peaches, sugar, cinnamon and almond flavoring in a bowl and stir until well mixed or coated. In oven, melt butter in a deep baking pan (7 x 12). In a medium bowl, stir remaining ingredients together except peach mixture. Pour batter over melted butter. Make sure the batter is evenly distributed, but do not stir. Carefully place peaches on top of the buttered batter. Any sugar that is left should be sprinkled evenly over the peaches. Do not stir. Bake for 1 hour at 350°. Surprise! The peaches go to the bottom and the crust rises to the top. This recipe can be doubled. If you like an extremely thick crust, use a slightly small pan.
Yield: 6 servings   *Bruce Goode Boling*

Dutchess Blackberry Cream Pie

1 (9-inch) pie shell,
unbaked
1 quart fresh or frozen
blackberries, (may
substitute blueberries)
1 cup thick sour cream
1¼ cups sugar

1 cup flour, sifted
¼ teaspoon salt
2 tablespoons fine dry
breadcrumbs
2 tablespoons sugar
1 tablespoon butter,
melted

Preheat oven to 450°. Sort, rinse and drain berries and put into pie shell. Place sour cream in bowl. Sift sugar, flour and salt together; gradually add to sour cream. Spoon mixture over berries, spreading into an even layer. Mix bread crumbs, sugar and butter together; sprinkle over sour cream. Bake at 450° for 10 minutes. Reduce heat to 350° and bake 30 minutes longer. Cool before cutting and serving.

Yield: 6 to 8 servings
Jeanne Powell Orman

Fudge Pie
Sinfully delicious

½ cup butter
2 squares semi-sweet
chocolate
2 eggs
1 cup sugar
¼ cup flour

1 teaspoon vanilla
Pinch of salt
1 cup pecans, chopped
Vanilla ice cream or
whipped cream
(optional)

Preheat oven to 350°. Melt butter and chocolate in microwave until soft. Beat eggs until light; gradually add sugar, beating until fluffy. Add flour, vanilla and salt. Stir in melted butter and chocolate. Add pecans. Pour into ungreased 8-inch pie plate; bake at 350° for 20 to 25 minutes. Serve warm with vanilla ice cream or a dollop of whipped cream. *Variation:* You may easily double this recipe. Bake in 10-inch pie plate at 350° for 30 minutes.

Yield: 6 servings
Betty Neel Cobb Lawton

German Chocolate Meringue Pie
Just what company needs!

Crust:
4 egg whites
¼ teaspoon salt
¼ teaspoon cream of
tartar
1 cup sugar

1 cup pecans, finely
chopped
1 teaspoon vanilla

Filling:
2 (4-ounce) packages
sweet German Chocolate
6 tablespoons water

2 teaspoons vanilla
2 cups whipping cream

Combine egg whites, salt and cream of tartar; beat until foamy throughout. Add sugar, 2 tablespoons at a time, beating after each addition until sugar is blended and mixture is stiff. Fold in nuts and vanilla. Spoon into a lightly greased 9 or 10-inch pie plate, reserving part for shell - like rim. Drop meringue by teaspoonfuls around rim of pie plate in the form of a teardrop. Bake at 300° (do not preheat oven) for 50 to 55 minutes. Cool. Place chocolate and water in a saucepan and melt over low heat (also can be done in a microwave oven). Cool; add vanilla. Whip cream to soft consistency; fold in chocolate and pile into shell. Chill 2 hours before serving.
Yield: 6 to 8 servings   *Cathy Sears Huff*

Gerry McCloud's Sweet Potato Pie
A Special Fall Treat

1 (9-inch) unbaked pie
shell
1½ cups sugar
3 eggs
1½ cups sweet potatoes,
cooked and mashed

1 teaspoon vanilla extract
½ cup butter, softened or
melted
1 small can evaporated
milk
Whipped cream (optional)

Preheat oven to 350°. Cream sugar and egg. Add potatoes, vanilla extract, and butter, mix well. Add evaporated milk and mix. Bake for one hour.
Yield: 6 to 8 servings   *Adrian Winship Pressley*

Japanese Fruit Pie

½ cup margarine
2 cups sugar
4 eggs
1 tablespoon vinegar
1 tablespoon vanilla
extract

1 (8-ounce) can crushed
pineapple
1 cup coconut, shredded
1 cup pecans, chopped
2 (9-inch) pie crusts

Preheat oven to 350°. Mix together first five ingredients. Add remaining ingredients and mix well. Pour into the 2 (9-inch) pie crusts and bake 30 minutes at 350°.
Yield: 2 (9-inch) pies

Lorene Orr

Katie's Old Fashion Lemon Pie

1 envelope unflavored
gelatin
½ cup sugar
½ teaspoon salt
4 egg yolks
⅓ cup lemon juice
⅔ cup water
1 teaspoon grated lemon
rind

4 egg whites
½ cup sugar
1 cup whipping cream,
whipped
1 baked pie shell
Whipped cream, kiwi,
strawberries or cherries
(optional)

In saucepan, mix gelatin, ½ cup sugar and ½ teaspoon salt. Beat together 4 egg yolks, ⅓ cup lemon juice, ⅔ cup water and stir into gelatin mixture. Cook and stir over medium heat just until mixture boils. Remove from heat and stir in 1 teaspoon grated lemon rind. Chill, stirring occasionally until partially set. Beat 4 egg whites until soft peaks form. Gradually add ½ cup sugar, beating until stiff peaks form. Fold in gelatin mixture. Fold in 1 cup whipping cream, whipped. Pour into baked pie shell. Refrigerate for at least 5 hours. Garnish with whipped cream and kiwi, strawberries, or cherries. *Variation:* Lime may be substituted for lemon.
Yield: 6 to 8 servings

Lynn Stiles Foster

Mama's Sour Cream Pie

Crust:

1¼ cups graham cracker
   crumbs
¼ cup sugar

¼ cup margarine, softened
Dash of cinnamon

Filling:

3 (3-ounce) packages
   cream cheese
⅔ cup sugar
2 eggs

1 teaspoon vanilla extract
1 cup sour cream
2 tablespoons sugar

Preheat oven to 350°.
Crust: Mix together crust ingredients, press into a 9-inch pie pan and bake 10 minutes.
Filling: Cream cream cheese and sugar together until smooth. Add the eggs and vanilla extract; beat until smooth. Pour into crust. Bake 20 minutes. Remove from oven and let cool slightly, then top with 1 cup sour cream mixed with 2 tablespoons sugar. Return to oven and bake 5 minutes longer. Chill well before serving.
Yield: 8 servings   *Marsha Brown Thomas*

Mom's Whiskey Pie
Delicious in winter, warmed and served with coffee

4 eggs
1½ cups sugar
1 tablespoon vinegar
4 tablespoons bourbon
6 tablespoons butter,
   melted

1 (9-inch) unbaked pie
   shell
Whipped cream, (optional)

Preheat oven to 325°. Beat eggs until light. Gradually add sugar until fluffy. Add vinegar, boubon and butter; mix well. Pour into unbaked pie shell; bake for 30 minutes until light brown on top. Serve with whipped cream.
Yield: 6 to 8 servings   *Betty Neel Cobb Lawton*

Marietta Mud Pie

Crust:
5 ounces Oreo cookies
2 tablespoons butter,
  softened

Filling:

15 ounces chocolate ice
  cream, softened
2 tablespoons coffee
  (ground)
2 tablespoons
  decaffeinated coffee
2 tablespoons whipped
  cream

2 tablespoons brandy
2 tablespoons Kahlua
1 (12-ounce) jar fudge
  sauce
1 (8-ounce) container
  whipped topping
1 (6-ounce) jar maraschino
  cherries

Crush oreos very fine, mix with butter and press into a 9-inch pie pan; freeze. Whip chocolate ice cream with ground coffee, decaffeinated coffee, brandy and Kahlua; fold in whipped cream. Fold mixture into pie shell and freeze until firm. Then cover surface with fudge sauce and return to freezer. To serve, remove from freezer and top with a dollop of whipped cream and a cherry.

Yield: 6 to 8 servings   *Susan Safran Potter*

Mother's Pecan Pie
A family favorite

2 (9-inch) pie shells,
  unbaked
½ cup butter, melted
1 (16-ounce) box light
  brown sugar

4 eggs
2 tablespoons water
2 tablespoons corn meal
2 cups pecans, chopped
1 tablespoons vanilla

Preheat oven to 375°. Combine all ingredients and pour into pie shells. Bake at 375° for 15 minutes. Reduce temperature to 350° and continue baking for 30 minutes. Check for doneness.

Yield: 2 (9-inch) pies   *Sybil Kendall Little*

Mocha Alaska Pie

Crust:

1 cup chocolate wafer
cookies, finely crushed

¼ cup butter, melted
1 tablespoon sugar

Filling:

1 quart coffee ice cream,
slightly softened

1 (5½-ounce) can
chocolate sauce
½ cup chopped nuts

Meringue:

3 egg whites
½ teaspoon vanilla extract

¼ teapoon cream of tartar
6 tablespoons sugar

Preheat oven to 350°. Mix together ingredients for crust. Press evenly over bottom and up sides of a 9-inch pie pan. Bake for 10 minutes, let cool.

Filling: Spread ice cream in crust and freeze until firm. Drizzle chocolate sauce evenly over ice cream. Sprinkle with nuts. Freeze until firm.

Meringue: With an electric mixer beat egg whites, vanilla extract and cream of tartar until soft peaks form. Add sugar one tablespoon at a time, beating one minute after each addition, until soft peaks form. Swirl meringue evenly over pie, sealing to the edge of crust and return to freezer. When frozen, wrap lightly but air tight, at least overnight. To serve, place frozen pie, uncovered in a 450° oven for 4 minutes or until golden.

Yield: 6 to 8 servings   *Jill Harper White*

Perfect Pie Crust

4 cups unsifted flour	1 tablespoon white vinegar
1 tablespoon sugar	1 large egg
2 teaspoons salt	½ cup water
1¾ cups Crisco	

In a large mixing bowl, combine 4 cups flour, 1 tablespoon sugar and 2 teaspoons salt. Add Crisco and mix with a fork until ingredients are crumbly. In a separate small bowl, beat the following together with a fork; 1 tablespoon white vinegar, 1 large egg and ½ cup water. Combine the two mixtures, stirring with a fork until completely moistened. Divide dough into five equal portions. Shape each portion into a flat patty for rolling. Wrap each patty in plastic wrap and chill for at least 30 minutes, or overnight. When ready to roll pie crust, lightly flour both sides of patty and roll out. This recipe makes 5 to 7 crusts. The dough patties will keep a week or longer in refrigerator before cooking or rolling out. You may choose to roll out patties and put in aluminum pie pans for freezing. When ready to use, remove from freezer and allow to thaw. For flakier crust, lightly bake, but do not brown.

Yield: 5 to 7 pie crusts   *Paulette Riley Gebhardt*

Rum Pie

1 envelope unflavored gelatin	2 (8-inch) chocolate pie shells (may substitute graham cracker pie shells)
½ cup cold water	
5 egg yolks	
1 cup sugar	Whipped cream (optional)
⅓ cup dark rum	Unsweetened chocolate,
1½ cups whipping cream	shaved (optional)

Soften gelatin in ½ cup cold water. Place on low heat and bring almost to a low boil, stirring to dissolve. Beat egg yolks and sugar until lemon-colored. Stir gelatin into egg mixture and cool. Gradually add rum, beating constantly. Whip cream until it stands in peaks and fold into gelatin mixture. Cool until mixture begins to set, then spoon into crust and chill overnight. Garnish with whipped cream and shaved chocolate.

Yield: 2 (8-inch) pies   *Laura Phillips Lewis*

Whipped Strawberry Pie

1 (9-inch) graham cracker crust (reserve some crumbs to decorate top of pie, if desired)
3 eggs, separated
¾ cup sugar, divided
¼ teaspoon salt
2 teaspoons lemon juice
1 cup strawberries, crushed
2 tablespoons strawberry juice, heated
4 tablespoons strawberry-flavored gelatin
⅓ cup heavy cream, whipped
¼ teaspoon cream of tartar

In a saucepan, combine egg yolks, half the sugar, salt, lemon juice and strawberries. Cook over low heat, stirring constantly until the mixture boils. Remove from heat, and add the juice and gelatin. Chill until partially set. Beat with hand beater. Fold in whipped cream. Beat egg whites with remaining sugar and cream of tartar until stiff. Fold into strawberry mixture. Pour into pie crust; chill.
Yield: 6 to 8 servings

Virginia Jones Eubanks

Fat Man's Misery

14 Oreo cookies
½ cup butter
1 cup confectioners' sugar
1 egg
A few drops of almond flavoring
1 pint whipping cream
½ tablespoon sugar
1 teaspoon vanilla
1 cup pecans, chopped

Crush Oreo cookies. Line a 9-inch pie pan or an 8-inch square pan with most of the crumbs. Reserve a few for the topping. Cream butter and sugar; add egg and cream again. Add almond flavoring and spread mixture over cookie crumbs. Whip cream with sugar; add vanilla and pecans. Fold until well blended. Spread this over first mixture. Cover with remaining crumbs. Refrigerate for 24 hours.
Yield: 6 to 8 servings

Cathy Colquitt

Praline Pumpkin Pie
"A Thanksgiving Special"

1 (10-inch) pie shell, baked
¼ cup butter, melted
½ cup sugar
1 cup pecans, chopped
1 envelope unflavored gelatin
½ cup cold water
¾ cup light brown sugar
1 (1-pound) can of pumpkin (not pie mix)
¼ cup milk
½ teaspoon salt
1 teaspoon cinnamon
¾ to 1 teaspoon freshly grated nutmeg
¼ teaspoon ground allspice
1 cup heavy cream, whipped

Mix butter, sugar and pecans in skillet and sauté, stirring until golden (3 or 4 minutes). Turn onto foil or wax paper to cool, then crumble. Mix gelatin with water. Place over heat and stir until dissolved. Remove from heat. Add brown sugar, mix in pumpkin, milk and spices. Fold in whipped cream. Place half of the crumbled pecan mixture into bottom of baked pie shell. Add filling and refrigerate until pie is set and then add remaining pecan mixture to the top for garnish. Serve with a dollop of real whipped cream.
Yield: 8 to 10 serivngs

Pamela Croy Newton

Bananas Flambé

4 firm ripe bananas
¼ cup butter
½ cup brown sugar, firmly packed
½ teaspoon cinnamon
½ cup rum
6 scoops vanilla ice cream (about 1½ pints)

Peel bananas and cut in half crosswise, then cut each piece in half lengthwise, set aside. Combine butter, brown sugar and cinnamon in skillet; heat, stirring constantly over low flame until mixture becomes a smooth syrup. Add banana pieces and baste them with syrup for 3 to 4 minutes. Remove from heat. In a small pan, heat rum until warm. Pour over bananas and carefully light with a match. Using a long handled spoon, baste bananas with sauce until flame dies. To serve, place ice cream in individual dessert dishes and top with bananas and sauce.
Yield: 4 servings

Judy Thomas Ballard

Apple Apricot Almond Tart
Apple-Betty Bake-Off Winner, 1985

Pastry:

1½ cups flour, unsifted	1 tablespoon sugar
1 cup almonds (ground)	½ cup butter
pinch of salt	4 tablespoons ice water

Filling:

6 to 8 medium tart apples	2 tablespoons flour
1 small jar apricot jam	1 tablespoon water
1 lemon	confectioners' sugar

For Pastry, mix almonds, flour, salt, sugar, and butter. Add ice water until consistency forms a ball. (Pastry may also be made in food processor). Refrigerate. Cut ¼ of pastry and save for lattice on top. Preheat oven to 425°. Roll out pastry on floured board and place in 10-inch tart pan. Place foil over pastry and fill with beans or weights and bake at 425° for 10 to 12 minutes. Carefully remove beans or weights and cool.

For Filling, grate rind and squeeze juice of lemon into a bowl. Peel, core and thinly slice apples into the bowl. Sprinkle with flour and toss to coat apples with flour and lemon juice. Arrange apple slices over tart in pan. Dissolve apricot jam with 1 tablespoon water. Pour or brush ¾ of the jam over apple slices. Roll out remaining pastry and cut into ½ inch strips. Place slices 1½ inches apart to form a lattice effect. Glaze with remaining apricot jam. Bake at 375° for 30 to 40 minutes until golden brown. Serve hot or cold; dust with confectioners' sugar.

Yield: 8 to 10 servings   *Cathy Sears Huff*

Amaretto Ice Cream

1 cup whipping cream	⅓ cup toasted almonds,
1 pint vanilla ice cream	chopped
¼ cup Amaretto	

Leave ice cream in refrigerator (not freezer) for a couple of hours until soft enough to stir. Beat cream until stiff. Combine cream, ice cream and Amaretto. Freeze until firm (may be frozen in individual serving cups or stemmed glasses). To serve, drizzle additional Amaretto over the top of each individual serving and sprinkle with toasted almonds.

Yield: 4 to 6 servings   *Leckie Kern Stack*

Black Bottoms

Vanilla Batter:
1 (8-ounce) package cream cheese, softened
1 egg, beaten
⅓ cup sugar

⅛ teaspoon salt
1 (12-ounce) package chocolate chips

Chocolate Batter:
1½ cups flour
1 cup sugar
¼ cup cocoa
½ teaspoon salt
1 cup water

1 teaspoon baking soda
⅓ cup oil
1 tablespoon vinegar
1 teaspoon vanilla
1 egg

Preheat oven to 350°. Combine all ingredients in vanilla batter, except chips, until smooth. Add chips and refrigerate. Sift dry ingredients in chocolate batter and set aside. Mix wet ingredients with egg. Combine dry and wet ingredients and stir well. Fill small muffin pans with paper liners. Fill cups halfway with chocolate batter; dab on vanilla batter. Don't fill to top; will rise soon. Bake 15 to 20 minutes at 350°. Refrigerate to keep.
Yield: 7 to 8 dozen   *Judy Gorrell Harper*

Boiled Custard
The best ever!

1 quart half & half
1 cup sugar
5 eggs

3 tablespoons vanilla (not a misprint)

Scald half & half. Beat together sugar and eggs and add to half & half. Cook slowly over a low heat stirring constantly until thickened (about 15 minutes). Add vanilla, refrigerate several hours before serving. This custard makes a wonderful, creamy ice cream, is grand in an English trifle, and also served over strawberries and Kiwi fruit, or fresh raspberries. *Variation:* For strawberry or peach ice cream, decrease vanilla to 1 teaspoon, add 2 cups mashed fresh fruit mixed with ½ cup sugar.
Yield: 6 to 8 servings   *Lanier Scott Hoy*

Caramel Ice Cream Squares

Crust:
2 cups flour
¾ cup oatmeal, uncooked
1 cup margarine, melted

1 cup pecans, chopped
½ cup brown sugar

Filling:
½ gallon (rectangular shape) vanilla ice cream
½ gallon (rectangular shape) chocolate ice cream

1 (12-ounce) jar caramel sauce
1 cup pecans, chopped

Crust: Preheat oven to 400°. Mix together and crumble all crust ingredients and place on a cookie sheet. Bake at 400° for 15 to 20 minutes, stirring to brown evenly. Press half of the mixture in the bottom of a 9 x 13-inch pan. Set aside remaining crust.

Filling: Layer vanilla ice cream over crust by slicing it thinly and placing slices side by side to make a solid layer. (¾ of the half gallon will be used.) Pour caramel sauce, then nuts over vanilla ice cream. Layer chocolate ice cream in the same manner as vanilla ice cream (again, only ¾ of half gallon will be used). Top with remaining crumbs. Cover with foil and freeze for several hours.

Yield: 18 servings *Laura Phillips Lewis*

Kahlua Fondue

1 tablespoon butter
2 squares semi-sweet baking chocolate

1 pint marshmallow creme
¼ cup Kahlua
Assorted fruit for dipping

Melt the butter and chocolate. Add the marshmallow creme and Kahlua. Serve in fondue dish. Dip with fruit (strawberries, bananas, mandarin oranges, apples, pears, etc. Angel food or pound cake cut or torn into bite size pieces may be used also.)

Yield: 6 to 8 servings *Leckie Kern Stack*

Choco-Mint Freeze

1¼ cups crushed vanilla
   wafers (28)
4 tablespoons butter,
   melted
½ cup butter
1 quart peppermint ice
   cream, softened

2 squares unsweetened
   chocolate
3 egg yolks, well beaten
½ cup nuts, chopped
1 teaspoon vanilla extract
3 egg whites
1½ cups confectioners'
   sugar, sifted

Toss wafer crumbs with 4 tablespoons of butter, reserve ¼ of the mixture for the top. Press into a 9x9x2-inch pan. Spread softened ice cream over crust and freeze. Melt chocolate and ½ cup butter over low heat. Beat egg yolks, gradually add chocolate, sugar, nuts and vanilla. Let cool. Beat egg whites; fold into the chocolate mixture. Spread over ice cream and sprinkle with reserved crumbs. Freeze for several hours or overnight. Allow to thaw slightly before cutting into squares.
Yield: 8 servings
Carolyn Cobb Anderson

Chocolate Velvet

Crust:
1½ cups chocolate wafers,
   crushed

⅓ cup margarine, melted

Filling:
1 (8-ounce) package cream
   cheese, softened
½ cup sugar
1 teaspoon vanilla extract
2 eggs, separated

1 (6-ounce) package
   semi-sweet chocolate
   chips, melted
1 cup whipping cream,
   whipped
¾ cup pecans, chopped

Crust: Combine chocolate wafers and margarine, press into the bottom of a 9-inch square pan.
Filling: Combine softened cream cheese, ¼ cup of sugar and vanilla. Stir in 2 beaten egg yolks and melted chocolate. Beat 2 egg whites with the remaining ¼ cup of sugar until the whites form peaks. Fold into chocolate mixture. Fold in whipped cream and chopped pecans. Freeze.
Yield: 9 to 12 servings
Susan Workman Yielding

Easy Chocolate Mousse

⅓ cup hot coffee
1 (6-ounce) package
   semisweet chocolate
   morsels
4 eggs, separated (at room
   temperature)

2 tablespoons cream de
   cacao
Whipped Heaven
(optional-see recipe
below)
Fresh strawberries or kiwi
(optional)

Put coffee and chocolate morsels into blender or food processor and process until smooth. Add egg yolks and creme de cacao and process for about 1 minute. Take egg whites (which should be at room temperature) and beat until stiff peaks form. Fold chocolate mixture and egg whites together by hand. Spoon into stemmed glasses or put entire mixture into a stemmed trifle bowl. Refrigerate until the mousse sets. Before serving top with Whipped Heaven and return to refrigerator to reset. If you like, accompany with a bowl of fresh fruit to the side and let your guests make their own dessert.
Yield: 4 servings

Whipped Heaven:
1 (12-ounce) carton
   whipped topping
1³⁄₁₆ ounce English Toffee
   Bar

3 tablespoons creme de
   cacao

Place whipped topping in large bowl and set aside until soft enough to stir. Place toffee bar in food processor and process until crumbled. Add toffee bar and creme de cacao to whipped topping and stir. Place back in freezer to thicken or until spreading consistency. Use in place of whipped cream. It is good on mousse or try in coffee. Be creative and find new uses or use a different liqueur. *Variation:* Use 1½ tablespoons creme de cacao and 1½ tablespoons brandy for a stronger flavoring, or add more English toffee bar to make it richer.
Yield: 16 ounces   *Bruce Goode Boling*

English Trifle

1 quart custard (recipe follows)
4 tablespoons orange liqueur
3 packages of lady fingers (36) or
2 (9-inch) cake layers
1½ to 2 cups frozen raspberries (drain if not using fresh frozen)
½ cup red raspberry preserves
¼ cup sherry, sweet
1 dozen crumbled almond macaroons
1 cup heavy cream
1 tablespoon sugar
1 teaspoon vanilla extract
toasted sliced almonds

Custard:
7 egg yolks
¾ cup sugar
1 cup hot milk
2 cups heavy cream
1½ teaspoons vanilla

Custard: Beat egg yolks and sugar. Add milk, cream and vanilla and cook in double boiler (uncovered) until thick, stirring constantly. Strain and cool. Add orange liqueur to custard. Line a trifle compote or a crystal bowl with ladyfingers; line bottom of bowl, rounded side of ladyfingers down, then circle ladyfingers with the rounded part to the outside of bowl. Combine raspberry preserves with sherry. Brush cake or ladyfingers with preserves mixture. Pour half of custard over ladyfingers, top with macaroons, then with frozen raspberries. Pour on remaining custard. Top with remaining ladyfingers and brush with preserve mixture. Whip cream with sugar and vanilla. Spread on top of ladyfingers and sprinkle with toasted almonds.
Yield: 12 servings
Pamela Croy Newton

Homemade Fruit Ice Cream
No Cooking!!

4 eggs
½ pint whipping cream
1 cup sugar
1 tablespoon vanilla
2 cans sweetened
  condensed milk

2 cups fruit of your choice,
  mashed, puréed or
  chopped (fresh fruit is
  best, but frozen which
  has been thawed may be
  used)
1½ quarts milk

Combine eggs, cream, sugar and vanilla in bowl; mix thoroughly with electric mixer. Stir in condensed milk and fruit. Pour into 4 quart ice cream mixer. Add dairy milk to the fill line. Churn until frozen.

Variations: Peppermint Candy Ice Cream: Add 1 and ½ cups crushed peppermint stick candy to ice cream after it has churned about 15 minutes. Continue freezing as directed.

Chocolate Chip Ice Cream: Add 1 and ⅔ cups grated semi-sweet chocolate or semi-sweet chocolate morsels to ice cream after it has churned about 15 minutes. Continue freezing as directed.

Yield: 4 quarts   *Meredith Webb Dykes*

Kahlua Mousse

1 cup sugar
1 cup water
1 (12-ounce) package
  semi-sweet chocolate
  pieces
4 eggs
⅓ cup Kahlua

¼ cup brandy
3 cups heavy cream,
  whipped or 16-ounces
  Cool Whip
Shaved chocolate,
  optional

On the top of a double boiler combine sugar and water; stir until sugar is dissolved. Place chocolate and eggs into a blender and blend on low speed. Add the sugar syrup in a steady stream and blend until the mixture is smooth; cool. Add Kahlua and brandy and beat well. Fold into the whipped cream and place in individual souffle dishes. Decorate with shaved chocolate. Place in freezer several hours before serving.

Yield: 10 to 12 servings   *Judy Thomas Ballard*

Lemon Charlotte Russe

This is pretty done in a crystal container.

1 tablespoon unflavored
  gelatin
½ cup cold water
4 large eggs, separated
1 cup sugar

½ cup fresh lemon juice
Grated lemon rind
1 pint whipping cream
2 dozen ladyfingers
¼ cup toasted almonds

Soften gelatin in cold water and dissolve over hot water. Set aside. Beat egg yolks until thick and lemon colored. Add sugar slowly while continuing to beat until stiff. Add lemon juice and grated rind. Continue beating. Add gelatin to egg mixture. Beat egg whites until light and fluffy. Fold into lemon mixture. Whip cream and fold into lemon mixture. Pour into a bowl that is lined on the side and bottom with ladyfingers. Fill bowl half full of custard, add another layer of ladyfingers and fill with custard. Sprinkle top with toasted almonds. Refrigerate 24 hours.
Yield: 10 servings   *Phyllis Royster Rivers*

Nut Torte

3 egg whites
1 cup sugar
½ cup pecans, chopped
¾ cup graham crackers,
  crushed
1 teaspoon baking powder

½ pint carton whipping
  cream
2 teaspoons sugar
Drop of lemon juice
Grated chocolate, optional

Preheat oven to 350°. Grease a 9-inch pie pan and set aside. Stiffly beat the egg whites. Gradually add sugar and pecans. Stir in cracker crumbs and baking powder. Pour into prepared pan and run a knife through batter to release any bubbles. Bake at 350° for 20 to 25 minutes. Combine whipping cream with 2 teaspoons of sugar and a drop of lemon juice. Whip to soft peaks. After torte cools, top with whipped cream and grated chocolate.
Yield: 8 servings   *Marsha Brown Thomas*

Lemon Sherbet
Great for pool or patio!

2½ cups sugar
⅔ cup lemon juice
Grated rind of two lemons

1 quart of milk
1 cup half & half

Mix all together and pour into electric ice cream freezer. Crank away! Garnish with fresh mint.
Yield: 1 quart   *Ginger Byrd McPherson*

Tropical Ice Cream
Perfect for bridge club!

1 quart coffee ice cream
1 package slivered
  almonds, toasted
1 (8-ounce) container
  whipped topping

8 large coconut
  macaroons, toasted and
  crushed
¼ cup Tia Maria (may
  substitute Kahlua)

Mound coffee ice cream by scoops into a dessert bowl. Sprinkle with toasted almonds. Cover with whipped topping. Sprinkle with macaroons and then with Tia Maria. Place in freezer. This recipe can be made in 8 individual dessert bowls. Just divide the ingredients evenly between them.
Yield: 8 servings   *Margaret Seawell Barfield*

Strawberry Sauce

2 cups fresh strawberries
3 tablespoons sugar

3 tablespoons brandy

Wash and hull strawberries. Place in electric blender; blend until smooth. Add sugar and brandy; blend thoroughly.
Yield: 1½ cups   *Claudia Mitchell Owens*

Frosted Oranges
Rich and refreshing!

6 large navel oranges
1 quart vanilla ice cream,
  softened

6 teaspoons Amaretto
4 egg whites
½ cup sugar

Cut bottom of oranges to make them stand level; be careful not to cut through the rind so as to make a hole in the orange. Cut ¾ inch slice off top and clean out membrane. Firmly pack orange shells with ice cream. Make an indentation and add 1 teaspoon of Amaretto. Freeze 4 hours or until firm. Preheat oven to 450°. Beat egg whites until foamy. Gradually add sugar, beating until stiff. Spread over ice cream, sealing at edge. Bake at 450° for 2 to 3 minutes or until lightly browned. Serve immediately.
Yield: 6 servings

Martina Goscha

Frozen Mocha Toffee Dessert

10 to 12 ladyfingers, split
2 tablespoons instant
  coffee crystals
1 tablespoon boiling water
1 quart vanilla ice cream,
  softened

6 chocolate-covered toffee
  bars, frozen and crushed
  (about 1½ cups)
½ cup whipping cream
2 tablespoons white creme
  de cacao

Line the bottom and 2 inches up sides of a 10-inch springform pan with split ladyfingers, cutting to fit. Dissolve the coffee crystals in the 1 tablespoon boiling water. Cool. Stir together coffee, ice cream, and crushed candy. Spoon into springform pan; cover and freeze till firm. Before serving, combine whipping cream and creme de cacao; whip to soft peaks. Spread over top of frozen ice cream layer. Garnish with pieces of additional broken candy bars. *Note:* Substitute flavored instant coffee for regular coffee, if desired.
Yield: 8 to 10 servings

Susan Thomas Burney

Pecan Crunch

½ cup sugar
1 cup pecans, finely
   chopped
1 egg, beaten
1 (3½-ounce) package
   instant vanilla pudding

1 cup sour cream
1 cup milk
1 (8-ounce) carton
   whipped topping
4 bananas, sliced

Preheat oven to 350°. Combine sugar, pecans and egg. Spread onto a cookie sheet which has been lined with foil and greased. Bake at 350° for 15 minutes or until brown. Watch carefully to avoid over-browning. Cool and crumble. Mix pudding, sour cream and milk; add whipped topping. Place half of pecan mixture in bottom of 9x13-inch baking dish. Layer bananas over pecan mixture. Pour pudding mixture over bananas and top with remaining pecan crunch mixture. Cover and refrigerate until ready to serve.

Yield: 8 to 10 servings   *Jane Waters Stoddard*

Spiked Apple Crisp

5 cups apples, peeled and
   diced
½ teaspoon ground
   cinnamon
1 teaspoon grated lemon
   peel
1 teaspoon grated orange
   peel
1-ounce Grand Marnier

1-ounce Amaretto
¾ cup sugar
¼ cup light brown sugar
¾ cup flour
¼ teaspoon salt
½ cup butter, softened
Vanilla ice cream or
   whipped cream

Preheat oven to 350°. Arrange apples in a greased 2-quart casserole. Sprinkle cinnamon, lemon and orange peels, Grand Marnier and Amaretto on top of apples. Combine sugars, flour, salt and butter until crumbly. Spread this mixture over apples. Bake 1 hour or until apples are tender and top is brown. Serve warm with vanilla ice cream or whipped cream.

Yield: 8 servings   *Trish Rogers Elliott*

Sour Cream Banana Crêpés

12 (7-inch) crêpés	4 large ripe bananas
1 cup sour cream	1 cup apricot preserves
2 tablespoons	1 tablespoon brandy
confectioners' sugar	Whipped cream
½ teaspoon cinnamon	

Combine sour cream, sugar and cinnamon in small bowl. Slice 3 bananas and toss with sour cream mixture. Fill each crêpé with about 4 banana slices and about 1 tablespoon sour cream mixture. Roll up and place in baking dish. Refrigerate until serving. Preheat oven to 325°. Heat filled crêpés at 325° for 10 to 15 minutes. Heat apricot preserves until warm, add brandy, slice and add the remaining banana. Serve over crêpés. Top with whipped cream.

Yield: 12 (7-inch) crêpés *Mary Pressley Clayton*

Basic Crêpé Batter

4 eggs	1½ cups flour, sifted
2 cups milk	1 teaspoon salt
2 teaspoons liquid	Liquid margarine
margarine	

In medium bowl beat eggs until foamy; stir in milk and 2 teaspoons liquid margarine. Beat in flour and salt until smooth. Heat 7-inch skillet or crêpé pan until very hot. Brush lightly with liquid margarine. Pour in batter, a scant ¼ cup at a time; quickly tilt pan so batter spreads and covers bottom. Cook over medium to medium-high heat until edges brown; turn and cook about 1 minute longer or until bottom browns. Turn crêpé out onto cookie sheet by flipping pan upside down. Repeat with remaining batter. Crêpés may be frozen between pieces of wax paper.

Yield: 18 crêpés *Emilie Morris Markert*

Strawberries And Cream (My Way)

2 pints fresh strawberries
¼ cup sugar
½ pint whipping cream
½ pint vanilla ice cream,
  softened, but not
  melted

4 tablespoons orange
liqueur
Mint (optional)

Cut berries and sprinkle with sugar early in the day before serving or the night before. Whip cream and mix with ice cream until stiff. Add liqueur and freeze. Serve in sherbet dishes and top with berries. Garnish with mint. (You may double or triple the recipe to have on hand in the freezer and fix berries as needed)
Yield: 6 servings   *Pamela Croy Newton*

Strawberry Tart

4 small baskets of fresh
  strawberries
1 cup butter, softened
½ cup sugar
2½ cups flour
Pinch salt

¾ cup apricot preserves
2 tablespoons water
3 tablespoons Grand
  Marnier
Whipped cream (optional)

It is best to buy the strawberries a day or so in advance, take them out of the baskets, and place them in a bowl to breathe. Preheat oven to 325°. Soften butter; add sugar, flour and salt. Combine into a ball in a bowl and press into the bottom and sides of all 11-inch tart pan. Bake crust at 325° for 30 minutes or less or until lightly browned. After the crust has cooled, wash and hull strawberries. Place them on the crust, flat side down. Heat apricot preserves, water and Grand Marnier to a boil. Strain. Brush or spoon over strawberries, using all of the glaze. Chill 2 hours. Serve with a dollop of whipped cream.
Yield: 10 to 12 servings   *Mary Pressley Clayton*

Hot Fudge Sauce

1 cup sugar
2 tablespoons cocoa
¼ cup milk
¼ cup whipping cream
2 tablespoons light corn
 syrup

1 tablespoon butter or
 margarine
½ tablespoon vanilla
 extract
Pecan pieces, optional

Combine sugar and cocoa; gradually stir in milk. Add cream, syrup and butter; mix well. Bring to a boil over medium heat, stirring constantly; reduce heat, and simmer 10 minutes without stirring. Remove from heat, and stir in vanilla. Serve warm over vanilla ice cream. Top with pecans if desired.
Yield: 1 cup   *Marilyn Simon Massey*

Peach Sauce
Makes a great housewarming gift.

6 cups fresh peaches,
 sliced
1 cup water

⅓ cup sugar
⅛ teaspoon ground
 cinnamon

Combine peaches and water in a large saucepan; cook over medium heat 5 minutes. Reduce heat; cover and simmer 10 minutes. Cool. Combine peaches and remaining ingredients in blender. Process until smooth. Chill. Serve over ice cream.
Yield: 3 cups   *Patricia Rusinek Macchia*

Praline Sauce

1 cup light corn syrup
½ cup sugar
⅓ cup butter or margarine
1 egg, beaten

1 tablespoon vanilla
 extract
1 cup coarsley chopped
 pecans

Combine first 4 ingredients in a heavy saucepan; mix well. Bring to a boil over medium heat, stirring constantly; boil 2 minutes without stirring. Remove from heat; stir in vanilla and pecans. Serve warm or at room temperature over ice cream.
Yield: 2 cups   *Anna Ferguson Tucker*

Sunday Night Suppers And Menus

Sunday Night Suppers

Sunday evening…the weekend's hectic pace is slowing down; across the South families are coming together for a special Southern tradition. The time for those tried and true favorite recipes has arrived! Enjoy these simple, yet delicious examples of Sunday suppers and begin your own family traditions.

Broiled Tuna Sandwiches

6 hamburger buns, split
3 tablespoons butter, softened
1 (6½-ounce) can tuna, drained and flaked

1 cup Cheddar cheese, grated
¼ cup green pepper, diced
2 tablespoons onion, minced
½ cup mayonnaise

Spread each half of hamburger bun with butter; set aside. Combine remaining ingredients, mixing well; spread mixture on bottom halves of buns. Place on baking sheet. Broil about five minutes or until hot and lightly browned. Cover with bun tops.

Yield: 6 servings   *Jennie Ingelsby Adams*

Cheeseburger Pie
(A Child's Favorite)

1 pound ground beef
1 small onion, chopped
1 (6-ounce) can tomato paste
1 teaspoon salt

½ teaspoon Italian seasoning
½ teaspoon pepper
1 can crescent rolls
1 (8-ounce) package mozzarella cheese

Brown meat and onions in a medium skillet. Add tomato paste, salt, Italian seasoning and pepper. Simmer about 10 minutes. Line a pie plate with the crescent dough. Add meat mixture and top with cheese. Bake at 375° for 25 to 30 minutes.

Yield: 4 to 6 servings   *Laura McLean Powell*

Chef's Special

1 to 1½ pounds ground beef
1 clove garlic, chopped
  or ¼ teaspoon
  garlic powder
1 teaspoon salt
1 teaspoon sugar
Dash pepper
2 (8-ounce) cans tomato
  sauce
1 (8-ounce) package small
  egg noodles, cooked
5 green onions, chopped
  fine
1 (8-ounce) package
  cream cheese
1 cup sour cream
½ cup sharp Cheddar
  cheese, grated

In skillet, brown ground beef; drain. Add garlic, salt, sugar, pepper and tomato sauce. Stir and simmer 15 minutes. In small bowl blend onions, sour cream and cream cheese. Lightly grease a 3 quart casserole. Layer ingredients as follows: noodles, meat sauce, cream cheese mixture; repeat. Top with Cheddar cheese. Bake at 350° for 25 minutes.
Yield: 6 servings   *Melanie Brannen*

Chicken In A Hut

2 cups chicken, cooked
  and cubed
4 ounces cream cheese,
  softened
2 tablespoons milk
¼ teaspoon salt
⅛ teaspoon pepper
1 (8-ounce) package
  crescent rolls

Combine all ingredients except rolls. Set aside. Divide rolls into 4 sets of 2 rolls each. Press seams together of 2 rolls to form a square. Spoon ¼ of chicken mixture onto the middle of the square. Fold corners up to make the "hut." Place seam side down on foil covered cookie sheet. Bake according to crescent roll package directions.
Yield: 4 servings   *Judy Singletary Davis*

Crab on English Muffins

1 (6½-ounce) can lump
   crab meat
¼ cup celery, diced
2 tablespoons onion,
   finely diced

½ cup sharp Cheddar
   cheese, shredded
¼ cup mayonnaise
4 English muffins–halved

Mix first five ingredients and spread on each muffin half. Broil until cheese melts and muffins are lightly brown.
Yield: 4 servings
Susan Workman Yielding

Crunchy Chicken Casserole

½ cup milk
2 (10¾-ounce) cans
   cream of chicken
   mushroom soup
3 cups chicken, cooked
   and diced

¼ cup onion, minced
¼ cup celery, minced
1 (5-ounce) can water
   chestnuts, chopped
1 (3-ounce) can chow mein
   noodles

Preheat oven to 325°. Combine all ingredients, except noodles and place in a 2 quart casserole. Top with noodles. Bake for 30 minutes.
Yield: 6 to 8 servings.
Jeanne Powell Orman

Easy Chicken Pot Pie

Filling:
1 (3-pound) chicken,
   cooked, skinned,
   boned and cubed
1 (10¾-ounce) can cream
   of chicken soup

3 cups chicken broth
1 (16-ounce) can peas and
   carrots, drained
salt and pepper to taste

Crust:
¾ cup melted butter
1½ cups milk

1½ teaspoons baking
   powder
1½ cups self-rising flour

Preheat oven to 425°. Combine filling ingredients and place in a 9x13-inch greased baking dish. Mix crust ingredients and pour over chicken mixture. Do not stir. Bake in preheated oven for 45 to 60 minutes or until crust rises and browns.
Yield: 8 servings
Jane Waters Stoddard

Creamy Chicken Casserole

3 large chicken breasts, cooked, skinned, boned and cut into bite size pieces
1 (6-ounce) box long grain wild rice
1 (10¾-ounce) can cream of chicken soup
1 (3-ounce) can sliced mushrooms
½ cup mayonnaise
½ cup sour cream
2 cups grated Cheddar cheese (optional)
2 cups crushed butter flavored crackers (optional)

Preheat oven to 350°. Mix all ingredients together, except cheese and crackers. Place in a 2-quart buttered casserole. Top with grated Cheddar or crackers if desired. Bake for 30 to 40 minutes until bubbly.

Yield: 6 servings

Georgie Keller Valentino

Easy Hamburger Quiche
You will have lots of requests for this one!

1 (9-inch) pie shell, partially baked
½ pound ground beef
½ cup mayonnaise
½ cup milk
2 eggs
1 tablespoon cornstarch
½ pound Cheddar cheese, grated
⅓ cup green onions, sliced (may use white onion)

Brown meat and onion in skillet over medium heat. Drain fat and set aside. Blend mayonnaise, milk, eggs and cornstarch until smooth. Stir in meat, cheese, onion and a dash of pepper. Turn into a partially baked (not browned) pie shell. Bake at 350° for 35 to 45 minutes, or until golden brown and a knife inserted in center comes out clean.

Yield: 6 to 8 servings

Patricia Weaver Bringardner

Hot Brown Grill

Sauce:

2 tablespoons butter
2 tablespoons flour
salt to taste
dash of cayenne pepper
¼ teaspoon curry powder
   (optional)
1 cup milk

1 (3½-ounce) can sliced
   mushrooms, drained or
   ¼ pound fresh
   mushrooms, sliced and
   sautéed
1 chicken bouillon cube
1 tablespoon sherry

Melt butter in a small skillet; blend flour, salt, cayenne and curry. Remove from heat; stir in mushrooms and bouillon cube. Cook until bouillon cube is dissolved and sauce is thickened; add sherry.

Sandwiches:

4 slices bread, lightly
   toasted
4 chicken breast halves,
   cooked and sliced or
   8 large slices cooked
   turkey

4 slices bacon, partially
   cooked and cut in half
1 cup Cheddar cheese,
   grated

Place toast on 4 ovenware dishes; cover with sliced chicken or turkey. Pour sauce over chicken, sprinkle with cheese and place pieces of bacon crisscross on top. Place under broiler and broil slowly until bacon is crisp.

Yield: 4 servings   *Charlotte Wells Lamm*

Sunday Night One Dish Meal

2 pounds round steak, 1
   inch thick
1 cup hot water
1 (3-ounce) can sliced
   mushrooms

1 package onion soup mix
1 cup dry red wine

Preheat oven to 350°. Remove a little fat from steak to grease a frying pan. Brown meat slowly on both sides. Transfer to casserole dish. Mix together in the frying pan onion soup mix, water, wine and mushrooms. Pour over browned steak. Cover and bake for 1 hour. Remove cover and bake 15 minutes longer or until steak is tender.

Yield: 4 servings   *Sis Shemwell Eastland*

Honey Chicken
Economical and Easy!

4 boned chicken breasts
½ cup honey
¼ cup butter
cooking oil

1 teaspoon curry
⅓ cup yellow mustard
1 teaspoon salt

Preheat oven to 325°. Melt butter. Stir in honey, curry, mustard and salt. Set aside. Brown chicken in frying pan with a little oil. Drain oil. Put chicken in casserole and pour mixture over it. Bake for 30 minutes in 325° oven.

Yield: 4 servings   *Carol Feledik Templeman*

Five Hour Beef Stew

4 pounds beef, cubed
3 onions, sliced
5 carrots, sliced
2 potatoes, sliced
1 can peas, drained
½ cup tomato soup

½ cup cream of celery
  soup
1 bay leaf
salt
pepper
½ can liquid from peas

Combine all ingredients in a large baking pan. Cover tightly with foil and bake 5 hours at 275°. An easy recipe which NEVER fails and is great for large family gatherings.

Yield: 8 to 10 servings   *Pam Duncan Balsley*

Egg Salad In A Pocket
"Great for Tailgate Party"

3-ounces cream cheese,
  softened
¼ cup mayonnaise
¾ teaspoon dill weed
½ teaspoon salt
½ teaspoon dry mustard
6 hard boiled eggs,
  chopped

½ cup celery, chopped
1 cup ripe olives, sliced
2 tablespoons onion,
  chopped
3 pita pocket breads,
  halved or quartered

Blend cream cheese, mayonnaise and seasonings. Add eggs, olives, celery and onions and stir. Stuff mixture into pita bread.

Yield: 3 to 6 servings   *Louise Hetherwick Hunter*

Husband's Delight
Simply add a salad

1 pound ground beef
½ (14-ounce) jar Ragu
  spaghetti sauce
1 package dry spaghetti
  sauce mix
½ (5-ounce) package egg
  noodles

1 (8-ounce) carton sour
  cream
Cheddar cheese, grated
Parmesan cheese

Brown ground beef in medium frying pan; drain. Add spaghetti sauce to meat. Stir in ½ jar Ragu spaghetti sauce. Simmer for several minutes; set aside. Add ½ packages egg noodles to boiling water and boil until tender. Drain. In 1½ quart casserole dish, layer ½ noodles, ½ ground beef mixture, ½ sour cream, ½ shredded Cheddar cheese. Repeat. Sprinkle top with Parmesan cheese. Bake at 350° for 30 minutes or until hot and bubbly.

Yield: 4 servings   *Dell Cochran James*

Pastichio

1 (8-ounce) box spaghetti,
  cooked according to
  package directions
Your favorite spaghetti
  sauce recipe or 1
  (32-ounce) jar
  commercial spaghetti
  sauce

½ cup margarine
½ cup flour
3 cups milk
3 egg yolks
1 (2½ to 3-ounce) jar
  shredded Parmesan
  cheese

Preheat oven to 400°. Grease a 10 x 15 x 2-inch casserole dish. Place cooked spaghetti in casserole. Pour spaghetti sauce over spaghetti. In top of a double boiler, melt margarine; add flour and stir until well blended. Slowly add milk, cooking until moisture thickens. Add egg yolks, one at a time, beating with spoon after each addition. Add cheese and cook until thick and fluffy (about 3 or 4 minutes). Spread cheese mixture on top of spaghetti sauce like frosting on a cake. Bake for 20 to 30 minutes until top is brown.

Yield: 8 servings   *Natalie Roy King*

Mexicali Casserole

1 pound ground beef
1 large onion, chopped
1 teaspoon salt
½ to 1 tablespoon black
  pepper, to taste
1 (16-ounce) can tomatoes
1 (8-ounce) can tomato
  sauce
1 package chili seasoning
  mix
1 (16-ounce) can chili
  beans, drained
½ pound sharp Cheddar
  cheese, grated
½ (8-ounce) bag corn
  chips

Preheat oven to 350°. Sauté beef and onion, drain fat. Add salt, pepper, tomatoes, tomato sauce and chili mix. Cook, uncovered, over medium heat for 30 minutes. Add chili beans and pour into a 2 quart casserole. Top with cheese and corn chips. Bake, uncovered, for 20 minutes.
Yield: 6 servings
Allyson Ray Murphy

Mexican Meatloaf
Georgia's answer to South of the border.

1 tablespoon plus 1
  teaspoon vegetable oil
1 cup onion, chopped
1 cup green pepper,
  chopped
2 garlic cloves
1 packet instant beef broth
2 teaspoons
  Worcestershire
1 teaspoon chili powder
1 pound ground veal or
  lean ground beef or
  ground venison or
  ground turkey
4 ounces Cheddar cheese,
  shredded
¾ cup plain bread crumbs
½ cup tomato sauce
¼ cup plain yogurt
2 tablespoons fresh
  parsley
Dash of pepper

Preheat oven to 350°. Heat oil in 9-inch skillet. Add onions, peppers, garlic and broth; sauté until onions are translucent. Remove from heat and mix with remaining ingredients. Shape into loaf and place in 8 x 8-inch loaf pan. Bake 45 minutes at 350°.
Yield: 4 servings
Joanne Cooper Davis

Vidalia Soufflé

A great alternative to quiche.

6 ounces stale or day old
French or Italian loaf (cut
into chunks)
½ cup butter or margarine
3 large sweet onions, cut
into thin slices *
1 cup Swiss cheese,
grated

1 tablespoon fresh thyme
or ½ teaspoon dried
thyme
3 eggs, beaten
1 pint light cream
Salt and pepper, to taste

Preheat oven to 350°. Place bread chunks in a 1½ quart soufflé dish. Melt butter in a large skillet. Cook the onions until slightly limp, or translucent. Pour butter and onions over the bread. Scatter thyme and cheese over the top. Blend cream into eggs until mixture is light and frothy. Add salt and pepper if desired. Pour over mixture in soufflé dish. Press down to make sure bread is thoroughly soaked. Bake 45 minutes or until knife inserted in center comes out clean. Serve with a salad. Add ham or bacon for a different flavor, or * more onions, if you like!
Yield: 6 to 8 servings   *Stephanie Threlkeld Gill*

Pita Bread Stuffed
With Avocado And Turkey

6 pita rounds
2 avocados, sliced
2 cups cooked turkey
1 head Bibb lettuce, torn
into bite size pieces

3 tomatoes, sliced
Salt and pepper to taste
6 slices of bacon, cooked
crisp and crumbled

Dressing:
½ cup mayonnaise   ½ cup taco relish

Fill pita bread with ingredients. Pour 1 tablespoon of dressing over all. Serve with homemade squash pickle and melon slices.
Yield: 6 servings   *Louise Hetherwick Hunter*

Pork Chops For the Family

6 medium pork chops
1 small onion, diced
1 (3-ounce) can
   mushrooms, drained
1 (10-ounce) can cream of
   mushroom soup

1 cup of milk
5 cups potatoes, thinly
   sliced
5 tablespoons prepared
   mustard
3 to 4 tablespoons oil

Preheat oven to 350°. Spread both sides of the pork chops with mustard; brown in oil. In the same skillet, add onion mushrooms, soup and milk. Simmer 5 to 6 minutes. Layer potatoes and pork chops, beginning with chops. Pour soup mixture over layers; cover and bake at 350° for 1½ hours.
Yield: 6 servings   *Beverly Webb McCollum*

Reuben Rollups

Pastry:

¼ cup shortening
1 (3-ounce) package cream
   cheese
1 cup flour
2 teaspoons caraway
   seeds

½ teaspoons salt
2 to 3 tablespoons cold
   water

Filling:

¼ cup 1000 Island
   dressing
1 (3-ounce) package sliced
   corned beef

1 cup grated Swiss cheese
½ cup drained sauerkraut

Pastry: Cut shortening, cream cheese, flour and caraway seeds into crumbs. Add salt and water. Roll pastry into 2-11 x 9-inch rectangles. Set aside.
Filling: Spread dressing on pastry. Top with beef, cheese and sauerkraut. Fold in ends of pastry. Roll up jelly roll fashion. Seal. Place on ungreased cookie sheet. Bake at 450° for 15 to 20 minutes. Slice according to desired serving size.
Yield: 2 to 4 servings   *Susan Bolan Sappington*

Quick Brunswick Stew

1 (8-ounce) package
frozen barbecue pork or
beef
1 (7-ounce) can whole
kernel corn
1 (8-ounce) can lima beans

1 (14½-ounce) can
tomatoes
Pepper to taste
1 tablespoon
Worcestershire sauce

Thaw barbecue. Combine all ingredients in a large saucepan and bring to a boil. Simmer for 15 minutes to blend flavors. This is a good lunch served hot with cornbread or crackers.
Yield: 4 servings   *Mary Ellen Miller Trippe*

Salmon Loaf

1 cup soft bread crumbs
½ teaspoon salt
Dash pepper
½ teaspoon dry mustard
2 tablespoons melted
butter

⅔ cup milk
1 (16-ounce) can of salmon
2 eggs, beaten

Combine crumbs, seasonings and butter. Add milk, liquid and oil from salmon and the beaten eggs. Mix well. flake salmon and add to egg mixture. Turn into shallow pan and bake at 350° for 45 minutes.
Yield: 6 servings   *Ann Hite Benson*

Sloppy Joes For A Crowd

3 pounds lean hamburger
meat
3 cups onions, chopped
3 tablespoons cider
vinegar
1½ cups ketchup

Dash of salt
Dash of ground pepper
3 tablespoons prepared
mustard
3 tablespoons sugar

Brown hamburger and onions in a Dutch oven. Drain fat and return to Dutch oven, add remaining ingredients. Mix well and simmer for at least 45 minutes. (When you reheat leftovers add a little more ketchup if it seems too dry.)
Yield: 12 to 15 servings   *Gail Kirk Stahl*

Sausage Casserole

1 cup rice, uncooked
1 pound hot sausage
1 small onion, chopped
1 (3-ounce) can
mushrooms, drained
1 (10½-ounce) can creamy
chicken mushroom soup
Tabasco
Chili powder
Salt
Pepper
1 (8-ounce) can water
chestnuts, sliced and
drained

Cook rice. Cook sausage, crumbling as it browns. Remove sausage and sauté onions and mushrooms. Combine sausage, rice, onions, mushrooms and soup. Blend well. Add Tabasco, chili powder, salt and pepper to taste. Add water chestnuts. Place in greased 2-quart casserole dish; bake 30 minutes at 350°. This freezes and reheats well.
Yield: 6 servings
Nancy Marlow

Soufflé Sandwiches

8 slices American cheese
8 slices ham
16 slices bread, trimmed
6 eggs
3 cups milk
½ teaspoon dry mustard
½ teaspoon salt
1 teaspoon Worcestershire
sauce
¼ teaspoon Tabasco
3 cups cornflakes, crushed
½ cup butter, melted

Put bread in greased 4 quart baking dish, top with ham and cheese. Cover with bread. Mix eggs, milk, mustard, salt, Worcestershire sauce and Tabasco. Pour over sandwiches and refrigerate overnight. Bake at 350° for 30 minutes. Combine cornflakes with butter, sprinkle over sandwiches and bake another 30 minutes until done. Cool 10 minutes before serving.
Yield: 8 servings
Susan Thomas Burney

Peppersteak

1 pound round steak, cut
　into bite size cubes
2 tablespoons bacon
　drippings
1 (4-ounce) can
　mushrooms, drained
Salt and pepper to taste
½ teaspoon ground ginger

½ teaspoon thyme
2 tablespoons soy sauce
1 cup water
1 medium onion, cut into
　rings
2 medium green peppers,
　cut into strips

In skillet, brown steak in bacon drippings. Add next 6 ingredients; cover and simmer for 20 minutes. Add onion and peppers; cover and simmer for 10 minutes.
Yield: 4 servings   *Yvonne Mullen Newman*

Taco Salad

1 pound ground beef
1 package taco seasoning
　mix
1 can chili beans,
　undrained
¾ head lettuce, chopped
3 medium tomatoes,
　chopped
½ pound Cheddar cheese,
　grated

1 medium bag of corn
　chips
1 (16-ounce) bottle
　Catalina salad dressing
Optional toppings: green
　onions, black olives,
　sour cream, Jalapeño
　peppers

Brown ground beef and drain off excess grease. Add the taco seasoning mix according to package directions. Add the chili beans. Simmer 20 minutes while you prepare the other ingredients. In a large salad bowl mix the lettuce, tomatoes and cheese. When ready to serve mix the ground beef and salad together, add the corn chips and Catalina dressing. Toss and serve with toppings, if desired. Serve immediately.
Yield: 12 to 15 servings   *Inez Pou Bennett*

Menus Suggestions

NEW YEAR'S EVE BUFFET

Mushroom Logs 24   Caviar Supreme 12

Apricot Wine Soup 43

Spinach Salad with Warm Bacon Dressing

Elegant Beef Tenderloin 94

Roasted Potatoes 167

Ice Box Rolls 217

Milk Chocolate Cheesecake with Custard Sauce, 268

Champagne

FIRESIDE DINNER FOR SIX

Hot Spiced Wine 36   Bacon-Cheddar Mushrooms 20

Charlie's Caesar Salad 71

Castiglione Family Meatballs and Spaghetti Sauce 95

Patsy's French Bread 214

Mom's Whiskey Pie 301

TRADITIONAL GEORGIAN DINNER

Ercelene's Baked Ham

With Blackberry Mustard Sauce 118

Ercelene's Spoon Bread 202

Southern Style Green Beans 150

Aunt Fanny's Baked Squash 245

Deep Dish Peach Cobbler 297

Southern Mint Tea 38   Coffee

EASTER DINNER

Mandarin Salad 75

Butterflied Grilled Leg of Lamb

with Mint Jelly 114

Herb Rice 172   *Velda's Carrot Custard* 157

Whole Wheat Potato Rolls 220

Mama's Coconut Cake

garnished with Jelly Beans 275

Ice Tea   Coffee

California - Rhine Wine

SPRING LUNCHEON

Shrimp Salad Masterpiece

served in a Cantaloupe Ring

garnished with mint 69

Marinated Asparagus 76

Blueberry Muffins 212

Special Occasion Ice Cream Cake 276

Chardonnay

ALTA TENNIS TEAM PICK-UPS

Ranch Cheese Spread 31   *Vegetable Mold* 33

with assorted crackers

Taco Dip with Corn Chips 19

Tipsy Fruit Dip with Fresh Fruit 20

Black Bottoms 308   *Tennis Team Cake* 277

Fuzzy Navels

40TH BIRTHDAY DINNER

Phyllis' Pickled Shrimp 13   Parmesan Crowns 16

Seven Layer Salad 83

Marinated London Broil 97

Veggie Kabobs served over Steamed Rice 185

Quick Company Rolls 216

A Classic Cake 261

California - Gamay Beaujolais

4TH OF JULY BARBECUE

Back Porch Lemonade 34

Jezebel Sauce with Cream Cheese and Crackers 13

Bacon Wrapped Shrimp 21

Marinated Country Ribs 121

Crunchy Peanut Slaw 80   Baked Vidalia Onions 163

Cheddar Cheese Bread 214

Peach Pound Cake 242   Homemade Fruit Ice Cream 313

Iced Tea   Cold Beer

BEACH IN THE BACKYARD

Frozen Lime Slush 39

Pizza Dip 22

Bahama Grill 135

Korean Salad 74

Delmonico Potatoes 166

Onion Lover's Twist 222

Caramel Ice Cream Squares 309

LABOR DAY BASKET PICNIC

Gazpacho 50

Egg Salad in a Pocket 328

Marinated Pork 124

Fresh Fruit Kabobs

Butterscotch Brownies 281

Iced Tea Punch 37

TAILGATE PARTY

Bloody Mary Mix 34

A Crowd Pleasing Shrimp Dip 15 *Poppy Cheese Sticks* 15

Crusty Parmesan Chicken 108

Marinated Tomaotes 76 *Sour Cream Potato Salad* 81

Carrot and Celery Sticks

Lillian's Sweet Georgia Brownies 238

PORTABLE DINNER

*Prepare in disposable containers
for a new neighbor or a sick friend*

Easy Chicken Pot Pie 325

or

Best Ever Beef Stew 94

Apricot Nectar Salad 55 *Cream-Style Cornbread* 200

Chess Bars 282

BOARD MEETING BRUNCH

Country Morning 225

Cheese Grits 222

Holiday Apples 186

Sour Cream Biscuits 197   *Lemon-Blueberry Bread* 210

Cranberry Tea 35

THANKSGIVING FEAST

Raw Vegetables with Cucumber Dip 18

Easy Spiced Pecans 13

Congealed Coca-Cola Cranberry Salad 56

Roasted Turkey

"Thanks Mama" Cornbread Dressing 201

with Giblet Gravy

Supreme Sweet Potato Soufflé 170

Favorite Broccoli Casserole 152

Beau's Yeast Rolls 216

Praline Pumpkin Pie 306

Wine - Pouilly Fuisse

CHRISTMAS DINNER

Wassail 40   *Nancy Varella's Cheesies* 14

Romaine Salad with Mustard Creme Dressing 78

Christmas Quail 111

Yorkshire Pudding 215   *Baked Fruit Compote* 189

Brazilian Rice 172   *My Grandmother's Rolls* 218

Mother's Pecan Pie 302

Wine - Fumé Blanc

INDEX

GEORGIA ON MY MENU
League Publications
P.O. Box 727
Marietta, Georgia 30060
(404) 422-5266

Please send me_____copies of **Georgia On My Menu** @ $15.95 each

$ _____

Add postage and handling @ $2.00 each $ _____

Georgia residents add 5% sales tax @ $.80 each $ _____

Total enclosed $ _____

Mail to:

Name _____

Address _____

City _____ State _____ Zip _____

Gift card to read_____

Please make checks payable to LEAGUE PUBLICATIONS

— —

GEORGIA ON MY MENU
League Publications
P.O. Box 727
Marietta, Georgia 30060
(404) 422-5266

Please send me_____copies of **Georgia On My Menu** @ $15.95 each

$ _____

Add postage and handling @ $2.00 each $ _____

Georgia residents add 5% sales tax @ $.80 each $ _____

Total enclosed $ _____

Mail to:

Name _____

Address _____

City _____ State _____ Zip _____

Gift card to read_____

Please make checks payable to LEAGUE PUBLICATIONS

Reorder Additional Copies